Georg Berner   Management in 20XX

The author

Georg Berner has held the following positions:

- Designer and project manager working on the development of the 1-Mbit memory chip at Siemens Corporate Research and Development
- Assistant to the management and sales manager in the Siemens Semiconductors Group
- Segment sales manager for Germany at Texas Instruments Deutschland
- Account manager and project manager at Siemens Corporate Projects
- Head of strategic planning and collaboration at Siemens Network Systems
- Head of global marketing in Siemens Nixdorf's IT Networks division
- Head of the Innovation Sector for Information and Communication at Siemens Corporate Technology
- Head of the Executive Office of the Siemens Corporate Executive Committee for the Information and Communications segment

In several of these jobs he successfully launched new business ventures or projects or optimized existing ones. Three children educate him in his rare leisure time.

Management in 20XX

What will be important in the future –
a holistic view

by Georg Berner

Publicis Corporate Publishing

Bibliographic information published by Die Deutsche Bibliothek
Die Deutsche Bibliothek lists this publication in the Deutsche Nationalbibliografie;
detailed bibliographic data is available in the Internet at http://dnb.ddb.de

Background of cover illustration: Celestial Fireworks, courtesy NASA/JPL-Caltech.

The author and publisher have endeavored to specify sources as fully and accurately
as possible. However, since this book emerged out of the experience and ideas gained
by the author in his day-to-day working life as well as from lectures, articles in
specialist publications and knowledge gained in discussions with others, and only
to a very limited extent from citable sources, it was not really possible to list all sources
systematically. To the best of his knowledge, the author has therefore made
reference in the bibliography to all books containing elements that he may have
incorporated into this book.

http://www.publicis-erlangen.de/books

Contacts:
gerhard.seitfudem@publicis-erlangen.de (copy editor and publisher)
georg.berner@web.de (author)

ISBN 3-89578-241-6

Editor: Siemens Aktiengesellschaft, Berlin and Munich
Publisher: Publicis Corporate Publishing, Erlangen
© 2004 by Publicis KommunikationsAgentur GmbH, GWA, Erlangen

Printed in Germany

Equipped for the future

We live in a time of sweeping, global changes. Triggered by fundamental innovations in microelectronics, modern information and communication technology has revolutionized our working lives and is increasingly also leaving its mark on our private lives. High-speed, efficient and, above all, low-cost communication and the associated vastly increased availability of information have accelerated the process of market globalization and consequently intensified competition and increased the pressure on companies to improve productivity. Technological change has led to changes in the industrial value chain and to the conditions under which innovation takes place: Time and knowledge are increasingly becoming decisive factors. Consequently, corporate structures and management methods are having to change. The trend is toward open, networked, collaborative structures and a working world whose most salient features are greater flexibility and individual responsibility. The information age's effects on society are already immense, and it is increasingly difficult to strike a balance between previously undreamed-of technological possibilities and what economies and societies can withstand.

In this time of change, one is reminded of the words of Charles Darwin, who said: "It is not the strongest of the species that survives, nor the most intelligent, but rather the one that is most adaptable to change." This is now widely known simply as the concept of the "survival of the fittest". The great challenge facing us today and in the future is best described as continuous renewal. This is an imperative that applies not only to business but also to science, government and society as a whole. Innovations change the world, yet innovation cannot flourish without change.

The ability to change, to respond quickly and – even better – to be involved in shaping the changes that are taking place is thus more important than ever. But the questions as to how this is to be done and which direction to take simply raise further questions. An important first step to take if these questions are to be answered is to take a systematic look at the future, in all its many aspects, and to examine what the implications are for today's strategies. This book makes a contribution to this – in terms of methodology as well as content – in a new and unconventional way: It brings utopian and in some cases amusing visions up against the realities of the various spheres in which we live our lives. And it provides all decision-makers – not just those in companies – with a fund of new ideas, strategies and ways of thinking. Moreover, it is also richly illustrated and attractively presented. This is a combination that distinguishes it from many other books about the future, and it thus conforms to the innovator's maxim to do it differently, not just better.

This book is certain to appeal to a wide readership – not just to those in marketing, sales and R&D departments.

I wish you an enjoyable read.

Prof. Dr. Claus Weyrich

Member of the Managing Board of Siemens AG and head of Corporate Technology

Preface:
Looking back at tomorrow

We are living in an exciting, innovative time in which much of what we are used to is being turned on its head. You need only think of the transformation we have undergone to become an information society: Within a very short space of time, life without mobile phones and PCs has become unthinkable. The world around us has changed more in the last few decades alone than in the previous two hundred thousand years since homo sapiens first appeared.

When we turn our attention to the future, we often make the mistake of drawing conclusions about tomorrow on the basis of what we know about today.

This often results only in small improvements to products, as has been the case with video recorders and CD players. While progress is made, there is no big breakthrough. However, there are also other approaches. One of them is being pursued by the manufacturers of DVD players, for example. Wherever possible, they use inexpensive computer components to keep development and manufacturing costs as low as possible. The more recent video recorders also make use of computer technology and are thus based on a completely new set of technical concepts.

When we develop new products and services on the basis of a vision of the future, we take into account customers' future needs and desires as well as the technology of the future.

This book will help you to examine your company's objectives and strategies with a view to finding out whether they are likely to make it fit for the future.

Figure 1 illustrates the different approaches that can be taken. Since we are going to make inferences about the present from the future, it should be read from right to left. We will begin by examining longer-term general and technology trends and describing possible scenarios for the future before turning our attention to the needs and wishes of our customers.

In the first half of the book we will make inferences about tomorrow on the basis of what we can assume about the day after tomorrow. We will thus be analyzing today's business and its processes from a new angle. Looking only at the months ahead simply will not give us the perspective we need. Only when we have an idea about what the distant future may bring will we begin to think about innovations that we have so far been scarcely aware of. By thinking in this new way, we will be able to strike out in completely new directions.

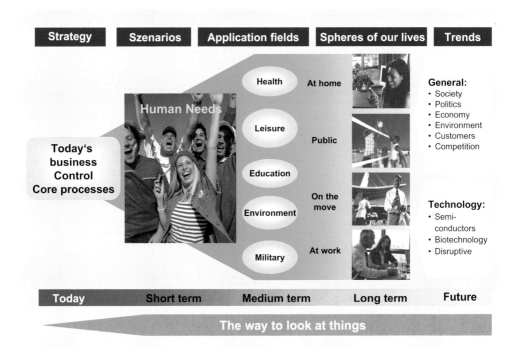

| Strategy | Szenarios | Application fields | Spheres of our lives | Trends |

Human Needs

- Health
- Leisure
- Education
- Environment
- Military

Today's business Control Core processes

At home

Public

On the move

At work

General:
- Society
- Politics
- Economy
- Environment
- Customers
- Competition

Technology:
- Semi-conductors
- Biotechnology
- Disruptive

| Today | Short term | Medium term | Long term | Future |

The way to look at things

Looking back at tomorrow   **Figure 1**

The second half of the book deals with the effects of our findings on every-day working procedures. We may then set ourselves different or new goals. The strategies used to achieve these goals will also be put to the test. This part of the book examines the consequences for companies' core business processes. Reflecting on the future in this way should make it easier to take the entrepreneurial decisions that will lead to good, profitable business tomorrow.

So let's embark on a journey through time ... to return to the present with new energy, ready to go about our work in new ways.

Looking at the future on the basis of current trends

It is generally assumed that analyses of the past are sound, even when – in the absence of reliable documentary evidence – they may be highly speculative. Looking into the future, on the other hand, is associated with crystal balls and is thus often not taken seriously. Nevertheless, we are going to take that risk here and examine the future in a little more detail. After all, it is into this future that we are aiming to successfully steer ourselves and our company.

Technology trends are important guides to progress. Long-term trends in development will emerge on the basis of products that are already in our laboratories today and that are not subject to any physical constraints. We are now well into the information age, and the next few years will be characterized by developments in the field of information and communication technology. But progress is also being made increasingly rapidly in the fields of biology and medicine, and this will usher in a new age in a matter of a few decades.

General trends

Trends, currents and fashions abound in today's world. We are going to focus here, above all, on those trends that are relevant from a business viewpoint – trends affecting society, politics, economics, the environment, technology, customers and competitors, as listed in figure 1. The following are among the major trends that can be observed in these categories:

Society
- Continued strong growth in the world's population
- Growing health awareness
- Demographic change – more older people
- Higher costs of private provision for ill health and old age
- Global consciousness
- Increasing terrorism in a wide variety of forms
- An increasing need for security
- Life-long learning
- Edutainment – entertaining, technology-assisted learning
- Flexibility with regard to working hours and leisure time and in society as a whole
- Income polarization, double-income families
- Reduced constancy in our working lives, with some people having more than one job at the same time
- Fewer jobs for low-skilled workers
- Increasing mobility (with slower growth than before)
- Changing values

Politics
- Increasing liberalization and deregulation
- Decreasing importance of borders and distances
- Decreasing influence of local politics
- Growing constraints as a result of debt

- Increasing scope for different interpretations of statutory conditions
- Reinterpretation of intellectual property
- Improved resolution of international conflicts
- Improvement of conditions for business, leading to higher employment

The economy

- Increasing productivity
- Increasing automation
- Growth in service industries
- Greater capital mobility
- Increasing globalization
- More frequent relocation of businesses, depending on conditions for business
- Increasing vulnerability of stock markets to emotional responses
- Increasing service orientation
- Virtualization of companies
- Knowledge as the most important resource
- New business models through electronic and mobile business
- New forms of collaboration between companies of all kinds
- Continued reduction in the length of product life cycles
- Even shorter intervals between innovations

The environment

- Increasing environmental awareness
- Sustainability/regulation of all intermediate and end products
- Increasing importance of recycling – new laws and regulations
- Sparing use of resources
- Alternative raw materials and energies
- Renewable energies
- Worldwide regulation and monitoring
- Environmental disasters and new illnesses with widespread effects

Customers

- Individualization of lifestyles
- Growing consumerism
- Increased expectations as regards quality and service
- Standardized, process-based buyer-vendor relationships
- IT infrastructure as the new backbone for communication
- Increased efficiency as a result of intelligent solutions
- Well-informed customers
- Outsourcing/partnering
- Rapidly growing importance of electronic, mobile and real-time business
- New purchasing criteria (e.g. self-explanatory products, ease of operation and plug-and-play functionality)
- Changing mentality: ordered today, delivered tomorrow

- Reduced costs/increased productivity
- Lower barriers to entry in new fields of business as a result of electronic media
- Global marketing of small and medium-sized enterprises
- Improved knowledge management to steal a march on the competition
- New competitors from other industries
- Shorter life cycles of products and services
- Shorter duration and effect of unique selling points
- Many small, incremental innovations as incentives to consumers to purchase
- Intensive price wars for market share
- Growing importance of brand and image

The first and most fundamental of a long series of exponential developments with which we are faced is world population growth (see figure 2). Unsurprisingly, we have great difficulty dealing with exponential phenomena like this. We find it difficult to cope with their effects because for a long time their effects are barely noticeable. Then suddenly, apparently out of nothing, they bring about great changes. By looking at a longer period we should be able to keep track of developments better.

500 years into the future and 500 years into the past

This section lists the hypotheses and expectations of futurologists as well as past events and occurrences that seem to me to be relevant.

The further we look into the future, the more difficult it becomes, of course, to predict both the events themselves and the point in time at which they might occur. In fact, we need look no further than weather forecasters for an example of how difficult it can be to make predictions

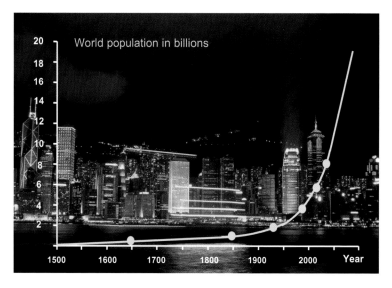

Figure 2
World population
growth

that go beyond the short term. Even a short period like five days is quite a challenge for them!

Take a few moments to consider when you think certain events might occur in the future. In the table below it does not matter so much how precise a prediction is; the important thing is to gain some distance from the present in order to think about what we and our company might be faced with in the year 20XX. Nor is the aim to come up with predictions that are a hundred percent realistic; the key thing is to identify trends. And if one or other of the predictions raises a smile, that's okay:

Smiling is fine, as long as you keep thinking as a visionary!

We should also take some time to consider the complexity of our universe and ask ourselves if – given that complexity – it is reasonable to assume that everything in it can be explained within our current mental and physical horizons. But let's begin by tackling the future a little more pragmatically:

Anybody tempted to think that the developments listed in the table are unlikely to take place very soon should pause to consider the fact that the speed of innovation is currently doubling every ten years.

And even this interval is getting shorter as time goes on. What used to take ten years to develop can now be done in five at most. But this is something we will return to later in the book. Acceleration of this kind is more than most people's imagination can cope with. After all, we are used to thinking in linear terms and making inferences about tomorrow on the basis of what we know today.

It's important when considering the future to concentrate on the work of the few good futurologists around rather than on those who take a populist approach. Good futurologists have access to a large number of databases in which trends are recorded, and they maintain good links to research institutes, universities and colleagues in relevant disciplines.

Anyone who would like to look more than 500 years into the future should refer to the work of J. R. Mooneyham. The effects on society of many of the predictions listed below will, of course, have to be discussed by society as they become imminent, but we will dispense with any such discussion here in the interests of producing a simple, chronological list.

2500   The first people settle on Mars

2450   The "United States of Earth" is founded

2400   Life expectancy has lost its meaning

2350   The species that come after humans develop the ability to change

2300   There are houses in the sky

2250   Hyper-intelligent life proliferates

2200   A software-based existence is no longer tied to computers

2150   There are many non-biological thinking beings

2100   Human minds are linked to the world of machines

2099   The century of conscious and religious machines begins

2098   Standard computers are as powerful as all human brains
       put together

2097   Rockets destroy meteorites

2096   Children learn via hyper-modems connected to the brain

2095   The world is controlled by artificial intelligence

2094   Robots and holographic displays have become ubiquitous

2093   The so-called "human" population reaches 12 billion

2092   Biorobots replicate themselves

2091   A computer-based religion develops

2090   Robots are sent to all the planets in our solar system

2089   Cryotechnology is developed for particularly long journeys
       through space

2088   Many new species are designed

2087   Ecosystems are rebooted to secure life on earth

2086   People contact their relatives by means of channeling and
       astral travel

2085   A nanobot species the size of insects runs out of control

2084   Improvements in bioengineering are demonstrated at the
       Olympic Games

2083   The aging population becomes an economic risk factor

2082   The moon becomes a new continent

2081   Cyborgs: People exist whose bodies are 90% machine and only
       10% organic

2080   The weather can be changed as required

2079   People can be altered psychologically to allow them to deal with
       new circumstances

2078   Virtual worlds become a drug to which many people are addicted

2077   People without neurological implants are discriminated against

2076   Projects are carried out in the further reaches of space using
       robots and new means of propelling spacecraft

2075   Synthetic nanorobot insects are used to support military
       operations

2074   A global justice center is set up to improve justice in the world

2073   Underground cities are built

2072	A new form of shamanism develops
2071	Methods of learning are adapted to suit people's genetic makeup
2070	Androids are available as consumer goods
2069	Implanted chips improve the functioning of the brain and senses
2068	A genetic Chernobyl takes place
2067	Statutory rights are granted to computer-based systems
2066	Machines claim consciousness
2065	Darwinist software reprograms itself
2064	Artificial brains are connected to computers
2063	Deep-sea power stations utilize new resources
2062	Pets with newly created DNA are given as birthday presents
2061	Radiation-contaminated areas are decontaminated by robots
2060	Human mutants are created
2059	Translators for communication between humans and animals are the most popular Christmas presents
2058	Artificial brain implants improve intelligence
2057	Implanted computers create a new interface
2056	Swarms of nanobots are sent in to help when disasters occur
2055	Old satellites orbiting Earth are removed
2054	Children's abilities can be programmed, and children are taught by computers
2053	Additional sensors are implanted in the body
2052	Nanotechnologies permit production facilities to be built into systems the size of suitcases
2051	Artificial eyes are implanted
2050	Vacations can be spent orbiting in space
2049	Houses in Japan are built deep underground
2048	Physical gene therapy is used extensively in developed countries
2047	Nuclear technology leads to the creation of new materials
2046	Direct brain-to-brain links are possible via computer network; a digital aura allows people to be linked up telepathically if desired
2045	International Internet immune systems go online; quantum computers provide high efficiency
2044	PCs create text, music and pictures that are comparable with what humans can do
2043	Artificial nerves are implanted
2042	Robots renew themselves
2041	There is a settlement the size of a village on the moon
2040	Life expectancy increases to 150; people can select the time of their own death
2039	Digital telepathy is used as a means of passing on information
2038	System startup times are strongly affected by software viruses
2037	NASA sends the first people to Mars

2036	Multi-sensory helmets are used in education to convey the material to be learned holographically
2035	A construction boom begins for satellites in orbit
2034	Super-jumbo jets carry over 1500 passengers
2033	Electronic agents learn without human intervention
2032	All the laws of physics are united in a single global formula
2031	Nanoprobes are connected directly to brain cells
2030	The capabilities of PCs are far in excess of those of the human brain
2029	Intelligent materials with sensors and effectors are present everywhere in the form of intelligent dust
2028	Chips and software programs repair themselves
2027	Wetware systems (biological systems) are combined with computers to produce neurocomputers
2026	In the developed countries there are more robots than humans
2025	Most communication no longer involves humans
2024	Machines know more than humans
2023	Computer programs obtain information, learn and develop on Darwinist principles
2022	Convoys of automobiles are linked together like a train and drive without human intervention on intelligent highways
2021	Ships without crews are able to navigate and dock automatically
2020	Consumer robots that understand speech go into mass production
2019	Chip production reaches the level of 50 million transistors per person per day
2018	Video recorders can (finally!) also be programmed by adults
2017	The world is represented virtually on the Internet
2016	Nomadic companies respond immediately to changes in local business conditions
2015	3D holographic displays the size of walls replace 2D displays
2014	Nanodevices carry out repair work in the human body; brainwave-based sensors worn in a cap permit telekinesis and speed up communication with computers
2013	The entire body of public human knowledge is available on the Internet
2012	Music for 6 days is available on a single chip
2011	Personal electronic agents help people with their everyday, routine work
2010	Real-time translations are introduced as a service; more machine-to-machine than human-to-human communication on the networks
2009	Virtual 3D reality is available for exclusive domestic use
2008	Electronic paper is used everywhere
2007	Optical cards replace floppy disks and tapes
2006	Quantum computer prototypes are created

2005	Nanocomputer elements are shown to be capable of functioning
2004	UMTS enables mobile and local online services to be made available everywhere; first human clone cell in a lab
2003	Wireless LAN emerges as a mobile alternative to the last few yards of wire from the telephone jack of the broadband landline network
2002	2 GHz computers are sold in supermarkets
2001	There is a boom in broadband Internet connections
2000	Mobile phones gain access to the Internet

The timeline below lists the most important innovations in the fields of information, communication and media technology. However, it begins not with the first cave drawings around 75,000 years before Christ but with the invention of printing by Gutenberg in the 15th century. The increased rate of innovation that took place in the 20th century can be clearly seen. Around 1980, digital technology began to make inroads in audio and video applications, leading to the kind of convergences that are taking place today, now that we have radio, music and videos available on the Internet, for example, and data can be downloaded via radio and television.

Five hundred years into the past

1448	Gutenberg invents printing
1453	Gutenberg prints the bible
1536	The first daily newspaper is printed in Italy
1544	The camera obscura is invented
1565	The pencil is invented
1609	The first regular newspaper is published
1663	Europe's first magazine appears
1710	Three-color printing is developed
1714	The first patent is granted for a typewriter
1770	The eraser is invented
1810	The first electromechanical telegraph is developed in Germany
1820	The first precursor of the pocket calculator is developed
1827	The first attempts are made at photography, and the first microphone is developed
1830	The first 5-needle telegraph is used on the railroad
1837	The Morse telegraph is invented
1838	The first 3D images are produced
1839	The first camera is developed (the Giroux Daguerreotype)
1843	The facsimile is invented by Alexander Bain
1847	The pointer telegraph is invented by Werner von Siemens
1855	The printing telegraph is invented in the USA
1862	Caselli, an Italian, sends the first pictures over a longer distance using a pantelegraph
1863	The first electric telephone is developed
1865	A communication cable across the Atlantic links Europe and the USA

Information, communication and media timeline

1867	The first typewriter is developed
1876	Edison invents the phonograph, and Bell invents the telephone
1884	Experiments with the first mechanical versions of the television are carried out by Nipkow
1887	Cellulose-based film is developed
1889	Strowger invents automatic telephone switching
1895	Guglielmo Marconi invents the radio, and the Lumière brothers invent the cinematograph
1896	Vitascope brings film projection to the USA
1897	The cathode-ray tube is invented by Braun; the shellac gramophone record is invented
1898	The first loudspeaker is developed
1900	Experiments are carried out with radio transmissions
1904	The first telephone answering machine is developed
1906	The vacuum tube is invented by Lee de Forest
1907	The first photocopier is marketed
1911	The first U.S. radio license is granted
1914	The first intercontinental telephone conversation is held
1919	Short-wave radio is invented
1922	The first 3D movie is produced (to be watched wearing red and green spectacles)
1926	Television transmissions are laboratory-tested
1926	The first television pictures are transmitted across the Atlantic
1929	Stereophonic sound is first produced in the cinema, the first experimental television station is set up in London, and the car radio is invented
1933	The first experiments are conducted into stereo transmission
1935	The first fully electronic television is developed
1936	Coaxial cable is invented
1938	Radio transmissions can be recorded and edited; the first live color television transmission is made
1940	The first regular television station is set up in the USA; stereo sound recording and playback emerges
1941	Microwaves are used for transmission
1947	The transistor and holography are invented
1948	The first Polaroid camera is developed
1954	Regular color television becomes available in the USA
1956	The first disk drive is developed at IBM; the first experiments are carried out with video telephones
1957	The USSR launches Sputnik
1958	The first stereo long-playing records appear; the first integrated circuit, the first photocopier and the ARPANET, the precursor to the Internet, are developed
1960	The first communications satellite is launched; the laser is invented

1962	The first high-speed digital cables are laid in telephone networks
1963	Philips develops the first stereo cassette recorder
1964	Moore publishes his law of processor development (Moore's law)
1966	Xerox sells the first fax machine
1967	The first floppy disk and the first cordless telephones are developed
1969	The first Intel microprocessor (4004) is developed, and the ARPANET is launched
1970	The prototype of a video disk is produced; it is suggested that optical fibers be used for communication
1971	The ARPANET is extended
1972	A satellite is used for a live television transmission for the first time; digital television is laboratory-tested
1973	Super 8 cameras appear; Ethernet is developed
1974	The first Dolby Surround Sound tests are carried out
1975	The first optical video disk is developed
1976	Dolby Stereo is first introduced in cinemas
1979	The first mobile-phone network is set up in Japan; the first Walkman is developed
1980	The first camcorders appear; the CD is invented
1981	The first IBM Personal Computer is released; the first designs for laptop computers are produced
1983	The first CDs go on sale
1984	CD-ROMs are invented
1985	The first 3D television that does not require the viewer to wear red and green spectacles and the first color photocopiers are developed
1986	The first laser printers are developed
1987	MPEG is first considered
1989	Digital photo editing becomes possible
1991	The Internet becomes available on a commercial basis
1992	Digital AM radio and MPEG-1 are developed, the World Wide Web is launched, and the first SMS messages are sent between mobile phones
1993	There is renewed testing of video phones, and the DVD (digital versatile disc) is invented
1994	Digital satellite television services appear
1995	The first laboratory CD-ROMs are developed that can contain an entire movie
1996	MPEG-4 is developed, and DVDs go on sale
1997	DVD players become popular
2002	DVD writers come onto the market

As you can see, we are in the midst of the information age. However, the preparatory work takes a considerable time, and a good many of the innovations that we think of as recent are actually older than we generally assume.

The information age will soon have peaked – as early as the year 2015, according to Kondratieff.

So the obvious question is: What will be the next wave?

We can safely assume that the fields of biology and medicine will play a decisive role in the next Kondratieff cycle. A timeline for biology and medicine – like the one for information, communication and media technology – shows the achievements of the past on which we can build in the future.

Timeline for biology and medicine	

1495 Syphilis is described for the first time

1564 The condom is invented

1590 The microscope is invented

1628 Blood circulation is observed

1658 Red blood cells are observed under the microscope for the first time

1683 Bacteria are observed for the first time

1733 Blood pressure (of a horse) is measured for the first time

1761 Pathology is established as a science

1771 The conversion of CO_2 to O_2 is observed in plants

1796 A smallpox vaccination is developed

1810 Homeopathy is developed

1816 The stethoscope is invented

1817 Chlorophyll is isolated

1818 The first successful blood transfusion is carried out

1836 An animal enzyme is isolated for the first time

1846 An anesthetic is used for the first time

1854 The cause of cholera and a prophylactic for it are discovered

1858 Virchow discovers that all cells develop from other cells

1859 Darwin's "The Origin of Species" is published

1861 Semmelweis recognizes the importance of hygiene

1865 Mendel's laws of heredity are published

1868 Multiple sclerosis is diagnosed for the first time

1869 Nucleic acid is discovered in the nuclei of cells

1874 Three-dimensional molecular structures are described

1879 Chromosomes are discovered

1882 The tuberculosis bacillus is discovered

1892 White blood cells are discovered

1895 X-ray radiation is discovered; psychoanalysis is developed by Freud

1897 The cause of malaria is discovered

1898 The first virus is discovered

1899 Aspirin is introduced

1901 Blood groups are discovered

1903 The electrocardiograph is developed

1906	Vitamins are discovered
1907	Pavlov carries out his conditioning experiments
1909	The cause of typhoid is discovered
1915	It is discovered that genes are located in chromosomes
1916	The first plastic surgery operations are carried out
1921	Insulin is used to treat diabetes
1931	The electron microscope is invented
1933	A vitamin (vitamin C) is artificially synthesized for the first time
1935	Lorenz describes the imprinting of young birds
1937	The first blood bank is established
1940	The first hormone therapies are introduced
1941	Penicillin goes into mass production
1944	DNA is recognized as being genetic information
1951	Cholesterol and cortisone are artificially synthesized
1953	The double helix structure of DNA is described
1954	The first kidney transplant is carried out
1955	DNA polymerase is isolated
1956	DNA is synthesized in vitro
1957	The first ultrasound examinations of pregnant women are carried out
1960	Chlorophyll is artificially synthesized
1961	An oral polio vaccination is developed
1964	The first heart bypass operation is carried out
1967	The first heart transplant operation is carried out
1969	In vitro fertilization is carried out for the first time
1972	Vitamin B12 is artificially synthesized
1973	The first recombinant DNA organism is created
1977	DNA is sequenced for the first time
1979	Smallpox is considered to have been eradicated
1982	Magnetic resonance tomography is invented
1983	The HIV virus is described; the first embryo is transferred
1984	A method of DNA fingerprinting is developed
1988	The Human Genome Project is set up
1995	The genetic code of a bacterium is sequenced for the first time
1996	Dolly, the cloned sheep, is born
2000	A working draft of the DNA sequence of the human genome is completed

As a result of his economic research, Kondratieff identified development cycles that last around 60 years each. The cycles are marked by radical advances in technology that bring about progress for humanity. The 19th century was characterized by the beginning of the population explosion, migration from the land and mechanization. The industrial revolution brought with it a huge tide of social change, as inventions and economic innovations were accompanied by political changes.

Kondratieff cycles

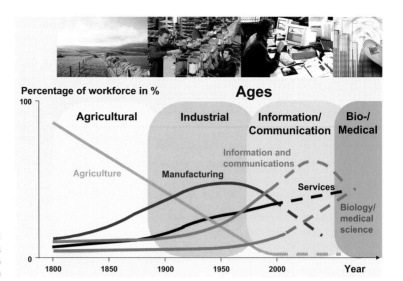

Figure 3
Employment trends
(according to
Leo A. Nefiodow)

At the beginning of the 21st century, we again stand on the threshold of a period of radical change, the full consequences of which are only slowly becoming apparent. The process of digitization is constantly gathering pace, and chips and computers are changing the world even more radically than steam engines, railroads, electricity and automobiles did before them. As a result of improved efficiency in agriculture, a much smaller workforce than before can now produce the same yield. And the improved productivity of industry manifests itself in the use of more machines and fewer people. The better the requisite basic technologies are mastered, the more efficiently processes run. Consequently, fewer people are now employed in both agriculture and conventional industry (see figure 3).

Fundamental innovations have in the past triggered growth cycles of approximately equal length and characterized entire ages. So far we have been through four of these Kondratieff cycles. In the first half of the 19th century, the steam engine was the fundamental innovation that triggered the first cycle. This was followed by railroads, shipping and steel production in the second half of the 19th century, which characterized the second cycle. The third cycle, from the beginning of the 20th century until the outbreak of the Second World War, was defined by electricity and the chemical industry, whereas the fourth cycle between 1945 and the early Seventies saw the automobile, aircraft and electronics industries come to the fore. Information and communication technologies dominate the fifth cycle, where we currently find ourselves, with the Internet emerging as a decisive driving force since the Nineties. As we have seen, a dominant industry or cluster of industries emerges in each of these cycles. Today it is the turn of the information and communication industry, which is now the world's dominant industry with annual global revenues of 2 billion euros (see figure 4).

At the beginning of the 21st century we have reached a turning point on the way to becoming an information and communication society. We are

Looking at the future on the basis of current trends

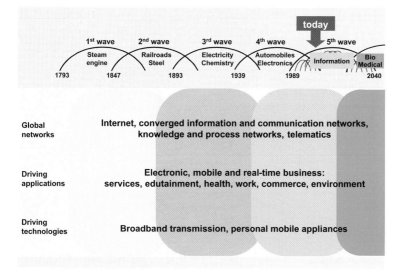

Figure 4
Kondratieff cycles

going through a phase in which many industries – in particular the IT, tele-communication, media and entertainment industries – are either about to undergo a process of fusion or have already done so. As a result, a large number of completely new business models are emerging.

Just as machines have become the servomotors of our muscles, the technologies of the Internet age help people with routine mental work.

As things stand, however, it is often still so complicated to work with these technologies that new problems are constantly appearing, and people find it impossible to work with them as a matter of routine. One need only think of the trouble people have with their PCs and video recorders.

The role of information, communication, biological and medical technologies is, of course, primarily to improve the quality of life. By looking into the distant future we can see that these technologies offer great potential but also present great challenges. And by looking at tomorrow's world from the starting point of the day after tomorrow we can come up with all sorts of new ideas.

Technology trends

Technology trends can be predicted more easily and with a greater probability of success than general trends because they are more independent of interfering factors. They are also reproducible and easier to get to grips with. But they change the world in just the same way as the general trends described in the previous section.

So let's take a closer look at technology trends. A word of caution is necessary at this point, however: It is wise to be careful when assessing business involving the latest technologies because market maturity generally develops in accordance with the hype cycle described by Gartner (see figure 5):

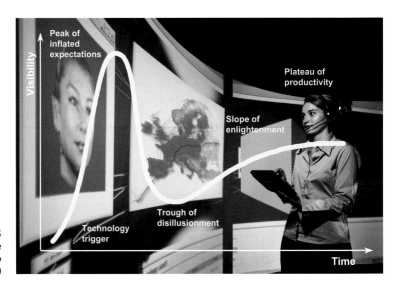

Figure 5
Hype cycle
(according to
Gartner)

It is not just those who come too late who are punished by the market. Those who come too early meet with a similar fate.

Moore's law

The pace of technological progress in today's industrial society is essentially dictated by microelectronics. Many of today's products now contain microprocessors and memory chips. Up to now the storage capacity and performance of microprocessors has doubled every 18 months. This rate was predicted by the former chief executive of Intel, Gordon Moore, back in the sixties, and has been known as Moore's law ever since.

Since virtually nobody is in a position to make an accurate assessment of the dynamics of this situation, we had simply best assume that the consequences, whatever they are, will be very dramatic, to say the least.

A Pentium PC from the year 2000 was a billion times faster than ENIAC, the first large electronic computer, which was built in 1946. By 2020 we can expect another increase in speed by a factor of up to a million. Thus, if we take one of today's computers costing around € 1000 as a starting point and extrapolate the development of processing and storage capacity into the future, Moore's law says that for the same price we will be able to buy a computer in 2020 that will have around the same number of transistors as the human brain has neurons (see figure 6). However, due to the high number of connections between brain cells – up to 10,000 per neuron – similar performance will not be achieved until some years later. Today, a computer this powerful would cost over a billion euros.

The computer of the year 2020 will be able to capture everything we read (20 GB), hear (300 GB) and see (100 TB) in a year. If Moore's law continues to apply beyond the year 2020, the processing power of machines will eventually exceed that of humans. Software alone will then decide whether computers also become more intelligent than us. This knowledge

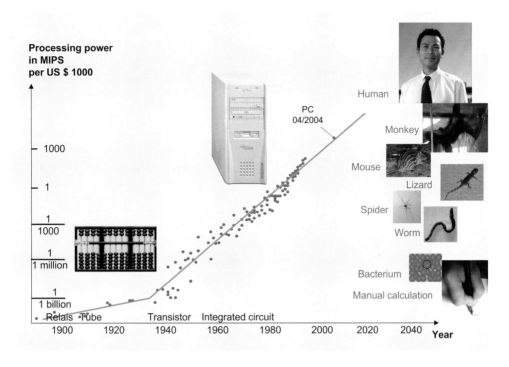

Processing power in MIPS per US $ 1000

1000

1

1/1000

1/1 million

1/1 billion

Relais · Tube · Transistor · Integrated circuit

Human

Monkey

Mouse

Lizard

Spider

Worm

Bacterium

Manual calculation

PC 04/2004

1900   1920   1940   1960   1980   2000   2020   2040   Year

Development of computer performance in relation to costs   **Figure 6**

has given new impetus to the development of artificial intelligence and self-learning systems.

In addition to Moore's law, there are a number of other laws regarding exponential technological progress that our linear imaginations essentially cannot grasp:

Examples of exponential technological developments

- The speed of integrated circuits/chips doubles every 18 months.
- The bandwidth of optical networks doubles every 12 months.
- The same applies to the storage capacity of hard disk drives.
- Internet traffic is currently quadrupling every 12 months.
- The resolution of computer monitors, on the other hand, is developing comparatively slowly, doubling only every 2 or 3 years.

Further exponential effects can be inferred from these developments, which, though the speed at which they are taking place is increasing in absolute terms, are often overlooked. The increasing speed at which the DNA sequencing of our genes is taking place is a case in point. There are also rapid advances being made in techniques for imaging the body – right down to the molecular level. When these two developments are combined, their effect on our understanding and decoding of biological systems and on our medical knowledge is multiplied.

Productivity in software development, on the other hand, is growing more slowly, doubling every six years or so, although the rate of growth is increasing.

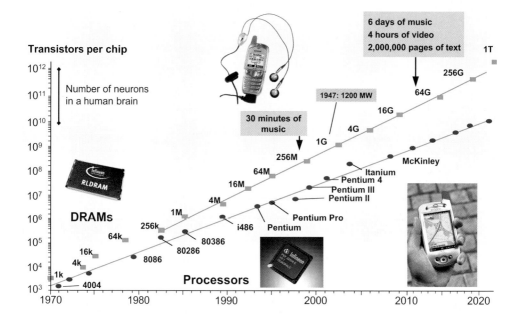

Figure 7 Moore's law (1970 – 2020)

We can expect Moore's law to continue to apply for the next two decades, so what does that mean for the consumer? Let's take a mobile phone from the year 2000, by way of example. Such a device was able to play back around 30 minutes of music stored on its multimedia card in high-quality sound, whereas in just a few years a device of a similar size will be able to play back music for days on end or, alternatively, store and play back several hours of video (see figure 7).

The low power consumption of modern chips is another interesting development. A 1-Gbit memory chip would use the power of an entire 1200-megawatt power station if it still had to rely on first-generation transistors. In 1947, each transistor used around one watt of power, which is actually not very much. Nevertheless, it is to be expected that power consumption per transistor will continue to decrease exponentially as time goes on.

And now for a useful, if unusual, tip for the consumer: Moore's law essentially applies to all products that contain integrated circuits. The more chips the product contains, the stronger is the effect of the law. Parents of technophile children should therefore avoid buying the very latest equipment and should instead upgrade when necessary; computers, in particular, lose a great deal of value within a very short space of time. With hi-fi components, on the other hand, it is different. It has long been known how these work, and their level of integration is not very high, so they lose very little value even over an extended period. A good amplifier – regardless of whether it is 10 or 40 years old – will generally still be technically excellent today. In this case, it therefore pays to invest a little more money because the benefit of doing so is long-term.

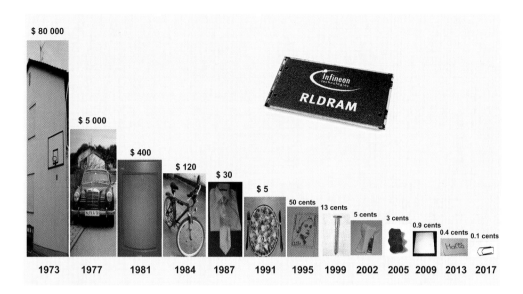

$ 80 000												
$ 5 000												
	$ 400											
		$ 120										
			$ 30									
				$ 5								

50 cents 13 cents 5 cents 3 cents 0.9 cents 0.4 cents 0.1 cents

| 1973 | 1977 | 1981 | 1984 | 1987 | 1991 | 1995 | 1999 | 2002 | 2005 | 2009 | 2013 | 2017 |

Prices for 1 Mbit of DRAM   **Figure 8**

Let's now take a look at how the price of the storage capacity of a 1-Mbit DRAM chip has developed over the last 30 years and what is likely to happen in the next few years (see figure 8):

In 1973, 1000 memory chips with a capacity of 1 kbit of DRAM were required for 1 Mbit. They would have cost as much as a decent-sized house. In the year 2017, 1 Mbit will amount to only a tiny part of a memory chip (probably 1/256,000) and cost no more than a paper clip. This fall in price will be a decisive factor driving forward the development of new applications in information and communication technology in the future.

There is scarcely another field in which advances are being made as quickly as in semiconductor technology, which is a real engine of innovation.

Integration replaces dedicated solutions

With its "Moore's law monsters" the PC industry is finding its way into all kinds of systems and – as a result of economies of scale – is superseding dedicated solutions.

At the Internationale Funkausstellung, a consumer electronics fair held every year in Berlin, it is possible to measure the advances made by the industry year by year, as CD and DVD drives have edged out record players and cassette recorders, for example. Hard disks are now encroaching into the territory of video recorders, televisions can now provide Internet access, and today's PCs can now do almost everything that hi-fi systems can do – and are thus making them superfluous. Similar developments can be observed in the automotive industry and in countless other industries, as well – which is why all companies should familiarize themselves with Moore's law and consider the consequences. The intelligent electronics of tomorrow implemented by means of Intel's new processor is not future-oriented, and it would be futile to try to defend it against the technology that will surely supersede it. It is thus wise to always keep a wary eye on new developments.

The transistor types used today will have been greatly reduced in size by the year 2017. According to the experts, for both technological and physical reasons we will then need new types of transistor. The question is: What other active components or computers will extend the applicability of Moore's law beyond the year 2017?

New components and computers

The information age was ushered in by advances made in chip technology, and further development depends critically on whether researchers succeed in developing even smaller components that are ready for production in the years after 2010.

At this point I would like to outline a number of new computing principles that have the potential to ensure progress beyond the foreseeable scope of today's chip technology.

Quantum computers

As far as physics is concerned, the logical development of the classical computer we are all familiar with is the quantum computer. Systems of this kind use the different quantum states of atoms or molecules for computation and storage. The process of miniaturization thus reaches the level of the smallest structures we currently know of. The only thing left to do then would be to produce control electronics of a similar size.

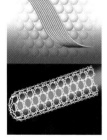

Figure 9
Carbon nanotubes – the replacement for copper conductors

Figure 9 shows a classical copper wire trace and a model of carbon nanotubes, which could be used for making connections in quantum computers. Superimposed on each other, nanotubes can function as tiny switches. Not only are they very stable; they are also able to transfer 1000 times more current than copper. With new algorithms for quantum computers, it will theoretically be possible to break through into totally new dimensions of computing power. These computers – once they are actually implemented – will be suitable for large simulations or applications in the field of encryption. Simplified laboratory tests have already been carried out successfully.

We will examine the new nanoworld in more detail in the section on disruptive technologies.

Molecular computers

Researchers from IBM and other companies are working on small molecules only a few nanometers in size that can take on switching functions. Power consumption is only a hundred thousandth of that of the equivalent semiconductor circuits. However, today these circuits only function at very low temperatures of 4 Kelvin ($-269\,°C$).

The effort required to cool these devices is considerable. The same applies to what are known as "Josephson junctions", which are a kind of tunnel for electron pairs across an insulating barrier, and consequently they are hardly ever used. This could change very quickly, however, as soon as supraconductors are discovered that work at room temperature.

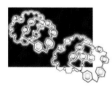

Figure 10
Molecular switch

Alternatively, there is also a single-electron tunnel transistor that could work at room temperature. This component uses organic molecules (a

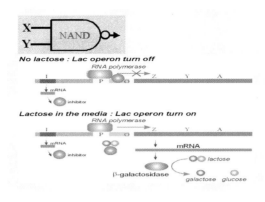

Figure 11
How DNA
computers work

carbon-oxygen compound). Figure 10 shows a model of such a molecular switch.

DNA analysis is already a widely used technology – and not just to establish reliably who is the father of a child. The analysis of the genomes of plants, animals and humans has reached an advanced stage.

DNA computers

Efforts are now being made to use DNA strands in computers, as shown in figure 11. However, computers using DNA strands rely on biochemical processes and can only work very slowly. Much more promising avenues for this technology are to use it to execute huge parallel algorithms or as a terabit data storage medium. The first successful attempts to solve complex problems with the help of "DNA cocktails" have already been made.

The first computing experiments with living neurons were initiated a number of years ago. Figure 12 shows such an experiment. Other research approaches involve inserting foreign genes into chromosomes and thus modifying or creating new flora and fauna, resulting in what are known as "biobots". The convergence between silicon technology and living organisms has already begun. The timeline for the next 500 years earlier in the book indicates the possible developments from this point onward.

Living computers

Figure 12
Computing with
neurons

As shown in figure 13, it will be possible, for example, to use neuron transistors for the interface to biological systems.

Researchers from Infineon and the Max Planck Institute of Biochemistry have developed a neuron chip that can receive electrical signals from nerve cells with a high degree of precision (see figure 14). They have also succeeded in transferring signals to the cells. This is a symbiosis that can remain stable for a period lasting months.

Figure 13
Neuron transistors

Such combinations are ushering in a new era of convergence between biology and machines.

Before long we will have grown accustomed to having autonomous computers all around us. These will collaborate and – as in biological systems – complement each other. If one computer fails, another will take on its work, which is exactly what happens in the human brain.

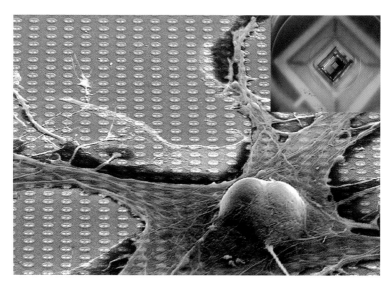

Figure 14
Neuron chips

Neural networks

Neural networks are electronic emulations of interconnected brain cells, so they are not computers in the classical sense, but their capabilities are already superior to ours for many tasks.

If, for example, there are three or more variables to be optimized in chemical or industrial processes, neural networks can manage a task like this with ease. They are also excellent when used for the purpose of forecasting. A neural network can even deal with the classification of complex interrelationships, as required in marketing and sales. When these capabilities are discussed later in the section on business processes, we should bear this technology in mind, since it can help us in our decision-making by doing valuable preparatory work for us.

Neural networks may also be used in the future to help us make more accurate predictions about the weather, the stock market or other important trends.

Ubiquitous computers

Particularly when compared with mechanical parts, the cost of computers these days seems negligible, and consequently they are now found in all kinds of applications. Our hope is that this is to our benefit and that, as time goes on, the machines around us will understand us better and better. For this to happen, an interactive approach is required, and men and machines must be able to communicate with each other.

Storage media

In the previous section we looked at how dynamic memory chips might develop in the future. Although these semiconductor chips are fast, the downside is that their memory is volatile. In other words, when the power is switched off, they immediately forget everything. Ferroelectric semiconductor memory chips are better in this respect because they are just as fast but can retain data over the long term. PCs and other terminal devices equipped with these chips no longer have to be powered up; instead, they are immediately ready for operation. The storage capacities of today's ferromagnetic products lag behind those of other storage media, however, and this is why we still need non-volatile mass storage devices such as hard disks, CDs and DVDs. Figure 15 shows the development of the storage capacity of different media. In the appendix you will find a table that will give you a better understanding of the orders of magnitude involved.

More storage capacity will certainly be needed in the future:

• Industry will need it for databases, archiving, simulation and control purposes.

• Consumers will need it for videos, images and music.

8000 songs compressed in MP3 format require around 30 GB on a hard disk, which is barely enough for a LAN party of ten gamers. For a music collection this size we used to need around 500 LPs or CDs. Now, on the other hand, all of Germany's 100 local telephone books, for example, can be stored on a single CD. Thus, high-capacity storage media not only save costs, they also save resources.

However the various storage systems turn out in the future, storage capacity is unlikely to be a bottleneck to progress.

As far as components are concerned, there are thus virtually no limits to the development of processing power and storage capacity. As we shall see later, the same applies to the transfer of data.

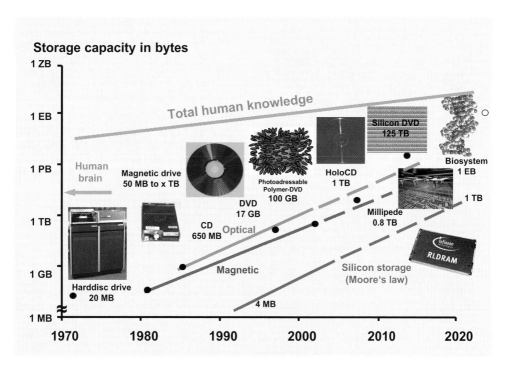

Capacity of mass storage devices soon to be measured in petabytes   **Figure 15**

Further disruptive technologies

There are a number of new developments that have the potential to bring about paradigm changes in technology – with the result that the old technology is no longer required. Let's take a look at a selection of these disruptive technologies.

Automation of development
Automated development: Is that just a favorite pipedream of work-shy researchers? Far from it. In development just as in other fields, results have to be obtained quickly and cost-effectively. In striving for this, researchers adopt an evolutionary approach borrowed from nature, namely to create diversity and then select the best results.

This Darwinist principle can also be applied in automated experiments, in which computers modify variables randomly and calculate the results. The more powerful computers become, the more complex are the problems that can be dealt with.

Software
Nowadays, virtually nothing works without software. We need software to communicate with computers and give them instructions. It is the software that decides what the essential attributes of systems are. Man-machine interfaces, error tolerance, learning capability, simulation, forecasting, self-modification and decision preparation are just some of the expectations that have to be met by artificial intelligence.

Programming code for software has to be written increasingly quickly and be free of errors, while software packages have to be modular and well structured, use standard interfaces and run on all widely used systems. The current trend is toward implementing software as Web service packages and thus enabling users to access them regardless of whether they are in the office or at some other location. In this way, the development of virtually identical software in parallel can be avoided, distribution channels can be made shorter, and software that is only used once every so often does not have to be stored locally.

The demands placed on software products are increasing all the time. As customers, we expect them to adapt to our circumstances and assist us with routine tasks. These include filtering unwanted information such as cybertrash, spam and junk mail, performing tasks such as automatic scheduling both in our private and working lives or shopping for us on the World Wide Web. Agent technologies are setting the pace here. The level of intelligence of products, systems or processes essentially depends on the software.

Cheap production of integrated circuits
A number of companies are now looking into low-cost ways of developing integrated circuits cheaply (see figure 16). They aim to make the production process and raw materials of these ICs as simple and cheap as they are in letterpress printing.

This should make it possible, for example, to apply intelligent, flexible labels to the surfaces of products and other objects, which would allow retailers to implement better theft protection systems, for example, or simply to debit the accounts of customers as they pass the "cash till" and automatically send them their bills.

Figure 16
Integrated circuits

In the long term, it will be possible for radio-frequency identification labels like this to give any physical object a unique ID. And by means of the appropriate sensors, mold or other symptoms of deterioration or contamination will be automatically detected and a corresponding alarm triggered. Disposable games or intelligent, monitorable packaging materials (see figure 17) are other examples of possible applications.

LEDs, the small, filament-free lamps are familiar to everyone. What is less well known is the story of their success. Every ten years since they were first manufactured their luminous efficiency has increased by a factor of ten, and since the nineties, it has been possible to produce them in any color by mixing red, green and blue (see figure 18). If treated properly, these little semiconductor lights will last 100,000 hours, which corresponds to a continuous operating time of almost 12 years. LEDs are now being used in traffic lights, the tail lights of cars and the first designer lamps.

LEDs

Minimal manufacturing costs are also the declared goal for organic LEDs. Films that shine brilliantly in all colors would enable displays to be manu-

Organic LEDs

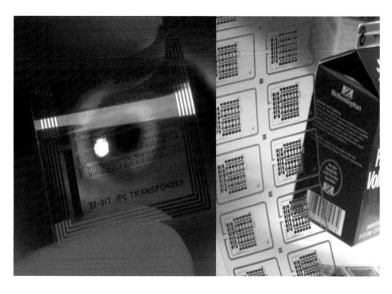

Figure 17
Radio-frequency
identification labels

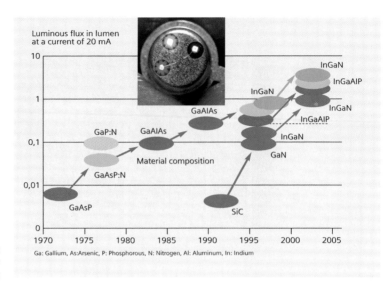

Figure 18
Luminous efficiency
and colors of LEDs

Luminous flux in lumen
at a current of 20 mA

10

1

0,1

0,01

0

1970   1975   1980   1985   1990   1995   2000   2005

GaAsP

GaAsP:N

GaP:N

GaAlAs

Material composition

SiC

GaAlAs

GaN

InGaN

InGaN

InGaAlP

InGaN

InGaN

InGaAlP

InGaN

Ga: Gallium, As:Arsenic, P: Phosphorous, N: Nitrogen, Al: Aluminum, In: Indium

factured extremely cheaply (see figure 19). Using the same production process as for the printable circuits described above, it may be possible to produce intelligent circuits for a few cents a time. A wealth of new applications would become possible with these new materials, such as light emitting wallpaper televisions or flexible electronic newspapers, to name only a couple of examples.

Electronic paper   A number of companies are involved in the race to produce the first reusable electronic paper, adopting a variety of different approaches in the process.

One solution is to use thin, lightweight films that are flexible, bendable, deletable and rewritable. The high-contrast image would be preserved even without power.

Other solutions employ toner or colors that are rearranged and distributed to suit each image. This electronic paper is designed to replace paper or boards and could be used for electronic daily newspapers, for example (see figure 20).

Figure 19
Fluorescent films

Looking at the future on the basis of current trends

Figure 20
Electronic paper

Sensors

Sensors connect machines, systems, robots and agents to the world around them. In complex production procedures or in the biomedical field, practically everything depends on these sensors working reliably. The same often applies in our everyday lives. Pilots, for example, put their trust in a collision warning system to prevent plane crashes. The demands placed on sensors are thus particularly high and frequently safety-related, unlike those placed on navigation systems in cars, for example, which are (still) merely designed to be an aid and thus are not safety systems. In fact, it is not unknown for a driver to follow his navigation system blindly into a river.

When more and more sensors are used to carry out increasingly complex measurements of substances, radiation and statuses, suitably precise analysis methods are required. Neurocognitive systems, which are emulations of biological systems, will soon enable computers to understand and interpret images. So in future when we come home in a bad mood, our intelligent home will be able to pick up the signals immediately and play us our favorite music to relax to.

Smells

Companies aim to appeal to all a customer's senses, even the sense of smell, and there are a number of different approaches to the question of how to produce suitable smells for each situation. Unfortunately, unlike with color, it is not possible to identify three primary smells that can be mixed to make all the others. However, the techniques used to make the fragrances sold in stores today may tomorrow be used to enhance PC games, television or cinemas with situation-dependent smells.

Multimedia interaction

If you aim to appeal to all the senses, you have to include the sense of touch as well. The input devices used for this are gloves and suits with countless integrated sensors. Force feedback already exists as a form of output for PC gamers, whose controls and chairs move in response to the situation in which they find themselves in a computer game. Further haptic components will be introduced in the future to make virtual reality elements tangible as well as visible. This is an important step along the way to making feeling and touching an aspect of virtual shopping.

The voice input and linguistic understanding of computers will continue to improve, as will their interpretation of our gestures and their ability to read what we want from our eyes. Computers will learn to recognize their environment and then behave appropriately in response to their surroundings and situation.

The next step would be the contact-free transmission of brain activity on the "your wish is my command" principle. Fast response times on the basis of EEG measurements of brainwaves can be expected. After all, thoughts are much quicker than speech or gesture.

Developing the man-machine interface remains the central challenge at the next stage of development. The trend is toward adapting machines to suit people rather than people adapting themselves to suit machines. The better computers become, the fewer excuses developers will have for making machines that are difficult to handle and interact with.

This multimedia interaction also raises questions of ethics, such as "how far can you go, and what can be justified?" We won't go into that here, but one thing is clear:

There will be a dramatic increase in the number of ethical questions raised when decisions have to be taken for or against new technologies.

Battery technology and fuel cells

Integrated circuits will in future increasingly merge into objects in the form of "intelligent dust", so the question of how to supply them with power will become a key issue. The distinguishing feature of storage batteries is that they can store energy from other sources. However, the current situation and prospects for further developments in the field of battery technology are not exactly enthralling.

Figure 21 shows the specific energy storage capability of different battery types and their future potential. The fuel cell stands out, but then it is not

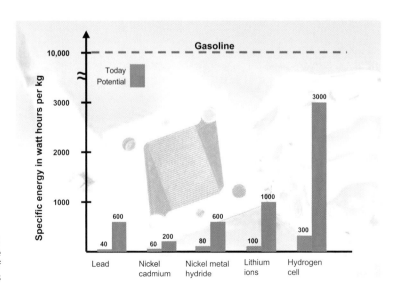

Figure 21
Energy storage capability of batteries

a storage battery in the conventional sense; it is a rechargeable supplier of electricity that, in much the same way as a cigarette lighter, can be refilled with methanol or hydrogen (see figure 22).

Besides from a power socket – in other words, from one of the classical types of power station – electricity can also be obtained from a hydrogen tank, light, heat or movement. Solar cells, wind generators, nuclear technology, piezoelectricity and thermoelectricity are well known alternatives, whereas tidal turbines and geothermal power stations are not so well known.

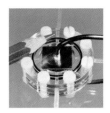

Figure 22
Hydrogen fuel cell

One interesting question for the future is the extent to which we will be able to supply our mobile devices with electricity ourselves. Given that the human body gives off an average of 100 W of heat, quite a few milliwatts of that could be used to operate an electronic device. Additional milliwatts could be gained from our arm movements and the movement of the air we breathe. Alternatively, we could install generators in our shoes. Men would have to learn to wear higher heels, of course, but what would that matter? Fashions change, after all.

Hydrogen has been suggested as a form of energy for cars, homes and industry for around 100 years now. However, for cost-related reasons it has not yet been implemented on a large scale, except in a few isolated cases.

The more mobile people become, the more they need mobile forms of energy. This applies both to the various means of transportation we use and to our mobile devices. No sharp increases in energy capacity are expected from battery technologies in the foreseeable future – which is why all the more hope is invested in the potential of small fuel cells to cover the energy requirements of PCs and mobile phones.

Huge progress is likewise being made in mechanical engineering. New materials are being used for engines, gears and other mechanical systems, and these are helping to improve their efficiency. Ever smaller systems and more powerful chips require smaller and smaller actuators and motors (see figure 23). Approaches ranging from motors etched into silicon to nanostructures are currently being examined. Indeed, over extended periods the process of miniaturization can be represented by an exponential curve similar to that for Moore's law.

Micromechanics

Figure 23
Micromechanics

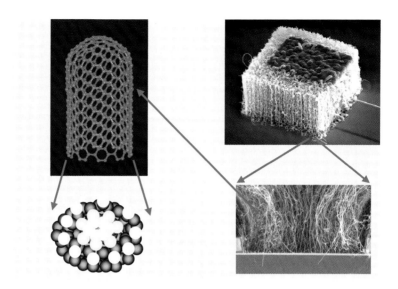

Figure 24
Nanotubes

Nanostructures

We should also expect a few surprises from the field of materials research. The development of nanostructures is still in its infancy, but already much progress has been made, and the first products have already appeared.

Nanostructures (see figure 24) are tiny structures consisting of individual atoms with extraordinary characteristics such as extremely high thermal conductivity, flexibility and current-carrying capacity while also being mechanochemically robust and extremely light. Their values for these characteristics are in some cases many times better than those of conventional materials. There will be many new applications for these materials, of which only a few are mentioned here: strong, molecular-scale motors, wiring on chips, new electronic components, new displays, new sensors, dirt- and liquid-repelling surfaces (see figure 25) and new materials for building and construction. In principle, it will be possible to build tiny nanosystems to emulate the processes that take place in living cells.

Figure 25
Dirt-repelling surfaces

Nanotechnology will also lead to countless radical innovations in the fields of electronics, biology, medicine, energy, environmental technology and construction. In fact, it will be the number one disruptive technology of the 21st century. Simulation programs will allow us to examine the behavior of atomic building blocks. If the properties of materials can then be predicted, a great deal of time will be saved that would otherwise have to be spent carrying out experiments. The rate of progress will thus further increase.

Piezoelectric transmitters

The piezoelectric effect, which we have known about for many years, is used in cigarette lighters, for example, to create an ignition spark by means of mechanical pressure. In response to a change in temperature or pressure, piezoelectric crystals give off electrical energy. If these pulses of energy are picked up by electronic sensors, corresponding signals can be sent to a recipient by a small transmitter unit (see figure 26).

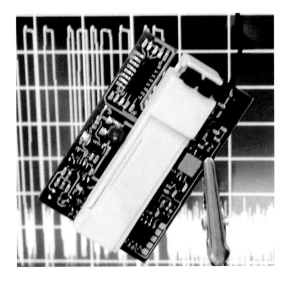

Figure 26
Piezoelectric
transmitters

This allows us to implement switches or sensors that do not require wiring or batteries. Whether you are measuring tire pressure, moisture in a wall or temperature in a construction, a small module – either integral, built on or stuck on – will report the required ambient data.

As radio-controlled switches become more and more miniaturized, they are expected to conquer new fields of application in mechanical engineering and medical technology. Radio technology will then be incorporated into miniature switches and sensor modules that will be integrated in machine parts and supplied with energy from the machine's vibrations. In the medical field, doctors will be able to use a plaster that will use an energy transducer to exploit the temperature difference between the skin and the ambient temperature, and body temperature or blood pressure will be measured by means of sensors and then transferred for analysis by means of wireless communication technology.

Robots and agents

You may be a little surprised at the heading of this section, but robots and agents really do belong in the same category, since both work independently once they have been trained or programmed.

The main field of application for robots today is in manufacturing. Robots are also increasingly being used in situations that are dangerous for humans, such as exploration, military operations or operations in dangerous zones or disaster areas. Once they can do cleaning and other useful work in the home or the workplace, as shown in figure 27, the use of robots will increase significantly.

We can expect to see service robots that will do the vacuum cleaning, mow the lawn, operate the television or even use the telephone. There is huge potential for growth in this field of application.

Figure 27
Cleaning robots

Even Sony's Aibo, a robot pet (see figure 28), has attracted much interest despite the fact that it is as yet not much more than an expensive toy. Perhaps the key to its success lies in its appeals to the emotions.

Star Wars fans will no doubt remember R2D2 – an astromech droid, basically a maintenance engineer robot that could speak, understand what was said to it and take appropriate action. They will also remember how amusing it was to see how it dealt with emotions and difficult situations.

Further advances in robotics will depend very much on progress in the development of sensors, process software for image and signal analysis and chip and battery technologies.

Robots must learn to analyze their environment even better and find their way around in it.

In addition to industrial production – principally automotive manufacturing – new, more complex fields of activity for robots can now be considered, such as food preparation, hospital work, provision of assistance to the disabled, warehouse and excavation work. Let's not forget our cars

Figure 28
Aibo robot from
Sony

here either: The more intelligent they become, the more they take on the characteristics of robots.

Agents differ from robots in that they are immaterial and programmed in software. They can already compare prices on the Internet, make appointments or take on administrative tasks.

We can save time by delegating increasingly complex tasks to our agents.

In future, as our personal assistants on the Internet, they will be able to help us with a wide variety of tasks or even carry them out for us autonomously. The central point about agents is that they reduce the routine mental work we have to do and increase efficiency.

Agents

Information and communication

As we make our way into the 21st century, we can no longer shut ourselves off from the innovations of the information age. Its effects are evident in all aspects of our lives, and many people are asking what it has in store for us next. It is useful in this context to begin by considering the demands placed on networks, because the evolution of networks is driven by the information and communication requirements of people and machines.

Human, man-machine and machine-machine communication

Most consumers are not terribly interested in network technology; they take as little interest in the digital nervous system as they do in our own. When they use the Internet, people primarily just want to communicate reliably with others, obtain information or engage in secure transactions. Basically, they just want everything to work without them having to concern themselves with the underlying technology (see figure 29).

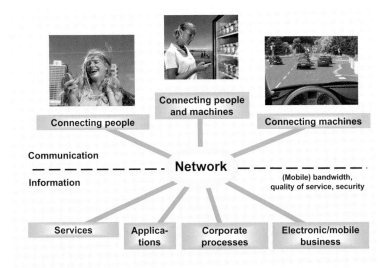

Figure 29
Demands on the network

But it is not just people who need to obtain information and communicate. In our everyday life there are more and more situations in which there is an information chain between machines. Take a drinks machine, for example. Wouldn't it be nice if the machine notified the supplier before its supplies ran out? The supplier's computer would then automatically work out a route for the delivery vehicle, taking in all the empty drinks machines. Banks are already beginning to move in this direction with their automatic teller machines. This example provides a good illustration of how communication between machines can make our lives easier by relieving us of routine work.

Regardless of whether we are talking about communication between people, between machines or between people and machines, the essential prerequisites are security, reliability and broadband networks. The latter are required in order to handle the high levels of data traffic involved. Unfortunately, the Internet of today is still unstable, unreliable and insecure.

The table below shows the requirements that the various interest groups will have of networks up to the year 2020 or so.

However, further advances in communication networks depend on more than just our requirements. In addition to technological progress, as out-

Table   What we can expect from communication networks in the next 20 years

	Bandwidth	Access	Quality of service	Payment	New services
Con-sumers	Realistic virtual worlds with interactivity	Access from anywhere, the last few meters often wireless, multifunctional applications	Immediate, uninterrupted connections, bandwidth as required	A simple, easily understood invoice, some free services	Multimedia services, communication from anywhere, unlimited mobility, multiple broadband connections per household
Corporate customers	Extremely high demand for broadband capacity, simulation of alternative solutions	Wireless access in the building, integration of wireless and wired intelligent devices and users	High availability on high-speed connections, use of technologies that are always ready for operation	Simple, comprehensible display of outgoings, linked to the bookkeeping system	New electronic and mobile business models, virtual presence/ meetings
Providers of telecom applic-ations	Rapid increase in high bandwidths, bidirectional interactive entertainment and interaction, more communication between machines	Networked portable devices commonplace, high bandwidths with high mobility through virtual reality	High quality of services for all applications, high service availability	Growing demand for more complex accounting and bookkeeping, payment per bit, basic monthly charges, payments through third parties possible	Services always ready for use, cheap access for large sensor and control networks, new, sophisticated applications (providing medical assistance, for example)

Looking at the future on the basis of current trends

Vendors of telecom accessories	Typically follow the demands of the market and applications	Timely testing of new equipment and technologies soon after development, financial support for applications with multiple access through providers	Systems that demand high-quality services	Little difference to today	Support of current market developments with new devices
Strategies of telecom service providers	More bandwidth probably needed, but will attempt to exercise sophisticated control over capacity utilization	Will try to support a diverse range of multifunctional devices	Will deliver perfect quality to enable bundled and higher-value services, will attach greater importance to the security of services	Will offer invoicing for complex services, possibility of free services, basic charge and hidden costs will increase this requirement	Will offer services that bring higher income, will create greater network intelligence to control service offerings
Content providers	Will force demand for bandwidth up, initially little need for interaction	Will penetrate the market for computers and devices with their content, content will extend beyond the entertainment sphere	Normal to high demands in terms of service quality	Will strive for accurate, automatic tracking of usage (necessary because of the increasingly complex situation as regards rights, fees, charging and subscriptions)	Interested in services where utilization is high and regular

lined in the previous sections, the development of the kind of applications that will demand such advances is also essential.

Human perception has an important role to play in discussions about the requirements placed on networks because it is a critical factor in the shaping of future access networks.

Human senses

What kind of bandwidths are required for human communication? Let's take as our starting point the five senses: vision, hearing, smell, taste and touch.

The capacity of our senses is in no way overtaxed by new technologies, as shown in figure 30. If you add up the maximum possible bandwidths that can be picked up by each of our senses, you get a total bandwidth of around 200 Gbps, but when it comes to transmission from the senses to the brain, we can "only" manage a bandwidth of around 250 Mbps. Signals that go beyond the capacity of our senses and cannot be passed to the brain are simply omitted. Technologies such as MP3 for music and MPEG2 and MPEG4 for video permit similarly high rates of data compression for transmission.

Only at speeds lower than 240 Mbps does our brain notice an information deficit. Music sounds a little flat, for example, colors are no longer brilliant, and virtual reality is no longer perceived as such. Our ears can already be supplied with a sufficient flow of information electronically, but it is

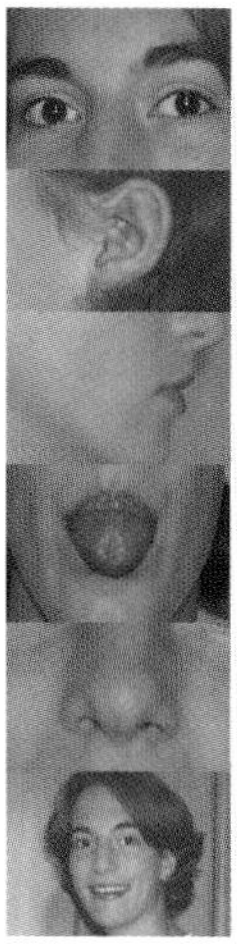

Senses	Bandwidth of receptors	Neural transmission
Eyes	200 Gbps	200 Mbps
Ears	4 Mbps	2 Mbps
Skin	1,5 Gbps	10 Mbps
Tongue	150 Mbps	11 Mbps
Nose	20 Gbps	30 Mbps
$\Sigma =$	Approx. **200 Gbps**	Approx. **250 Mbps**

Figure 30
The capacity of
human perception

our eyes that are particularly demanding: even high-quality 3D cinema films leave them relatively unimpressed. This is why work on developing improved forms of projection is being carried out around the world, involving large, high-resolution screens, projectors or displays built into spectacles.

Theme parks and high-quality PC games are moving in the direction of appealing to as many senses as possible. In addition to pictures and sound, PC control devices are now available that provide feedback, thus involving the sense of touch, while many theme parks now offer simulations of motorbikes, surf boards and so on that actually move, thus intensifying the experience.

The following conclusions can be drawn from the figures presented above:

- If you were simply interested in the best possible sound quality, there would be little point in going to a concert.

Unless you are sitting in the middle of the front row, the audio signals you receive do not match the quality of a CD. And the other senses are hardly involved. As far as your senses are concerned, it is more worthwhile to go to the opera or the ballet because then your eyes also take in information, resulting in higher utilization of the bandwidth available to your senses. And if you round off the evening with a meal, your senses of taste and smell also get something out of it.

- New computers are not being bought just for rational reasons.

A processor with a clock speed of no more than 1 GHz is sufficient for most office applications; higher performance is only required for some of the more sophisticated games and videos. Consequently, it is our senses or those of our children that determine what we buy.

Network technologies

So now we have some idea of the bandwidth of human senses. If we want to transmit virtual reality between people, we can assume a maximum bandwidth of 250 Mbps per person, which is very high compared to the bandwidth of current transmission systems (see figure 31).

Broadband information and communication technologies increase productivity and improve the quality of life – just as electricity did when it was first introduced. By 2015, experts expect broadband connections to have reached 70% to 80% of households in the world's more advanced countries.

Broadband infrastructures, wherever they are in place on our planet, are a significant competitive advantage, driving forward the knowledge society and the development of digital markets, transactions and services.

The required bandwidth for access networks can be provided in a number of different ways: via ISDN (Integrated Services Digital Network), analog modems or cable modems for cable television networks, for example. Some companies also use satellite connections. The more recently introduced transmission technologies include GPRS (General Packet Radio Services), UMTS (Universal Mobile Telecommunications System) and wireless LAN (local area network) for mobile applications, as well as various DSL (Digital Subscriber Line) technologies. BWA, which stands for broadband wireless access, and WMAN (wireless metropolitan area network) can provide data transmission speeds in the two- to three-digit Mbps range. UMTS and wire-

Access networks

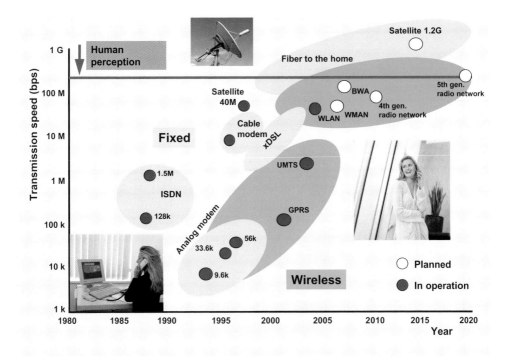

Networks go broadband   **Figure 31**

less LAN provide high-speed wireless access using the 5 GHz band for domestic connections, thus permitting both outdoor and indoor applications. Some access technologies have the characteristics of one-way streets, and these are adequate for radio and television, whereas communication and the Internet always require back channels.

From where we stand today it is not possible to see clearly which of the above technologies will gain widespread acceptance. Wireless LAN has had initial success but has no chance of being used by people on the move, regardless of whether they are on foot or driving a car. Blanket coverage is also a problem, as is transmission reliability. And on a different note, it is worth questioning the extent to which we are prepared to use electronic devices in our everyday lives just because it is possible to develop them.

As we have seen, the Internet is crucial to the information and communication industry. There are basically two ways of accessing it: by using a landline or by using wireless technology. Figure 32 illustrates the options available for each.

What direction will the development of access networks take? Economic factors will play an important role here. For operators the access networks are the most expensive part of the overall network, which is why they use existing networks for as long as they possibly can. A widespread business model involves leasing the lines of other operators. The copper networks of telephone operating companies can transmit data at speeds of up to 50 Mbps over short distances, and the average life expectancy of the copper cables used is 50 years. In view of the age of these cable systems, which were laid in the sixties and seventies, huge investments can be expected in access networks in ten to twenty years in most Western countries. By that time, investment in replacement cables will be necessary anyway, and the new networks will be primarily optical. Until that happens, however, the existing copper cable networks will continue to be used for data transmission, and only their capacity utilization will be improved.

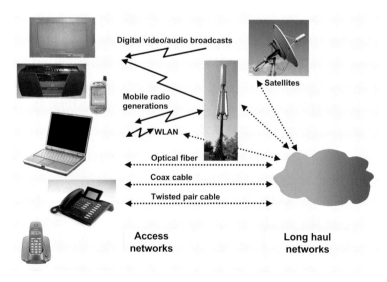

Figure 32
Different data transmission media

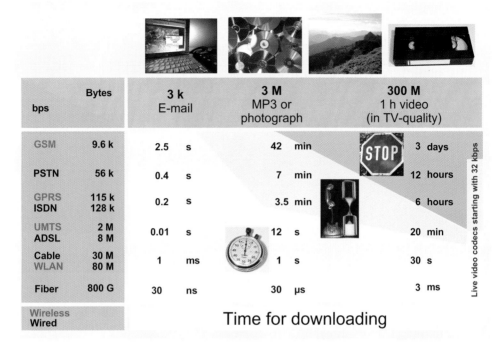

Download times using different technologies   **Figure 33**

A number of technologies have been developed for this purpose, providing access at different speeds. Figure 33 shows the different times required to download an e-mail, a song or a video lasting an hour using these different technologies:

- For a simple e-mail all the existing technologies are adequate.
- To download a song or a high-resolution image, you need to use at least ISDN on a landline connection or GPRS for a wireless connection.
- On the other hand, TV-quality videos can only be transmitted in sufficient quality using ADSL (Asymmetric Digital Subscriber Line) on a landline or UMTS without one. If you transmit moving images at lower transmission speeds, you have to accept a considerable loss of quality.

The number of networked machines is rising much more quickly than the number of networked people, and the associated additional communication on the various networks is boosting demand for bandwidth.

When it comes to data transmission, the issue is how much bandwidth can be transmitted across what distance. Those who work in the field will have heard of the Shannon theorem, which showed that physical limits restrict data transmission on a conventional telephone line to only a few Mbps, whereas the coaxial cable used for television aerials can transmit several hundred Mbps (see figure 34).

Transmission networks

The optical fiber, on the other hand, opens up the prospect of much greater bandwidths. In the field of optical networks (photonics), the performance

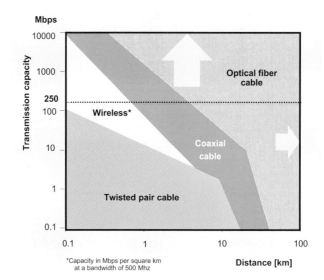

Figure 34
Limits of data
transmission

of systems has improved more quickly than in microelectronics. The transmission capacity of optical systems has, in fact, doubled every 10 or 12
months (see figure 35).

There are now optical-fiber products available that permit data transmission speeds of over 7 terabits per second along a single optical fiber. Yet
optical fiber is still a long way from reaching its limits.

Two- to three-digit volumes of terabits per second can be transmitted over
longer distances – which means the entire capacity of a human brain could
be transmitted in a second.

On the whole, optical transmission systems have so far been used only in
long-distance networks to connect large centers of population or countries.

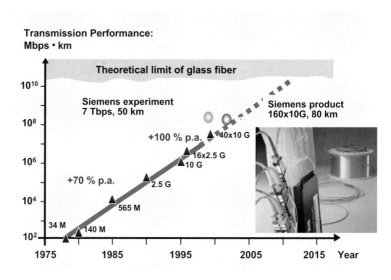

Figure 35
Performance
improvement in
photonics

Looking at the future on the basis of current trends

However, they are now beginning to penetrate urban areas. In industrial areas more and more optical fiber rings or metropolitan fiber-optic networks are being installed for business-to-business use.

In the next 10 years, optical systems will slowly begin to conquer access networks. But why not any quicker?

- To begin with, the existing copper lines have to be replaced with optical cables, which involves huge investments. After all, 70% of the investments made in telecommunication networks are accounted for by access networks, the main cost being for earthworks.
- Furthermore, optical switching technologies have not yet reached maturity. A closer examination of optical transmission systems reveals that signal processing is still entirely electronic. In today's networks the only active optical elements apart from laser transmitter diodes and optical receiver diodes are optical repeaters.

For the future there are visions of end-to-end optical networks in which the signals will only be processed optically and there will no longer be any place for electronics. However, it is still unclear when this vision will turn into reality. Today's optical components are large and still somewhat temperamental and the first purely optical transistor was only developed a few years ago. Electronics will therefore still be in use for many years to come for switching and signal processing, and it will be some time before the first fully optical long-distance network is developed and put into operation.

The transmission capacities of wireless systems are also really quite impressive. Given a cell size with a diameter of 200 meters, for example, 7.5 Gbps can be transmitted per square kilometer.

Corporate LANs (local area networks) are having to meet growing requirements. The network hardware is often designed to meet maximum bandwidth requirements, which make it expensive to purchase and operate.

Corporate networks

By making use of "computing on demand", a company can operate more efficiently and cost-effectively. Sometimes referred to as grid computing, this involves the use of high-speed networks inside and outside the company. The computers and servers involved cooperate to distribute the load intelligently and thus improve the efficiency of computer deployment. In much the same way as utility companies distribute power, this involves collaboration between geographically distributed resources.

As far as software is concerned, we are moving in the direction of Web services – universal software programs that can be used directly and made available to anyone either inside or outside the company. Large software companies have agreed on standardized protocols and interfaces for these. Consequently, in the future it will be possible to call programs as Web services over the Internet rather than have them stored locally on our PCs.

The latest generation of mobile networks is characterized by broadband access, efficient utilization of the entire frequency and global multi-standards.

Mobile networks

In the field of mobile access networks, in particular, there are a number of technologies to consider, such as GSM, GPRS and UMTS, as well as their subsequent generations. If you are moving slowly and within a limited area – in a hotel or an airport, for example – other technologies such as WLAN (Wireless Local Area Network), BWA (Broadband Wireless Access), BRAN (Broadband Radio Access Network) or MMAC (Multimedia Mobile Access Communication Systems) are also an option. Figure 36 provides an overview of these technologies.

Technologies for short distances measured in meters, such as radio tags, Bluetooth, DECT and WLAN, enable all intelligent devices to be networked. The intelligent homes of the future will be based on these standards. Terminal devices will also be able to set up an ad hoc network in order to work together. So far, Europe has been the driving force behind these technologies, with the USA still lagging behind a little (see figure 37).

There are already more mobile phone users than landline users, and surveys of trends indicate that in future we will be surfing the Internet more from our mobile phones than from our computers.

The first applications for UMTS networks are already upon us: location-based services, video telephony, improved WAP (Wireless Application Protocol) and video streaming. Mobile office services, online games and video surveillance are also available. Other trend-setting applications are local television programs, video conferences, chat and music streaming.

Although there are still some doubts about the business plans for UMTS, work is already underway on the next mobile network generation. The 4th generation mobile network is expected after 2012, promising speeds of

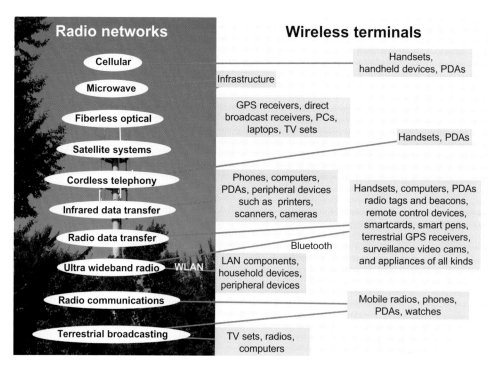

Figure 36 Mobile networks

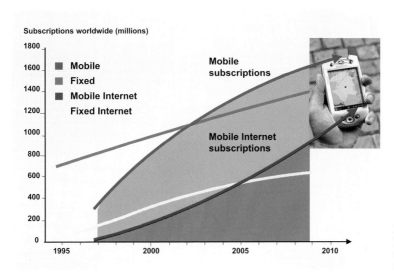

Subscriptions worldwide (millions)

Mobile
Fixed
Mobile Internet
Fixed Internet

Mobile
subscriptions

Mobile Internet
subscriptions

Figure 37
Mobile Internet
access will domi-
nate

10 to 100 Mbps. This only needs to be increased by a factor of two to reach "hi-fi" quality for all our senses.

The ad hoc networks mentioned above are a really clever idea, involving mobile devices that network with each other autonomously and exchange information. So don't be surprised in the future if your increasingly intelligent equipment starts talking about you!

Internet

The Internet is the most important platform in the information and communication industry, and, as such, it is accelerating the process of fusion taking place between the previously separate worlds of information technology, telecommunications, media and entertainment. In the next ten years it is likely that the world's entire stock of public knowledge, including all its historical documents, will have gone digital. All the world's books, pieces of music, pictures, publications and so on will be available on the Web (see figure 38). And in order to cope with the immense flow of information this will entail, we will need powerful, reliable networks.

If we compare the development of landline and mobile applications since the nineties, we can see that landline applications have always appeared before the equivalent mobile applications. The reason for this is that landline networks have always had a lead over mobile networks in terms of functionality, speed and costs. Thus, in each case, the transmission of text, pictures and audio and video files became possible over mobile networks 3 to 5 years after landline networks. But mobile networks catch up.

We live in a fast-moving age. Daily we learn about new technologies, products, company startups, mergers, joint ventures and alliances.

The rate of change is increasing day by day.

It may be difficult for us to grasp the consequences of this increasing rate of change, but it is illustrated clearly in figure 39. New media catch on

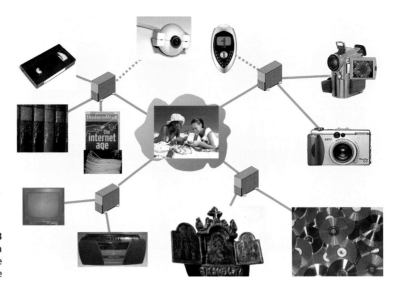

much more quickly now than they used to. It took 90 years before the telephone had 50 million users. The mobile phone, on the other hand, reached the same total in eleven years, while the Internet took only five.

Some suspect that the Internet age is already beyond its peak following the industry's slump in 2001 and 2002 and the slower growth in Internet hosts, as shown by figure 40. The number of Web pages was obtained on the basis of a comprehensive analysis of domain names and includes the pages of organizations and companies as well as private individuals. The statistics

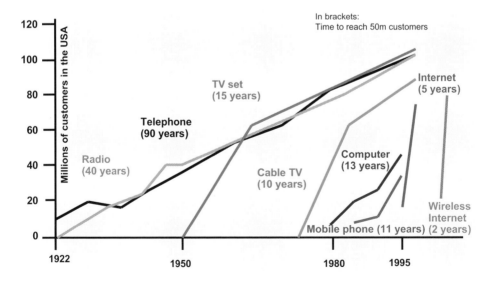

Figure 39   Penetration of the US market by information and communication technology

Millions of Internet domain hosts

Old	
Adapted	
New	

Source: http://www.isc.org/

Figure 40
Internet growth

are published by the Internet Software Consortium, a non-profit-making organization.

Even when all public domain knowledge is digitized, the Internet will still be far from complete. It will still be a number of years after that before broadband access is available everywhere.

Next-generation networks

Building the Internet of the next generation will require expertise in voice transmission (i.e. telecommunications) in addition to the existing expertise in data transmission that we already have from the Internet.

There is no doubt that voice transmission will set the standards for the convergence of data and voice networks. This is because it is much more difficult for today's data specialists to transmit voice traffic using the Internet Protocol (IP) than it is for voice specialists to transmit data. The reasons for this are historical.

Switching technology in telecommunications has developed at a terrific rate since the invention of the telegraph in 1840. In 1884 telephone calls were still switched by hand, but the first automatic switching systems came onto the market as of 1935, which marked the advent of electromechanical switching systems. Analog switching technologies dominated the market for a short time in the mid-seventies, but once digital switching became available at the end of the seventies, the revolution of modern, packet-oriented router systems kicked in. Data packet-oriented networks such as Ethernet emerged in the field of computer networking. So as far as stability, reliability and security are concerned, the Internet does not yet come up to the standards of the telephone.

We need a better Internet – the Internet of the next generation – that is as reliable as the telephone, as powerful as the computer and, perhaps, as mobile as the mobile phone.

Expertise in the field of voice transmission is of crucial importance because it is voice transmission rather than data transmission that will set the standards – both technical and commercial – for the convergence of voice and data transmission. Standards – in terms of reliability, service quality and real-time transmission – are significantly higher for voice transmission.

What are the forces shaping the networks of the next generation?

- To start with, there are the technological advances in multiplexing, computer performance and intelligent systems, for example.
- In addition, optical networks and the growing scope of wireless communication are raising network capacities.
- However, with their increasing demands for mobility and greater bandwidths, consumers are also playing their part.
- Governments and regulatory authorities are demanding general access to networks, which they want to achieve through deregulation and privatization.
- Further driving forces are applications, services and interactive multimedia services, since new applications will have to be developed for communication between machines in the course of the conversion of all data and voice traffic to IP.

Convergence In spite of all the efforts being made to achieve convergence between data and voice networks, a supernetwork to meet all needs cannot be expected to emerge in the near future. If experience is anything to go by, there is no reason to expect that one network technology will replace all others. As history has shown, electronic media have not replaced print media, for example. Similarly, televisions and video recorders have not replaced the cinema, television has not replaced radio and so on. But one thing is certain: all media will be digital.

Instead, different technologies exist side by side and may even complement each other and lead to new cases of media convergence: cameras that can work as telephones, for example, televisions that can surf the Internet or telephones that can also shoot films. This principle of coexistence also applies to the field of telecommunications.

In the final analysis, only what meets the needs of consumers and businesses will really catch on. And generally that is something simple that works reliably.

Today's Internet is a cheap version of what we can expect in the future. The Internet of the future will bring entirely new qualities to the table. Ultimately, it will have to be characterized by the following attributes: always-on access, ubiquity, speed, multi-media, multi-sensor, reliability, simplicity, intelligence and, of course, intuitive handling.

Terminal devices

As already mentioned, networks are being further developed in order to provide us with a fuller sensory experience. Local output devices such as televisions, computers and game consoles provide good image quality on large screens, and large flat screens or beamers have now reached the home market. Although they are still relatively expensive, prices are falling. Moreover, their resolution and brightness will continue to improve, so they are serious contenders to supersede today's televisions. Based on these, the first really good 3D projectors are already emerging, taking us closer to virtual reality. The first virtual meetings and lectures have been well received.

Multifunctional mobile devices will soon be stealing the limelight (see figure 41). What will they look like? At first glance they may not be noticeable, as they are likely to be incorporated in a watch, a piece of jewelry or a jacket. This development illustrates how the information and communication terminal device industry has long since moved on from being simply a branch of the manufacturing industry into the sphere of consumer goods and even the fashion industry.

Multifunctional mobile devices

This has had a dramatic effect on the business models of manufacturers. Marketing costs, for example, are much higher for consumer goods and fashion, while product life cycles are shorter. In addition, mobile devices are set to gain market share compared to computers. It is conceivable, for example, that a consumer (or household) might have only one computer but a range of mobile devices: jacket with an integrated mobile phone and MP3 player, for example, a watch that includes functions for monitoring health data or mobile devices for playing games (see figure 42). However, we do not yet have any convincing solutions for the small screens of mobile devices.

Engineers throughout the world are working toward producing images that will do justice to our vision. As part of this, they will have to put high-resolution images on mobile devices.

Support through mobile devices

Take, for example, an aircraft repair engineer. A mobile device provides him with information from the operating manual on a small screen mounted right by his eyes. This leaves his hands free for the actual repair work. This is good news for all air travelers. It means the captain will no longer shut off the engine that is still working rather than the one that is on fire simply because the engineer wired two sensors incorrectly.

Figure 41
Innovative mobile devices

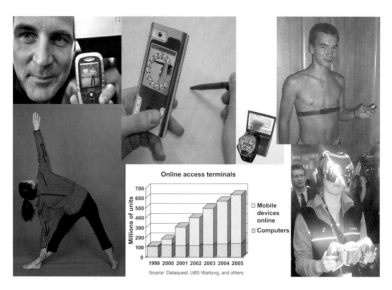

Figure 42
Mobile devices
become wearable

As this example shows, human skills will be supported by the full spectrum of information and communication technologies. Together with a number of other companies, Siemens has developed a concept for the specialists of the future. The aim of this project is to use information and communication technologies – augmented reality, for example, which involves overlaying text and graphical information onto the objects within your field of vision – to accelerate work processes and reduce errors (see figure 43).

3D devices

Mobile devices will soon be able to display 3D images. Helmets and consoles with 3D displays will enhance the effect of virtual reality games, for example.

Electronic boards

Electronic boards and pens are already in use. An electronic board can show what you yourself and another person perhaps many thousands of miles away are drawing. Changes are displayed immediately, and all those involved always see the same overall picture.

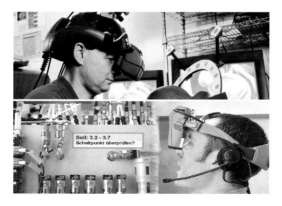

Figure 43
Wearable mobile
devices make it
easier to work

Looking at the future on the basis of current trends

Whereas in the nineties it was initially all about simply being able to use a phone on the move, the size of mobile phones subsequently developed into the critical factor. The smallest phones sold like hot cakes. The next big step was the addition of features such as SMS texting, games and personal organizer functions. As the phones began to make big inroads into the consumer market, prices sank and the brand became the key factor. Each new model seemed to follow another new fashionable trend. In the meantime, the applications have become an important criterion in the decision for or against a particular phone, and this makes it easier for manufacturers to differentiate their phones from those of their competitors.

Personalized devices

Mobile devices are becoming our constant companions. New functions will continue to be added to them: always-on online access, location-based functionality and new security and personalization features, for example. Network operators and service providers around the world are constantly on the lookout for profitable new services – "killer" applications – because the fact is that basic broadband services such as file downloading from the Internet simply will not earn the network operators what they need to finance the investments to be made in the networks of the next generation.

In addition to the sending of SMS (Short Message Service) text messages, e-mails and multimedia messages with pictures and sound, mobile devices will soon boast a wealth of additional functions. You will also be able to pay with them, for example. Whether you are in a restaurant, a shop or on the road, you will be able to settle the bill using your mobile phone. Mobile devices will also be able to function as a kind of identification, with jewelry such as rings, chains or watches having built-in intelligence and offering the functionality of keys, wallets or mobile phones.

As a result of improved sensors and increased processing power, terminal devices of all kinds will develop the capability to behave situation-dependently. Corresponding services will then be offered proactively.

Today's terminal devices will no doubt eventually be joined by devices that have not yet even been thought of. Meanwhile, devices that are already familiar to us will increasingly be networked. In addition to information and communication devices like telephones, PCs and PDAs, media devices such as televisions and video cameras will be among the first. But it will certainly not end there.

Growth of networking set to continue

In future it will be possible to connect up all kinds of devices, machines and objects, among them cars, trucks, containers, packages, diagnostic devices in medicine and household appliances.

You will be able to find out, for instance, whether the iron is switched off, whether the central heating is on or what you have in the refrigerator without actually having to be there. Today this is still a technical challenge; tomorrow it won't be.

Progress is being made all the time in the field of medicine. New, smaller analytical devices are constantly being developed and providing more accurate data (see figure 44). In the future they will be able to transmit important data from within the body by means of small transponders. And at some point in the future, as indicated by the timeline earlier in the book, it

Transfer of medical data

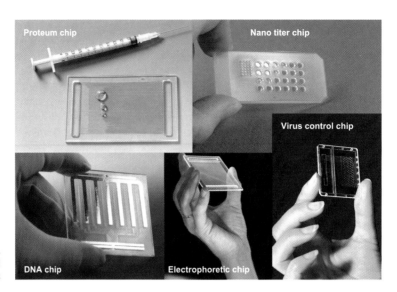

might be possible for us to have a digital aura, allowing us to communicate by telepathy.

It is difficult to say with any degree of certainty that a given object or device will not be networked as a terminal device in the future. What this means in effect is that the future will provide us with an increasingly accurate representation of reality online.

Digital photography and video technology

Much is changing in the world of photography and video as well. Figure 45 shows how the resolution of digital cameras and camcorders is improving. These form a platform for a new kind of personal communication, because increasingly we will be sending each other multimedia messages. Pictures and videos are already beginning to play a more significant role in communication. The trend is still only in its initial stages, and the huge volumes of data generated will have to be transported somehow, but it provides further evidence of converging functionalities.

IP convergence

It can already be seen that the functionalities of many terminal devices are converging. Sooner or later all of them – telephones, PCs, computers, televisions, radios, cameras, video cameras, game consoles, photocopiers, scanners, household appliances, hi-fi systems, medical devices, cars and robots – will be speaking the same language: IP.

Essentially, anything that can be connected to a power socket or run on batteries is a candidate for speaking IP. And the number of IP-networked devices is growing exponentially. There are now more processors in the world than people, and they will soon be computing and communicating with each other in every sphere imaginable. Hopefully we will reach a point where we will simply be able to tell our video or DVD recorders what it is we want in whatever language it is we speak.

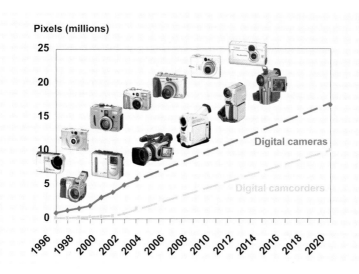

Pixels (millions)

Digital cameras

Digital camcorders

1996 1998 2000 2002 2004 2006 2008 2010 2012 2014 2016 2018 2020

Figure 45
Picture quality is improving

Biotechnology

Whereas chemists have been working at the molecular level for many years and physicists have been splitting and fusing atoms for over 50 years, it is only recently that biologists have started to look into such minute structures. Moving on from cellular and molecular biology, they are now immersing themselves increasingly in the analysis and composition of the basic building blocks of life – above all, DNA.

Some time this century we can expect a holistic approach uniting biological principles, chemical properties and physical laws.

Figure 46 shows some of the fields that will be associated even more closely with biotechnology in the future.

To make further progress in biotechnology, we will not only have to decipher the programming language of our genes, DNA, but also to understand it. Only then will we be able to make replacement organs in biological incubators and nip illnesses in the bud.

Other challenges present themselves in the field of biological operating systems and their applications in cells and groups of cells. The convergence of biological and information systems is already evident today, as we have seen with biochips and DNA computers.

Intelligent biotechnology is seen by many as an opportunity to solve power supply problems, free ourselves of much pollution and reduce suffering.

Biologists in different fields of research are attempting to answer a wide variety of questions, such as:

• Why should it not be possible to obtain hydrogen from bacteria?
• Why should biosystems not be in a position to filter CO_2 and other pollutants out of the air, water and ground?

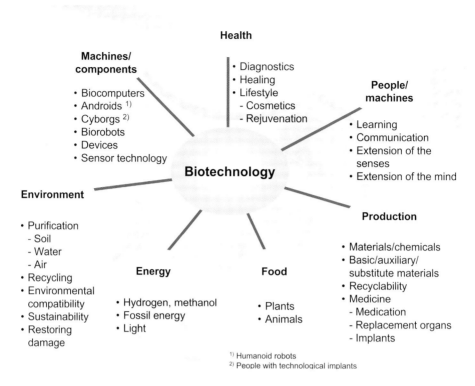

Health

- Diagnostics
- Healing
- Lifestyle
  - Cosmetics
  - Rejuvenation

Machines/ components

- Biocomputers
- Androids [1]
- Cyborgs [2]
- Biorobots
- Devices
- Sensor technology

People/ machines

- Learning
- Communication
- Extension of the senses
- Extension of the mind

Biotechnology

Environment

- Purification
  - Soil
  - Water
  - Air
- Recycling
- Environmental compatibility
- Sustainability
- Restoring damage

Energy

- Hydrogen, methanol
- Fossil energy
- Light

Food

- Plants
- Animals

Production

- Materials/chemicals
- Basic/auxiliary/ substitute materials
- Recyclability
- Medicine
  - Medication
  - Replacement organs
  - Implants

[1] Humanoid robots
[2] People with technological implants

Figure 46   Biotechnology: fields for the future

- Could non-desalinated seawater be used in desert areas to create new ecological cycles from which we could then obtain basic substances for which we need mineral oil today?

Biotechnologists will be seeking answers to these questions and weighing up the chances and risks involved.

At this point we come to the end of our journey into the future. It is worth emphasizing that it is not so important to be able to predict the future accurately; the important thing is to be prepared for the future in order to be able to play a part in shaping it.

Looking at the future on the basis of current trends – conclusion

- The rate of innovation is accelerating.
- The underlying exponential increase in the rate of change is beyond anything we have experienced before and is therefore generally underestimated.
- The previous boundaries between industries and research disciplines are fading.

- The range of possibilities for the use of new technologies is huge, and at the same time these technologies are converging. As disciplines come closer together, they benefit from mutual progress.
- Nanotechnology will create myriads of innovations across all technological disciplines.
- Moore's law is accelerating the process of deciphering DNA and thus the rate of progress in biology, which in turn has the potential to create a new era.

The challenge is to develop the right, sustainable products and services for both humankind and the planet. In the business world we inevitably have to ask ourselves what this means for our own company, leading us to form new objectives and strategies, followed by actions.

The different spheres of our lives

Our lives take place in a number of different spheres. We will be examining these briefly below and taking a look at what our lives might be like in these different spheres in the future.

Among the factors driving future developments are the desires for security and reliability, time and cost savings, increased convenience and improved quality of life. Factors hampering these developments include complexity, the absence of standards and poor service. The drivers of change are the technologies mentioned in the previous chapter and the continued development of these technologies.

It is safe to assume that consumers will have at their disposal an intelligent Internet providing location-based information. Internet search engines will answer users' queries precisely, without overwhelming them with a vast number of hyperlinks. We will each have a personal agent that knows our preferences. Routine, everyday mental work will increasingly be done by intelligent personal systems, and we will benefit from reliable protection and safety systems in our surroundings. Moreover, business hours will no longer be a limiting factor because nearly all transactions will be conducted electronically.

At home

As things stand, our homes are still really not very smart. They have virtually nothing that is system-supported or runs automatically. The home does not issue the homeowner with any warnings or report any faults. Although intelligent devices are now finding their way into our homes, they are not networked so while they may be getting smarter, they essentially remain what they were before: PCs, televisions with Internet connections, scales, central heating control systems, weather stations, refrigerators, mobile phones and so on – with the associated proliferation of cables. When something is broken, the repair man generally has to come more than once. After all, the device needs to be assessed and taken apart, and replacement parts need to be ordered before it can be repaired and possibly improved.

Gradually all this bother is going to be consigned to the past, although there are bound to be a few abortive attempts before the hurdle is finally cleared and the smart house actually becomes a reality, but there is every chance we will be there before the year 2020. Let's look at what that might involve for a fictitious character, who we will call John Smith.

Following a heavy fall of snow, John Smith's alarm clock rings 30 minutes earlier than usual because it has received all the latest information on the weather from an online weather report service and his barometer and thermometer. This gives John enough time to clear the snow from his drive and make his way to work bang on time. Before he has breakfast, the scales report his current weight to the refrigerator, which consequently keeps the butter tray locked. As he is leaving the house, he receives a short message telling him that the refrigerator has not switched off. When he investigates, he finds that the door was not closed properly. Once he is on the road in his car, he is not sure whether he switched the television off. He contacts the central control system, which informs him that the television is on standby. Thanks to his home's automatic central locking system, there is no chance of any windows being left open or doors being left unlocked. Lights are switched off automatically. Even when John is not at home, there is still much going on there: Robots vacuum the carpets or mow the lawn in summer; thanks to smart labels his stocks of food, drink and consumables are monitored and order lists created that he later merely has to confirm; thanks to biometrics, no strangers can get into the house – except any tradesmen or repair engineers with whom appointments have been arranged; and thanks to remote advance diagnostics, repair engineers come with the correct replacement parts and tools and quickly deal with any problem. If any new problems occur, the monitoring system contacts John Smith automatically so that he can take the necessary action as quickly as possible.

There is much more that could be said about the home of the future. We could, for example, talk about the large projection walls that can connect John to his colleagues at work or his parents in their living room, almost as if they were right there with him. The home can thus be transformed into a teleworking office, a telelearning workshop, a party venue, a virtual amusement arcade, an eldorado in which he can pursue his favorite hobby or a health center with diagnostic, preventive and treatment facilities. The home of the future will cater increasingly for our security, health and con-

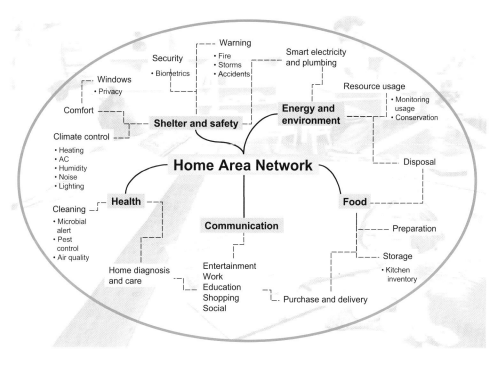

The networked home   **Figure 47**

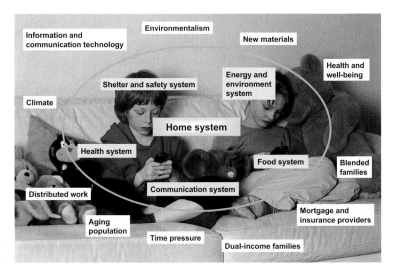

Figure 48
The smart home

venience as well as help us to make savings. It will also allow us the opportunity to enjoy mobility without losing contact (see figure 47).

Much of the convenience gained is the result of the fact that the house looks after both us and itself. The backbone of the smart home is formed by the networking of all the essential terminal devices, which can extend their sphere of activity by means of wireless communication with other products. An important prerequisite for this is, of course, the standardization of a common language for all devices. The current barriers between white, brown and gray goods (kitchen appliances, hi-fi systems and PCs) are impeding progress.

The house of the future will adapt itself to our needs as we grow older and help us with our hobbies, regardless of whether it is gardening, music or painting that we enjoy. The smart home will thus help us with our self-development as well as work-related activities (see figure 48).

New technologies will also influence how we spend our leisure time together. Only a few years ago an afternoon with the children might have meant a game of cards, monopoly, dominoes or chess (if we weren't watching television). Then came the GameBoy and PlayStation boom. What will the future bring? Interactive games with mobile devices that transport our children into virtual worlds?

At work

We'll deal later with the details of how the actual work that we do will change, but first we are going to take a closer look at the environment in which work will take place.

Let's accompany John Smith to work. On the way to the office he has his new e-mails and his schedule for the day read out to him. Thoroughly well prepared, he enters the office, which looks more like a landscaped garden and includes workspaces, communication zones and niches for meetings. In a few hours, John has to travel to a customer event at which he has to give a presentation. In the presentation he will have to give some time and attention to the various customers in attendance so he displays the personal profiles of his audience and adapts his presentation accordingly. He then loads the 5-GB presentation document onto his personal memory stick. Because his voice is a little hoarse today, he chooses the playback option, which plays back a recorded, audio version of the prepared text for the films and pictures should his voice let him down. This reassures him greatly. Less reassuring, however, is a preliminary meeting in preparation for an appointment with another customer. The service engineer on site puts on his stereo camera spectacles and shows the problems that have occurred to all those involved in the meeting, who see the pictures on a projection wall. It is unclear whether it is a hardware or software problem that has almost brought the customer's process chain to a standstill. John uses his electronic assistant to put a virtual ad hoc team together. The criteria for selection are that the people must have the key skills required and be available immediately. In a short video conference with the team, John explains the customer's activities and the importance of the project and distributes the service engineer's stereo video report. Everything he says in his explanation is simultaneously transformed into stylistically correct text and forms part of the project documentation. He then leaves the office to go to the airport.

So much for the working life of John Smith. Figure 49 shows some of the trends that will affect employees and the workplace and what their interrelationships will be. While not all the trends and groups of people involved are shown, you do gain an impression of the complexity of the relationships involved.

Some of the trends are already clear because we know how they have developed in the past and can follow their progress in the present:

- Mass production ➔ small production units
- Standardization ➔ production to specification
- Hierarchies ➔ teams
- Job security based on age ➔ job security based on capabilities
- Limited competition ➔ global competition
- Social benefits linked to employer ➔ flexible social benefits
- Payment on the basis of years of employment ➔ payment on the basis of performance and results
- Large, bureaucratic organizations ➔ smaller, more flexible organizations
- Competitive standards based on costs ➔ competitive standards based on quality and punctuality
- Homogeneous working class ➔ diversified specialists
- Learning for a limited period ➔ lifelong learning
- Integrated companies ➔ alliances of core competencies

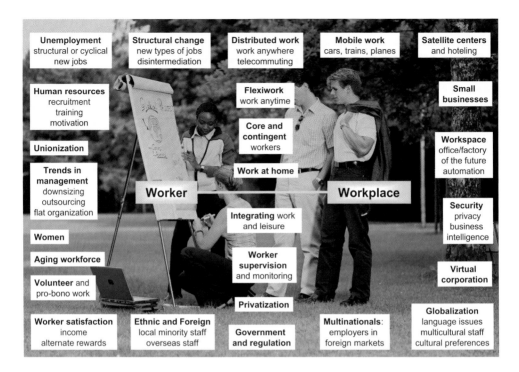

Figure 49   Employees and the workplace

As a result of increasing globalization and new, electronic ways of conducting business, company locations will become less fixed and jobs will become more flexible and less secure.

The same trend has been evident for some time now in global flows of capital. In future, conditions for business in different locations will play a central role in companies' decision-making. Hard factors such as infrastructure, legislation, taxes, personnel costs, flexibility to hire and fire, suppliers, customers and skills levels will, of course, affect the decisions of both individual companies and large corporate groups about where to do business. However, soft factors such as positive and inspiring government visions, the reliability of the authorities and business partners and the financial support available for new businesses are becoming increasingly important.

Countries that exert a positive influence on both the hard and soft factors can gain a competitive edge in the knowledge-based economy. High employment rates, low taxes and other statutory costs and a low level of debt are the virtually automatic result.

On the move

Around 20% of the world's energy consumption is accounted for by transportation. The reason for this is that all over the world, whether we are old or young, rich or poor, we spend an average of an hour a day on the move.

Most of us make three or four journeys a day. In addition, we go on three to four trips a year, spending between 11% and 14% of our annual income in the process – in the developed countries, at any rate. There are strong regional differences in the means of transportation used, but statistics tell us that Germans, for example, travel by plane once a year.

Means of transportation play an important role in our lives.

As materials become increasingly light, stable and recyclable, construction methods will change. The efficiency of engines will improve continuously (although there are clear physical limits). Consequently, fewer raw materials will be required in their manufacture, and less fuel will be required to run them. The use of hybrid engines in cars could reduce pollution in urban areas, where engines could be run entirely on electricity or hydrogen fuel cells. However, the costs of using such hybrid engines are still too high today.

As our means of transportation improve in efficiency, they will produce less pollution and noise. More precise information on traffic volumes and active traffic control will enable traffic flows and route utilization to be optimized.

Cars, planes, trains and ships are already very intelligent systems, but they are nevertheless still rapidly improving thanks to advances in microelectronics. Consequently, they are becoming increasingly smart and autonomous. Means of transportation such as ships and trains will soon make use of fully automatic navigation systems, following the trend set by autopilots in airplanes. The role of captains, train drivers and pilots will be restricted to one of monitoring operation and intervening in unusual traffic situations.

So how is John Smith doing on his way to the airport? Being something of a technology freak, he has all kinds of technical accessories in his car, and these are helpful to him today. To begin with, his car's navigation system suggests an uncongested route to him. It also checks whether it would be quicker under the present circumstances to head for the nearest train station and use public transportation. Since in this case it wouldn't be, John hands over control to the car's autopilot, which keeps a safe distance from the car in front, taking the weather conditions into account, and adheres exactly to the speed limits indicated on the road signs. There is thick fog and the road markings cannot be detected so the autopilot hands control of the steering wheel back to the driver. At the same time, an infrared camera projects an image of the road ahead onto the windshield. The car monitors the driver's attentiveness regularly and issues a loud warning sound immediately it detects any sign of fatigue. John wants to make better progress and overtake the car in front, but the steering wheel does not allow itself to be moved easily and a yellow exclamation mark flashes on the windshield. This means that the inter-vehicle communication system has either detected a vehicle overtaking from behind or a vehicle approaching at high speed from the opposite direction. John is well advised in this situation to listen to what his car is telling him.

Before John arrives at the airport, let's take a look at some of the other extras in his car. When driving at night, for example, the driver and passengers can enjoy photo-realistic displays of the environment. The anti-theft system is totally secure. The car knows John's mobile phone number and won't allow itself to be opened by anyone else. It also sends signals to approaching vehicles, thus enabling their drivers to respond. An automatic emergency calling facility and a system that provides an initial assessment of any damage complete the safety package. The on-board computer records any problems that occur or signs of wear that become evident during the journey. A mobile service engineer can be called at any time before a serious problem arises. Systems like this are already being developed.

John arrives at the airport and is guided to a free parking space. Because he is alone, he makes use of the fully automatic parking system, which most men tend to reject as a matter of pride. The fuel consumption indicator stands at 105 miles per gallon, which seems about right.

At this point we leave John Smith again to turn our attention to figure 50, which shows how many factors have an influence on the vehicle as a system.

By around the year 2010, cars will be able to prevent collisions, identify obstacles and help to avoid dangerous driving situations. Cameras and a proliferation of sensors will monitor the immediate and medium-range surroundings and communicate with them. The risk of accidents will thus be

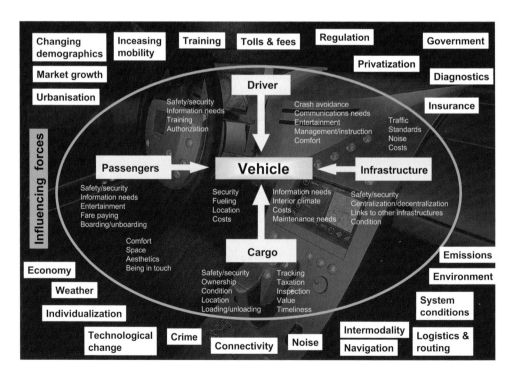

Figure 50   Variables affecting the road vehicles of the future

reduced, the allocation of parking spaces optimized, toll charges collected and goods/freight identified. But it will certainly take until the year 2020 or even longer for cars with autopilots to drive us around safely without any intervention from us. Drivers will still always bear the responsibility – at least for as long as we are required to have driving licenses!

In public

Facilities and institutions that are open to the public are already revamping their business models. It goes without saying that more people will visit museums, parks, zoos, shopping centers and theaters the more attractive they become. This is why sponsors can be found and why financing them thus becomes easier. Interactive solutions can bring an element of entertainment and fun, as well as taking into account safety requirements and health issues. Virtual reality, animation and dramatic simulations are the core elements of such solutions.

Let's go back to John Smith for the last time. In the airport lounge he identifies himself at his work portal using a voice recognition system. A short video mail informs him that the customer's problem has been localized and work is currently underway on the solution. He contacts his family via live video conference, and his daughter expresses a wish for new dancing shoes with batteries that recharge when you walk in them. He has his personal electronic assistant research prices and availability nationwide and finds out that for 150 euros he can either pick up the shoes at his destination airport or have them sent to his home. He makes his choice and continues on his way. On the plane he checks to see which friends he hasn't been in contact with for a long time and sends them his greetings together with a short film of his family's last weekend outing. Then he starts his personal learning program for Chinese. Shortly before landing he plans his evening. After viewing film clips of the current offerings at the theater, he decides on a musical and buys a ticket in the middle of row 10. In the taxi from the airport he watches a short video on the history of the city he's in on his PDA. He can use information from it in his presentation. But now it's time to leave John Smith, whose presentation actually went down very well with his audience in spite of his hoarseness.

Fields of application

Health

Health and medical care will benefit from huge technological advances in the years to come. Preventive medicine, health monitoring and aftercare will gradually be freed from geographical constraints. It will be possible to monitor certain aspects of our bodies while we are on the move in order to generate warnings in good time or indicate the need for preventive measures.

Mobile devices will become personal health managers that function as interfaces to medical services and databases as well as guides to pharmacies, doctors or health facilities. Mobile health management will allow us to access information, make appointments and contact call centers.

But it is not just patients who will become more mobile. As a result of the improved performance and, at the same time, further miniaturization of medical devices, the mobility of medical care itself will increase. And it is not just people in remote areas who will benefit from this.

As in anything else, costs do, of course, play an essential role in health care, since it is generally financed through a central organization or organizations (at least in Europe). As a result of cost pressure, some developments will proceed more slowly than is technically possible, but cost pressure will never actually stop new development. It may be appropriate to ask ethical questions, but they have to be answered by taking a global view, and while some countries – perhaps rightly – will struggle to prevent certain new technologies being used, others will gladly proceed with them. So the following is clear:

Technological development is oriented toward those who are ready to accept the new.

Figure 51 provides an outline of a healthcare system, giving some impression of its complexity.

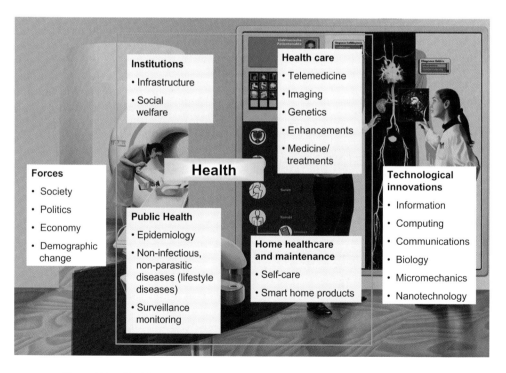

Figure 51   Healthcare system

The different spheres of our lives

Health management offers huge potential for making savings. For example, although the various institutions involved in healthcare now possess a physical network, this network is not used to optimum effect. The information flows between doctors, consultants, hospitals, insurance companies and patients are chaotic – more like a flood than a flow. Yet taking the step toward standardized, cost-effective processes would not be difficult. An institution could then access the health data it required and quickly take the necessary action. If telemedicine were implemented, the costs for frequent and labor-intensive examinations in hospital could be reduced and patients would remain in the care of their family doctor.

In many western countries we, the patients, are having to pay an increasingly large proportion of our health costs ourselves, so it is very much in our interests that processes are rationalized and thus become more cost-effective. As computers and application software become more powerful, it will become easier for us to carry out standard examinations ourselves at home. We ourselves notice changes in the state of our health sooner than anyone else, after all. Using a PC and the Internet, we could make our own diagnosis – or at least an initial diagnosis – in order to decide on further action and get some advice on suitable forms of treatment. In most cases involving minor complaints and everyday aches and pains, we would be able to treat ourselves.

So what does the future hold for us? Let's begin by taking a look at our life cycle in the year 2012 (see figure 52).

- Networked with OBGYN/ health center
- Bedside monitors and sensors for home prenatal care
- Home area network answers frequently asked questions (FAQ)

- Crib monitor for vital signs, infectious bacteria levels
- Two-way video link with work, day care
- Biofeedback for seizures and allergies
- Smart card for child kept by parents

- Wearable to track whereabouts
- Toys to detect developmental disorders
- Home health kits with interactive instructions for emergencies/ accidents

- Secure interactive sessions, e.g.: sensitive topics such as sex ed
- Smart card with health history, genetic profile

- Wearable calorie and cholesterol monitors
- Home scanning for common illnesses
- Monthly reports by monitors for health trends analyses

- Bed monitor for vital signs
- Ad lib contact with knowbots to answer health questions
- Smart pharmaceutical dispensers
- Control over life cessation via internal monitors

Life cycle in the year 2012   **Figure 52**

In addition to the forms of continuous health care described above, there will be an increasing number of health services available to consumers. Standard procedures to correct short-sightedness will be carried out at the local health store. Gene therapies will be used to rejuvenate the body. Individual organs will be replaced with new ones grown from the patient's own or stem cells. Many cosmetic operations will be carried out to ensure people continue to look younger than their years. The leaner, affordable healthcare systems described at the beginning of this section will also endeavor to ensure we have a healthy diet. Pill-sized microrobots will be able to report health-related values from inside our bodies. Other electronic pills with sensors will be able to administer drugs in the dosage required to achieve the optimum effect.

Prevention is always better than cure. In the field of diagnostics and prevention, in particular, there is a great variety of possible uses for modern biotechnology. However, there is also much demand for human replacement parts such as skin, lungs, livers, hearts, stomachs, intestines or spleens, as well as bones, joints, muscles and blood. Here the aim is to grow these parts either from the patient's own cells or stem cells or by using other host organisms (xenotransplantation).

The trend toward minimizing invasive surgery will continue. Microrobots in the body will take on analytical and therapeutic functions. NASA and Xerox PARC are already carrying out research into nanomachines that will be able to clean out our arteries or destroy tumors. In the field of drug research, the trend is toward smart pills that can administer the appropriate dosage of a drug independently, as required. Thus, everything possible is being done to increase our life expectancy as well as our quality of life in the longer-term future.

To speed up this development, it is time that healthcare providers looked upon us as customers rather than patients.

Doctors   Figure 53 illustrates the new developments affecting doctors.

Doctors will increasingly be faced with patients/customers who are knowledgeable about their state of health and symptoms and have already obtained relevant information on the Internet. A small, knowledge-based PC system may have already carried out an initial diagnosis of the customer's health problem by means of a series of standard questions. And a networked laboratory chip may have already examined a drop of blood and carried out initial analyses.

In the year 20XX the same rules will apply to the health-care industry as apply to other industries today. The industry will have to comply with global standards and will only achieve success by means of positive branding. A keen focus on customer and service orientation combined with a high degree of effectiveness and efficiency will be imperative in the future.

Leisure and entertainment

Let's consider for a moment how we spend our leisure time today. However old we are, there is plenty for us to do and enjoy with our friends and family. There are already many ways for us to amuse ourselves in the real world. At home we can watch TV or videos, browse the Internet, look

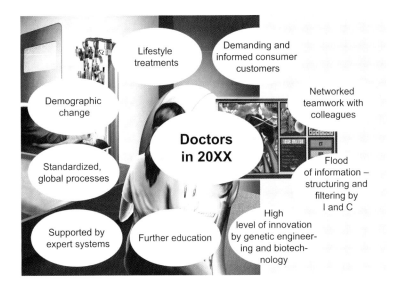

Figure 53
Developments
affecting doctors in
the year 20XX

at photographs, listen to music, read books or newspapers, eat and drink, play computer, card and board games, do crossword and jigsaw puzzles, improve our gardens or balconies, take a bath, shower or sauna, laze about, make music, sit around chatting or pursue any of a wide range of hobbies. Outside the home we can go for a meal or to museums, parks, cinemas, theaters or other attractions, go for a walk or play a huge variety of sports. Much of this will hardly change in the future.

As a result of the convergence of audio, video, media and PCs, the boundaries between the real world and virtual worlds are beginning to fade, as shown in figure 53. The home is developing into an information center, from where – thanks to webcams – we can, for example, observe the stork in its nest on the roof of the town hall or check out the weather at our weekend destination. Computer games offer us realistic simulations of the real world. Virtual aircraft, trains, cars and people move around in worlds that look increasingly natural as time goes on and the technology improves. In the future we may be able to play these games with robots.

The virtual world

Without leaving home, we will soon be able to cycle through astonishingly real-looking mountain scenery on our exercise bikes. We will feel the incline of the road in our legs, and the smells of nature will be produced by smell generators. If we want to play tennis at home, we will be able to put on an electronic sport suit complete with gloves, tennis shoes and many built-in sensors. The data corresponding to our movements will be recorded, and the virtual ball we hit will either fly into our opponent's court or land in the net, depending on how well we hit it. Whether we are faced with the court on a large projection wall or are wearing 3D projection spectacles will simply depend on the size of our house. We will have the option of keeping the physical effort we make within the optimum range because our bodies will be constantly monitored. The virtual coach's advice will be so good that the next time we step out on the center court in real life, we surely can't fail to win.

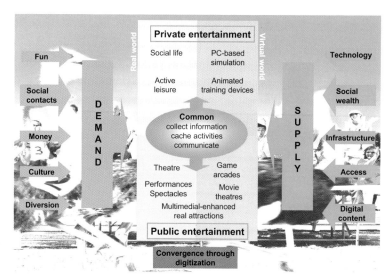

Figure 54
Some of the factors involved in the development of leisure and entertainment

If you visit an advanced amusement arcade, you can immerse yourself in a virtual world with life-sized models of racing boats, motorbikes, bobsleighs, Formula One cars or water skis, for example. Alternatively, you can overcome dark forces and fight evil like a Star Wars hero. Every year the special effects improve and the simulations appear more real. It's easy to imagine a time when they deceive us almost completely.

Museums will soon also become more attractive, with each picture and sculpture able to tell us the story behind it. In zoos there will be information kiosks showing pictures of animals' homes both above and below ground. Some animals will have cameras attached to them, thus allowing us to follow their movements. Trees and shrubs will also be able to tell you about themselves. The better these animations become, the more visitors will be attracted. The more customers pay, the more money there will be for reinvesting. To this can be added funding from sponsors and advertising revenue.

Figure 54 shows some of the factors involved in the development of leisure and entertainment.

Learning

We never stop learning as long as we live. Experiences, books, photographs, films and games broaden our horizons daily. The volume of new knowledge we are having to keep up with is growing all the time. In the next 7 to 10 years alone, as much new knowledge will be produced as in the previous 2000 years. As a result of the increasing rate of innovation and shorter and shorter development cycles, knowledge quickly becomes obsolete, while at the same time we are receiving more and more information via the Internet, radio, television and CD/DVD, often in a multimedia format.

We have to learn to process this deluge of information actively in order to draw any benefit from it. In this context, it becomes increasingly important to develop the ability to make connections, create knowledge out of information and deal pragmatically with contradictory data and facts. However, we are left with precious little time for conscious learning.

We can only solve this dilemma by developing well-targeted, effective and efficient ways of working, something that we will be looking at later in the section entitled "Me Inc." The information technologies that have put us in this difficult situation must now help us to master it.

There is no doubt they are perfectly capable of doing this, as figure 55 shows. The rate of progress today is being slowed, above all, by cultural mores, traditions and plain rejection. Educators, teachers, tutors and trainers are still using much the same methods as they did 50 years ago, and it is time to take a more modern approach.

It is becoming apparent that children are likely to start going to school at an earlier age in the future. And there will also be many different types of school to choose from. Education in schools, which is now largely the responsibility of the state, will move in the direction of becoming a profit-oriented "school industry". This will permit the financing of research programs into educational science and educational technologies. In addition, there will be a variety of schemes available to children for the time before and after school aimed at further developing their skills and abilities. Special programs of training will facilitate the transition from school to work,

New models of schooling

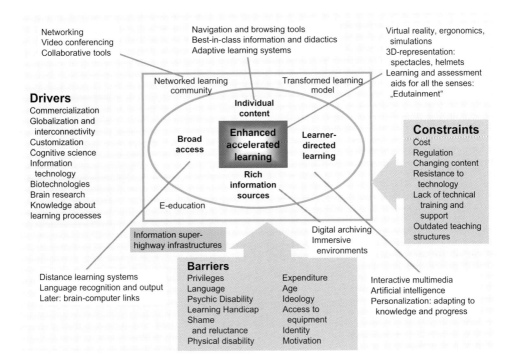

Technology-assisted education   **Figure 55**

while industry will participate in the education of its future workforce by setting up support schemes and entering into partnerships.

The shaping of balanced personalities that will enable children to come to grips with their lives as they grow older begins at the preschool level. And that's just the first of many stages. Children's adult lives will take place in another time, so it is very important to prepare them for that. As in the past, children today receive no training – or at least very little – that will help them in their everyday adult lives. Questions such as "where should I invest my money?", "how do I get the right insurance?" or "what is good for my health?" have been neglected. And there is still too little attention given to the most important aspects of everyday life, such as how to make effective use of PCs, the Internet and new media – to name but a few.

Training for individuals

However, it is not just a question of using new information and communication technologies. It is also important to implement immediately the latest findings of research into how the brain works and learning processes. Based on the findings of neurological research, we need new approaches that take due account of the differences between individuals, some of which are outlined briefly below.

Children these days come into contact with applications of the latest technology at a very young age. GameBoys are typical of the times. Increasingly, we will buy our children toys that foster the development of all parts of the brain, bears and dolls with perfect speech and exciting computer programs in the hope that these will increase their natural enthusiasm for learning. Later, brain-friendly, multimedia, interactive and team-oriented approaches will be used to foster personality development. The aim will be to target training toward minimizing weaknesses and developing natural skills and abilities. Later still, teenagers will be trained to take on responsibility and work with the latest technologies and services. A further learning objective will be to train them to find ways of solving conflict situations and overcome difficult challenges as part of a team.

These skills are all required by people working in multi-cultural teams – and later virtual teams – using global networks. In terms of their social skills, people will have to meet new and higher requirements.

It is already the case that school and university students ought to prepare themselves for a working life that involves several careers and working in a number of different spheres. By doing so they will be laying the foundations for their ability to come to grips with life in the future.

Professional training

If we are to successfully provide training that will prepare people to do new kinds of jobs on a networked planet, curriculums and syllabuses will need constant fine tuning. Electronic means can be used to allow technical or specialist subjects to be taught by the world's leading authorities, employing the most effective teaching methods. The processes involved in teaching and the jobs of teachers, professors and trainers will thus change. Globalization, competition and efficiency will play an important role here, too. Companies need to recruit the best people and keep them constantly up to speed. This applies to specialist and social skills alike. In many cases, it makes sense to train people in teams for the sake of the immediate feedback that is obtained. On the other hand, specialist subjects can often be studied alone at home or on the move. Smart learning programs will be able to adapt to the learning speed of the individual on the basis of progress made in order to ensure that the learner remains motivated and is successful.

The transition from conventional learning to the kind of learning required in the future involves the following changes:

- Teacher-centered "chalk and talk" → student-centered teamwork
- Passive learning → proactive, investigative learning
- A specialist approach → constant reference to the real world
- Listening, reading, writing → taking in, simulating, trying out
- Little use of different media → multimedia, multisensory learning
- Little appeal to the senses → a brain-friendly approach
- Teacher-student activities → teacher-student teamwork
- Referencing of the past → preparation for life in XX years
- Focus on conveying information → focus on acquisition and integration of knowledge and contextual thinking

More needs to be done to help people learn increasingly important social skills, but this will only work if people are prepared to invest time in learning them.

What modern means of communication primarily do is increase the efficiency with which we communicate information and facts; what they do not yet do is help us appeal to the emotions or build confidence.

Environmental protection

The more people there are on our planet and the higher their standard of living, the more critical the situation becomes for the environment. It is therefore essential that we do everything within our power to protect the environment and conserve resources. This includes examining every stage of a product's life cycle with a view to conserving resources and promoting sustainability and then adapting it. Figure 56 shows the stages involved in an environment-friendly product life cycle.

Satellite surveillance is useful in that it allows us to monitor changes to the earth's surface on land and at sea with increasing accuracy. Constantly improving sensors are being used that can detect forest clearing, types of cultivation und pollution of all kinds. Additional monitoring stations on the ground, in the water and in the air complete the overall picture we have of our world's ecosystem. The challenges of the future include automating the analyses that need to be carried out and coordinating the international action that needs to be taken by the relevant authorities. It is also important that serious efforts are made to predict changes to our living conditions so that we can initiate action to protect the environment as soon as possible.

Environmental monitoring

There are many sides to sustainable product design. Miniaturization saves materials. Modular designs allow faulty parts to be replaced subsequently. Platform concepts facilitate subsequent upgrading with more powerful components. Appropriate design creates durable and long-lasting prod-

Product design

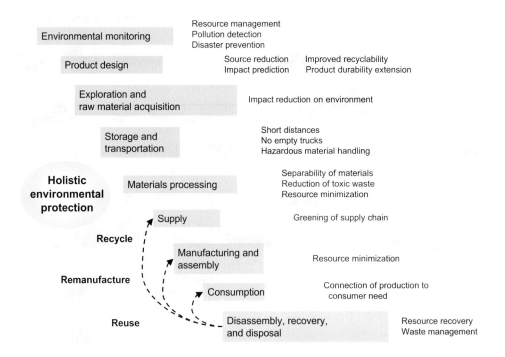

Figure 56   Environment-conscious product life cycle

ucts. The individual components of a product must be easy to replace, dismantle and separate and increasingly easy to recycle. It is also conceivable that materials could be detected automatically, e.g. by means of chips welded into them or automated material analyses.

Particular attention should be given to reducing consumption of energy, electricity, water, oil, chemicals and so on. Electricity consumption is given far too little attention today. More and more small appliances that consume electricity are leading to higher overall consumption of electricity per head. Devices that are not currently being used should not be consuming any electricity, but just try switching everything off or onto standby and then take a look at your electricity meter! The increase in per-capita electricity consumption caused by these small electricity consumers is so huge that you have to think in terms of power plant units to cover it. A few more wind turbines simply would not be enough.

Ecodesign means building more intelligence into both the product and the product development process.

Exploration   Exploration for new sources of raw materials can be electronically supported in a wide variety of ways. However, given sustainable product life cycles and closed material flows, it is relatively unimportant.

Transportation   Resources have been wasted up to now in transportation as a consequence of inadequate strategies and vehicles being sent on empty runs. Using information and communication technologies, runs can be bundled and optimized in interconnected local logistical systems.

Recycled raw materials can be prepared for reuse in production. The relevant legislation and environmental protection regulations will become increasingly stringent in the future. Large numbers of sensors (including new types) combined with more powerful computers will ensure adherence to these standards.

Material processing

The links between purchasing departments and suppliers will be improved as a result of improved networking and integration. Platforms, module outsourcing and the just-in-time concept are the key elements here. Outsourcing companies will have to meet new requirements stipulated by their customers. Additional pressure will be applied by environmental activists and ministries of the environment, which will audit manufacturers and their suppliers.

Outsourcing

In the next few decades, manufacturers will improve their production processes and take advantage of all the technological advances made. National environmental legislation, which still varies greatly from one country to the next, will converge as time goes on. Design, construction and production concepts will determine the extent to which products can subsequently be dismantled and reused. Residual waste will have to be recyclable or degradable. There is a great need for innovation here.

Production

In the future all products, secondary substances and residual waste will have to be recyclable.

Manufacturers will bear increased responsibility for how their products are used. We are already familiar with extended warranty periods, product liability and manufacturers' obligations to take products back, and, as time goes on, environmental issues and recyclability will increasingly have to be taken into account as well. The role of the manufacturer over the entire product life cycle is changing, and manufacturers' overall responsibilities for their products are increasing significantly – as we attempt to take a more holistic view and minimize the negative effects on the environment.

Product usage

The resources required for recycling or degradation should be limited, and the process should run automatically.

Recyclability

This imposes greater responsibilities on developers, designers, subcontracted suppliers and manufacturers, who have to work in close coordination with one another and the customer in order to fulfill all requirements. Sustainable product cycles with closed flows are imperative. For customers, this will become a new purchasing criterion – because if they buy ecologically unsatisfactory products, for example, they will have to take disposal costs into account. For manufacturers, on the other hand, it will become a new factor contributing toward success. New technologies and materials will ensure all this becomes feasible.

To conclude this section, it is worth making the point that if we are making an effort to protect the environment, we must not allow it to be destroyed as a result of countries' efforts to reach a position of domination.

Environment and wars

Military conflicts and efforts to develop biological weapons or other weapons with the potential to cause high levels of destruction must therefore be regarded as utterly reprehensible in the 21st century, not just from a moral and political viewpoint but for environmental reasons as well.

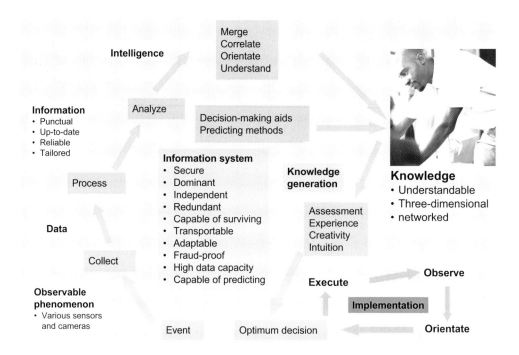

Figure 57   Knowledge generation and decision-making

Nevertheless, in the next section I would like to examine a number of interesting developments in the military field.

The military

You will no doubt be asking yourself what a section with a heading like this is doing in a book about management strategies for the future. But for technological and application-driven reasons, this is exactly where it belongs. Sometimes civilian life can benefit from progress made in the military field. After all, a technology is normally by definition neither civilian nor military.

What subjects might be particularly interesting to us here?

Information processing

Good decisions are made on the basis of the right information received at the right time. This process is illustrated in figure 57. The idea of knowledge-based decision-making support is an interesting one. An artificial intelligence system makes knowledge available and submits concrete suggestions as prioritized options for action. Artificial intelligence (AI) is understood here to be the interaction between heuristic searching, the modeling of interrelationships, general knowledge, the ability to make logical connections, language input and output, picture and video interpretation, problem-solving and advance planning.

An artificial intelligence system has to meet the following concrete requirements:

- It should take in and interpret the world around it.
- It should form plans and make useful suggestions designed to achieve an objective.
- It should communicate with other human or machine interfaces.

In military "projects" lasting a limited time, the ability to maintain an overview is an important prerequisite for survival. The situation is similar in complex civilian projects where a knowledge-based approach is required.

AI systems – physical robots and electronic agents – do, of course, proceed in a quite human way in order to complete their tasks in such projects. The difference is they are more accurate, quicker, more reliable and not affected by stress.

In the military sphere, of course, people are required to have additional, military skills. Figure 58 shows a military training model. The aim is not just to produce good soldiers; they need to be excellent. At the end of their training the trainees should be able to "do the right thing, in the right place, at the right time, for the right costs". This requires attributes such as fast reactions, flexibility, an awareness of costs and feasibility, powers of endurance, courage, the will to survive and an ability to communicate.

Training

The more complex the tasks that a soldier will later have to perform, the more often he takes part in training and simulations. This applies particularly to pilots and drivers but also to combat strategists. The objective of the training is to put military units in a position where they are able to at-

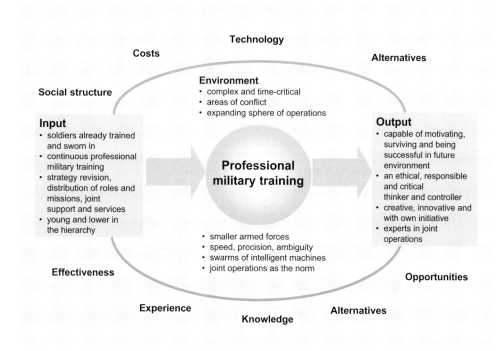

Training model for excellent soldiers **Figure 58**

tain military supremacy in the air and on the ground and carry out mobile operations throughout the world with a high degree of precision. To do this, they need superior information, logistics and systems. This can only be successfully achieved when excellent soldiers are brilliantly led.

The training of soldiers is based on real situations. This is something we can learn from in the civilian world.

Clothing · Intelligent clothing should be more than just dirt-repelling. Depending on their assignment, soldiers may have to carry a large amount of equipment and materials. The proportion of this equipment accounted for by intelligent systems is increasing rapidly. In the long term, their clothing will develop into a protective, intelligent second skin that enhances the senses – by providing a 360° representation of the surroundings, for example, allowing the soldier to obtain information about friendly and enemy positions and what others are doing.

All the soldier's equipment will be networked, keeping him in constant contact with his comrades and superiors. Sensors will monitor the environment and report any danger from ABC weapons. Enemy air and ground systems, whether manned or unmanned, will be detected and reported. The same will apply to weapons hidden in the ground or robots camouflaged as animals.

Sensors will also monitor bodily functions and the state of his personal equipment and forward all this information to the control center. If he gets wounded, his suit will automatically report an emergency and make an initial assessment of the position. The medical unit will then be able to take the necessary action immediately.

During their operations, soldiers will thus be transformed into a kind of new species with new attributes. They could also serve as a model for the industrial environment, since a similar approach would also be possible in plant engineering and construction and for maintenance activities.

New ways of doing business

The information age has by no means run its course yet. There is a great deal of homework still to be done and much unexploited potential. Indeed, most companies are not yet prepared for the globalized marketplace. The tricky points often lie within the companies themselves. There is much that is already done electronically in one form or another, but there is still also much unnecessary switching of media, and frequently end-to-end support for current processes is lacking. The terms "business intelligence" and "knowledge-based" are often little more than buzzwords that have no bearing on everyday practice. And it is revealing that companies are still using "search engines" rather than "find engines". The actual finding process does not begin until the results of the search have been obtained.

An example of how fast we can respond in other areas is indicated by the progress made in stock trading. Compared to ten years ago, what we have now is practically real-time business. We buy and sell stocks using a computer, thus conducting electronic business. The first services allowing us to do the same thing by mobile phone have now appeared, which is mobile business. It is no exaggeration to say that the future belongs to applications and services for electronic, real-time and mobile business.

Electronic business

One thing is certain, so we might as well prepare ourselves for it: We are going to depend increasingly on electronic equipment in both our working and our private lives. This is evident from the increasing number of cables running through our offices and homes and from the fact that we are spending more and more time in front of the computer screens that are now all around us. It has even been suggested that the toilets hired for rock concerts should be equipped with Internet access!

E-business is changing everything: how we work, learn, play, buy and sell, find our way around and act. As usage of the Internet increases, so does the number of electronic viruses and worms. Inevitably, comparisons are made with biological systems. Overall, however, viruses and worms hinder the spread of the Internet less than user-hostile technologies, programs and applications.

This brings us to the decisive lever that will propel electronic business forward: the focusing of applications and services on the needs of people. Individual consumers have the following expectations and requirements: that their lives should be made easier, that their quality of life should be improved, that the services they are offered should be personalizable and that overall they should get value for money. Corporate customers, on the other hand, want to reduce costs, increase their sales profitably and improve their image.

Functions of strategic concepts

These considerations make it clear that the subsequent development of e-business will not primarily be about the technology. All that matters is that the technology in the background works well. While it is important to invest in technology, investments are often made in the wrong technology. Coherent overall concepts are the key to success, not perfect standalone solutions. Important parameters that have to be taken into account in this context include return on investment (ROI), capital expenditure (CAPEX) and operating expenditure (OPEX). A further important aspect to consider is the long-term effect of an investment.

Figure 59 illustrates the potential development of electronic business over time. Whereas the first corporate websites generally consisted of a home page with a little information about the company, now they provide a wealth of multimedia information for customers, staff, analysts and journalists alike, including online shops with photographs and videos, electronic catalogs, interactive product configurators, e-mail addresses and call center numbers. At the beginning of the third millennium, "e-business or out of business" has become the slogan of the moment.

Portals as gateways to the world

Internet portals are having to meet increasingly stringent requirements, supporting or providing all of a company's links to the outside world for the purpose of communication and conducting business transactions. It is not necessarily what can be seen on screen that is important; what matters

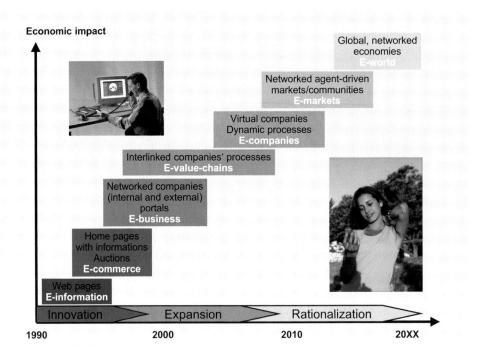

Figure 59   Development of e-business

is that the company's internal processes are connected to the world outside the company. Figure 60 makes plain the huge importance of networking.

Once shared processes are installed, a mere technical link using SAP or similar systems is not enough. Objectives, strategies, procedures, needs and desires all have to be shared through links in the form of services and applications, for example. How successfully this is done depends not on the Internet or information and communication technologies but on us and the companies involved.

We are the ones who have to exploit the potential of shared processes.

By participating in electronic business, a company becomes integrated in the global ecosystem of networked economic areas and thus defines its role in it, at least in technical terms. Whether this role is strategically the right one is a different question.

E-customer bonding   E-business, done correctly, enables closer bonds to be formed with customers and personalized offers to be made. It also saves time and money. The costs of office space, staff, paper, postage and payment handling are all reduced. Open 24 hours a day, 7 days a week and 365 days a year, the portal either clears up queries or allows them to be answered by e-mail, thus reducing the number of queries that have to be fielded by a company's staff. Companies are reducing staff numbers locally and relying on call centers and Internet portals instead. Call centers in different time zones allow incoming calls to be dealt with promptly – which is a significant criterion for success in the electronic marketplace.

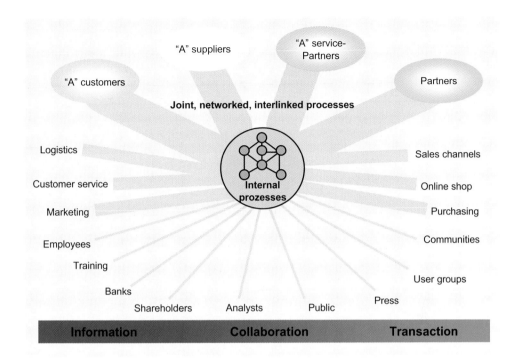

Further development of electronic integration   **Figure 60**

The way we do things in our everyday lives is also changing dramatically. It won't be long before we ourselves are configuring our next car on the computer, for example, trying clothes on virtually to see what suits us and strolling virtually down famous shopping streets. In the future we will decorate and furnish our houses on the computer first before finally deciding on the best furniture combination and colors. And we will plant our gardens virtually first to see which flowers bloom best in what sequence and at which locations.

As the influence of globalization spreads and the level of networking increases, smaller companies will increasingly also go online, trade globally and use information and communication technologies efficiently for distributed business processes and teleworking. Research and development work will increasingly be carried out on a distributed basis, involving a variety of different forms of collaboration. Meanwhile, the global employment market is already becoming a reality, and knowledge and its application are already key to success. The electronic marketplace will supersede regional markets in terms of importance, while e-business will foster the emergence of new, interactive processes.

E-business in every industry

Taking banking as an example, we used to have to keep to our local bank's opening hours and often had to wait in a queue until we were served, whereas now e-banking provides us with access to our accounts 24 hours a day, 365 days a year, and all transactions are conducted online and increasingly quickly.

A transition to a strong online presence is imminent in whatever sector you care to think of: consulting or agency work, knowledge-based services, legal services, accountancy, brokerage, insurance, architecture, the construction industry or the travel business, to name but a few. The face of retailing is set to change as well: Cars, appliances, gifts and luxury items will all be on sale online.

There used to be only two ways of contacting our company: by phone or fax. Now, on the other hand, we can contact our workplace via LAN access or mobile phone. Which is why, whether you are a software developer, a marketing specialist or a Web master, you can work from home or any other place from which you have access to your corporate network. In the future, access will be totally unrestricted: We will be able to contact our workplace via landline or the mobile network at any time. An increasing number of latter-day nomads are now working like this.

E-business is also changing the way the transportation industry works. Whereas, in the past, dispatchers managed the fleet from the office by phone or fax, today the vehicles can be controlled from a virtual control desk using an extranet or, alternatively, a mobile phone. Hard-wired industrial plants have been controlled in this way for some time now. UMTS or a similar technology will be used in future for fleets of vehicles with access via an extranet or mobile virtual marketplaces. A continuous flow of data is thus possible within the logistical chain.

A comparable transition can be observed in order processing and the management of customer data. In the past, customers placed their orders on the phone or sent them by post, and all customer data was kept on paper. Today we can also order online by e-mail or on the Web, customer requirements and data are processed immediately electronically, and automatic processes are increasingly being introduced for order processing, distribution centers and bookkeeping.

Revival of the marketplace

The marketplace of the Middle Ages is coming into fashion again – virtually speaking. As in the Middle Ages, there is direct contact with the customer, sales analyses can be carried out in real time, and dynamic pricing is possible, depending on product availability. There is competition for good sales locations, agreements are struck with those at neighboring stands, and not all the products are placed on the table at the same time. Trust is an important factor. There may be something extra offered for free or a sample of a new product. The goods can be viewed and inspected – on the Internet in 3D. On request, a short demonstration may be given. It is also possible for the customer to get references from other customers. After all, it is in the interests of both the stall owners and the portal operator to encourage the customer to come again. And the entire marketplace is, of course, interactive, responding situation-sensitively and flexibly, depending on requirements.

To continue the analogy of the medieval market, it used to be that the wealthy would sometimes send their servants shopping for them. This, too, will be happening virtually before long: electronic agents will go shopping for us, obtain information, arrange and rearrange appointments, place orders and do much else besides.

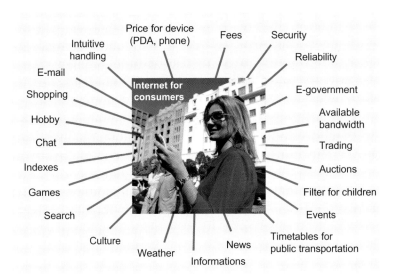

Price for device
(PDA, phone)
Fees
Security
Intuitive
handling
Reliability
E-mail
Internet for
consumers
E-government
Shopping
Available
bandwidth
Hobby
Chat
Trading
Indexes
Auctions
Games
Filter for children
Search
Events
Culture
News
Timetables for
public transportation
Weather
Informations

Figure 61
Private Internet usage

While companies in the foreseeable future will be internetworked to a large extent, the same will not apply to consumers for some time to come. In the year 2004, around 4% of the world's population will have Internet access, and 90% of Internet users will be in the industrial countries, which account for around 15% of the world's population. Even in countries on the leading edge of technological developments, the penetration rate of private Internet connections is rarely above 50%. And many people who are not Internet users today are not interested in starting. Conversely, people who have discovered the Internet no longer want to be without it.

There are, of course, many good reasons for using the Internet: entertainment, communication, shopping, fun and much else besides (see figure 61). These have to be taken into account if you want to use the general formula of "value = benefits minus outlay". Outlay in this case consists of time and money but also the energy and effort that have to be invested.

Real-time business

Real time in this context means very fast processing and up-to-the-minute information.

Someone planning a weekend away, for example, will be very impressed if, on entering a possible destination, he gets a connection to an online webcam showing him live pictures of the Eiffel Tower or Piccadilly Circus, together with a list of the available hotel rooms and a weather report for the next few days. Is the sun shining? Is it warm? A couple of clicks later everything is booked – at special low prices, of course, because he is told about all the bargains, as well.

Let's consider the company's internal processes for a moment. Do we understand these processes, its internal "bio-logic"? What happens in the ecosystem of the market economy that is all around us? Essentially, this is really of no interest to us as customers; it really doesn't matter to us how a particular company works:

All we want is for our questions to be answered immediately rather than in weeks or months.

Figure 62 indicates a number of areas where we seem to want things to go faster and faster.

It's not just in the private sphere that auctions are common. There are already examples of large companies inviting and awarding tenders for projects electronically. Real-time processes are required here to keep up with the bidding and manage the auction.

As more and more sequences of activities are carried out electronically and more and more content becomes available online, processes will be executed and products supplied increasingly quickly. The more global your business is, the greater the competitive pressure becomes and the quicker you have to act. Whereas previously a company's strategic direction had to be reviewed perhaps every few years, these days it has to be done several times in a single year. Product life cycles are being reduced from years to months, depending on the industry involved, while processing times are being reduced from months to minutes, again depending on the industry. Unless a company can seamlessly integrate all its business processes, it will be unable to keep up with the speed at which society, customers and the competition are now moving.

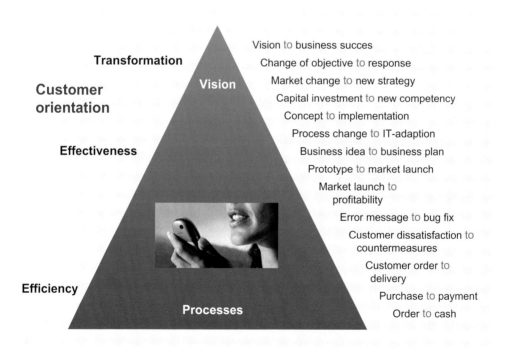

Figure 62   Speed is everything

If this all begins to get too much for you and you begin to lose your sense of direction, keep one thing in mind above all else: customer orientation. It is essential to make this your priority and maintain a constant dialog with the right customers.

Mobile business

Mobile business gives you even more freedom than electronic and real-time business on their own; in addition to all the features of the electronic, real-time Internet, it also permits location- and situation-dependent interaction. To find out where the next Italian restaurant is, for example, all we need to do is pick up our mobile device. The cellular network knows where we are and sends us the local information we need, allowing us to book a table and receive directions telling us how to get there.

Personalized and time-dependent services are also possible, thus enabling me, for example, to find out whether one of my friends, whose phone number is stored on my mobile phone, is nearby. I can then send him a quick message – perhaps he'd like to meet me at the Italian restaurant.

The i-mode service of the Japanese network operator NTT DoCoMO has been offering Internet applications on mobile devices for some time now – and has met with a very favorable response from customers. i-mode offers three different types of IP content: process applications (such as mobile banking), its own i-mode pages and Internet sites that have been adapted to suit i-mode. As far as the customer is concerned, the value of this lies, above all, in the mobile access provided to a large number of Internet sites. The high demand for attractive mobile video and game applications is leading to increasing demands for greater bandwidth.

The Internet on mobile devices

Thanks largely to the large number of Internet sites adapted for i-mode, subscriber numbers have rocketed. By 2002 there were 50,000 pages available to 30 million subscribers. As a result of its application orientation, which provides tangible benefits to customers, i-mode has established a lead over similar European approaches (see figure 63).

Outside Japan the world is not standing still either. In Europe and the USA, high growth rates are expected for multimedia applications, in particular for the Multimedia Messaging Service (MMS). This standard, which is available to all network operators and service and content providers, can already be used by customers to send photographs and videos by mobile phone in real time, thus giving network operators the opportunity to make profitable use of their available bandwidth.

MMS

Things will become really interesting when authenticated payment becomes a reality. Customers will then be able to pay for goods and services at a keystroke, which will considerably increase the value of a mobile phone or personal digital assistant (PDA). This raises the possibility of a vast array of new scenarios. We might, for example, be able to view a movie trailer, book seats and then pay for them – all from our mobile device. But, before that particular scenario can be implemented there are a number of security issues that have to be dealt with.

Mobile payment

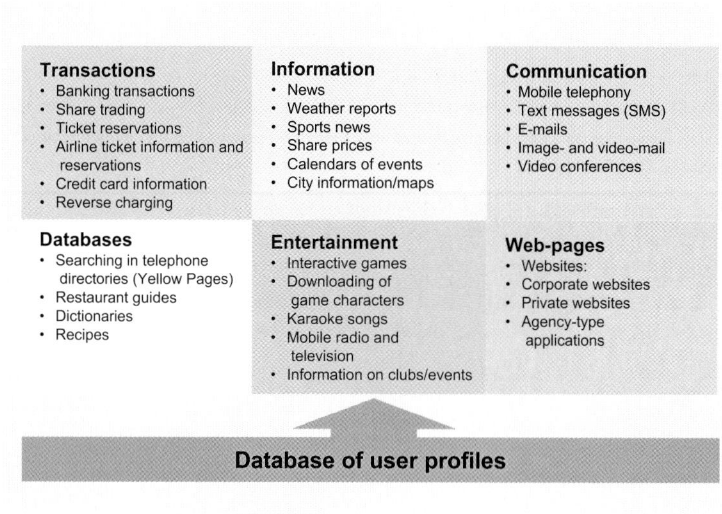

Transactions	Information	Communication
• Banking transactions • Share trading • Ticket reservations • Airline ticket information and reservations • Credit card information • Reverse charging	• News • Weather reports • Sports news • Share prices • Calendars of events • City information/maps	• Mobile telephony • Text messages (SMS) • E-mails • Image- and video-mail • Video conferences
Databases • Searching in telephone directories (Yellow Pages) • Restaurant guides • Dictionaries • Recipes	**Entertainment** • Interactive games • Downloading of game characters • Karaoke songs • Mobile radio and television • Information on clubs/events	**Web-pages** • Websites: • Corporate websites • Private websites • Agency-type applications

Database of user profiles

Figure 63
The i-mode portal

Customer requirements

Market researchers have asked consumers what new applications they would like and would be willing to pay for. What they have found is that, whereas young people would be prepared to pay for audio and video clips and interactive games, adults would pay for multimedia messages and up-to-the-minute traffic information that could be displayed to them in their cars.

Prodigious growth is expected in the numbers of "mobile" customers. The mobile Internet will gain widespread acceptance eventually, although it will have to struggle for a while yet with the problem of small displays. What this means for company portals is that they must be able to make the essential information available in a suitable form for a variety of screen sizes.

At this point we should not forget some of the potential applications of new technologies discussed earlier. It will be possible, for example, to use your mobile phone to check what is in your refrigerator and place an order with the supermarket to have what you need included in your daily delivery.

The different spheres of our lives – conclusion

There is much still to be changed in the world in which we live:

- Learning will play a greater role than before for working people.
- More than ever the customer will be king. There will be more available to us, what is available will be more personalized, and the success or failure of products will depend on what we decide we want.
- Customers will customize their electronic worlds to suit their individual requirements. Only companies that track these requirements will be able to come up with the right thing at the right time.

- Companies will only survive if their processes are fast and customer-oriented (i.e. if they conduct electronic, real-time and mobile business).

We have now examined possible future scenarios and seen how the ubiquity of the Internet and extensive digitization will change our lives and the way things are done. Geographical distances will become shorter, complex sequences of activities will take a fraction of the time to complete that they do now, our senses will be augmented, and our awareness of the world around us will be improved. Let's turn our attention now to what matters to us most, namely ourselves.

People as customers

Our mobile phone may still be working – but how can we allow ourselves to be seen with such an ancient old fossil? Did we ask ourselves before buying it exactly which functions we required and what priority they had? What specialist magazines did we browse through beforehand looking for test results in order to finally narrow our choice down to one particular brand and one particular model? That would have been the rational approach. Much more often, however, we allow ourselves to be guided by superficial aspects such as a product's appearance or by the products used by celebrities or friends we identify with or admire. And how does the new mobile phone fit with our roles in our private and working lives?

It is entirely normal that a purchasing decision should not be made on primarily logical grounds; after all, we have senses, feelings, needs and desires as well as a sense of logic. Let's begin by reflecting a little on our situation.

Our lives

In the course of our lives it is not just the kind of relationships we have that change but also the time we have available for them. And whereas communication used to be limited to direct person-to-person contact, we can now use electronic networks instead. In international companies, stable working relationships are built up between people in different continents without the need for them to pay each other frequent visits. Face-to-face meetings are being replaced by electronic terminal devices such as the telephone that allow us to exchange text, pictures and increasingly videos as well. Indeed, often it suits people to only have brief but intensive contact with other members of a team or community. Many find this is a very effective, time-saving way of working. Figure 64 shows what makes up the lives of the different members of my family at different ages, by way of

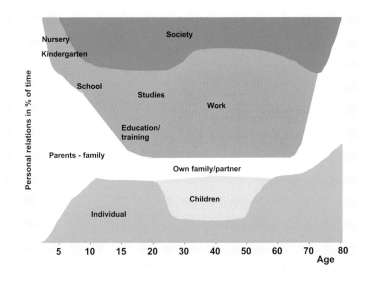

Figure 64
The changing
content of our lives

Figure 65
People play
different roles

example. Take a moment to think about what the chart would look like in your own case.

Our roles

When we look at Madonna, Shakira or other stars, we often envy them the variety of their roles: the successful singer, the dreamy girl, the bewitching goddess of the night, the caring mother, the water nymph, the seductive beauty or the jeans-wearing woman next door portrayed on CD covers, in magazine articles and on Web pages, which are, of course, full of such images.

It comes as a surprise to many that each of us also plays a variety of different roles – often much more authentically and genuinely than these stars (see figure 65). Depending on what phase of life we are in, there are all sorts of roles we may slip into and out of every day: the devoted family member, the man on a relaxing stroll through the town, the individualist out for self-fulfillment, the hard-working employee, the superior aware of his responsibilities, the consumer out to indulge himself, the ambitious athlete, the thoughtful adviser, the indecisive searcher, the good friend, the committed club member, and so on.

Having different roles means making adjustments, having different ways of behaving and different ways of dealing with people, facts and emotions, depending on the situation you are in.

Personalization of the moment

Though we take on many different roles, our day is still divided up into highly rigid blocks. Figure 66 provides an example of the kind of activities we are involved in over the course of a day.

Generally, a strict division is maintained between the time we spend working and the time we spend doing other things. On the whole, employers

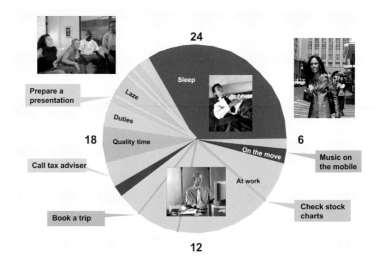

Figure 66
A day in the life

still like to keep it this way. However, information and communication technologies are giving people the flexibility to arrange their days to suit their personal preferences. The picture hints at this. When you are at work, you might very well check up on the price of a stock or book yourself a private trip – discreetly on the Internet. On the other hand, you might also sit down at home to put in some work on a presentation.

As described in the scenarios earlier in the book, office work can be done on the way to work or at home just as easily as at the office. And if more and more employees prefer to go through their e-mails, work on their presentations or draw up schedules in peace in the evening, then there is no reason why they shouldn't allow themselves a short break during working hours to take some air in the park or do some stock trading. The boundaries between our private and working lives are fading, and the new multimedia information and communication technologies have a lot to do with this development.

According to an interesting study carried out by the Henley Centre in England, people use their mobile phones and the Internet a third of the time for work-related reasons (see figure 67). In the other two thirds of the time, people use them to organize their lives, chat, relax or maintain important relationships.

We are still a long way from being able to do everything we might want to on the Internet, but that will change as more and more processes become electronic and digital. Broadband connections – whether via a landline or a mobile network – will provide integrated access to information and communication, which will give us further scope to arrange our working and private lives to fit our personal requirements. This is an idea whose time has come. Given that many people are being subjected to increasing pressure in their everyday working lives, it should be possible for them to allocate their time to suit themselves.

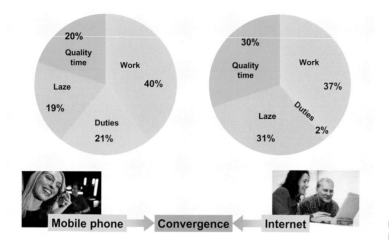

Figure 67
Mobile phone usage

Our needs and desires

This section examines the findings of Abraham Maslow, who drew up a hierarchy of human needs often represented as a pyramid, as shown in figure 68.

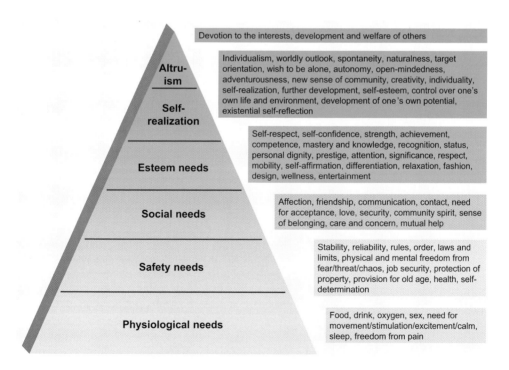

Maslow's hierarchy of human needs   **Figure 68**

Essentially, Maslow's theory states that we do not attend to needs higher up in the hierarchy until we have met the needs at the lower levels. Thus, solo pianists will interrupt their playing to drink when they are thirsty.

The needs of a higher level cannot motivate you until your lower-level needs have been met.

The accuracy of this theory is shown by how people behave after a war. In Germany in the period after the Second World War, for example, it was possible to observe successive consumer waves for food, clothing, apartments, houses, furnishings and, finally, waves characterized by the quest for self-fulfillment and individuality.

Each of us makes our way up and down Maslow's pyramid possibly several times a day (see figure 69).

The level of the pyramid at which we find ourselves at any given time depends on our situation and the extent to which we are in form on a particular day. Whichever level we are on, we look out for the kind of offerings that are currently important to us. Communication is more important to us than information – which is why we are more likely to accept a computer that crashes rather than a telephone network that goes down for a longer period of time. Our needs are strongly influenced by social trends and fashions.

We want to have fun, speak to our friends, have constant access to up-to-date information, do some shopping, be healthy, feel safe and be able to work, regardless of where we currently find ourselves.

The trick to targeting people as customers is to begin by considering which level of the pyramid they are on.

This is no simple matter. If you employ logic alone, it becomes quite impossible – as we shall see later – because products are increasingly used as a means of self-presentation.

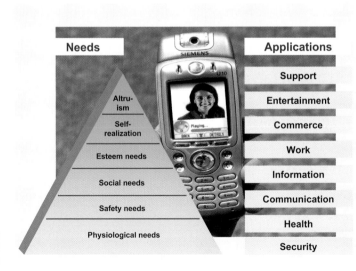

Figure 69
Maslow's pyramid
and its applications

Lifestyle is made up of the things we are prepared to pay for that go beyond satisfying our basic needs. Often we spend much more than is necessary. "It doesn't hurt to spoil yourself sometimes," is how we see it. While the factors that influence us here come to a certain extent from within us (have a look at the discussion of the iceberg syndrome in the next section), external influences also have a strong effect: the marketing and image of a brand, for example, or recommendations from people you know.

Researchers carrying out work into trends and consumerism are faced with a great many challenges here. For marketing and sales people, on the other hand, this means a constant stream of new opportunities.

The emotional versus the rational

Philosophers have postulated that a proper conversation really only takes place when both participants listen closely and make an intense effort to understand what the other is trying to say. Unfortunately, this is a rare occurrence, so we would do well to focus on what is really happening: Not only do icebergs sink large ships; in interpersonal relationships their hidden structures often thwart proper interaction between people, preventing them from taking in what others are really saying.

This is the only way to explain how several eyewitnesses often give quite different reports of a particular event, although each of them perceives the same thing and has the same bandwidth of 250 Mbps for transmitting information from the senses to the brain.

We each have our own personal filters; this means we interpret, look for and evaluate things very differently to others and thus cannot be objective.

Whenever people come together, there is communication between them. This is not just verbal; in fact, verbal communication accounts for only a small proportion of the messages we send out. In advertising, huge efforts are made to use all possible forms of expression – the voice as well as body language – to influence our purchasing behavior. Problems arise both when we try to consciously express what we are thinking by using language and gestures and when we receive and interpret the signals of others, thus leading to many avoidable misunderstandings and conflicts. We need only think of the many communication problems that occur between men and women to be reminded of this. It seems likely that our rational side simply cannot exist in isolation from our emotions.

The iceberg under the surface, in all its complexity (as shown in figure 70), is still far too often underestimated – in our private and working lives as well as in public life. By focusing more on what lies under the surface we can improve cooperation and trust between people and accelerate progress. These soft factors are in reality often the hardest. And they become even harder when functions are increasingly being taken on by electronic systems. It is thus all the more important for us to understand our emotional side and learn to deal with it. This is a question of getting

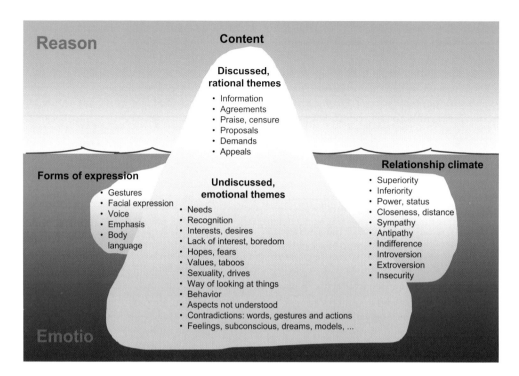

Figure 70   The iceberg principle

together with other people – our friends, colleagues and coworkers – to raise the level of our behavior, values and standards. By doing this we will be laying the foundations for success in the future.

Me Inc.

Let's begin by removing any possible confusion: Me Inc. is not the invention of a minister of employment; it's a concept that can be applied to each and every one of us, since we are all, in a sense, one-man or one-woman companies. We have visions, for example, of everything we want to have achieved, done and experienced by the time we retire and in the years afterwards. To translate these visions into reality, we set ourselves objectives and then search for the right strategies to help us achieve them. We make investments in our minds, bodies and souls and constantly try to improve ourselves (at least, most of us do). In the previous sections we have learned about what we may be faced with in the future – but will it also affect us personally?

The answer is a resounding "yes". Computers and networks will gradually take on more of our routine mental tasks as they become better at them than us (see figure 71). As a consequence of Moore's law and the development of improved software, their capabilities can in fact only rapidly improve, so they will take on the simpler tasks first, followed by the more

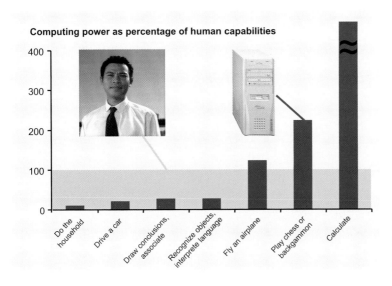

Computing power as percentage of human capabilities

Figure 71
Comparison of human and artificial intelligence in the year 2000

complex ones. These will be tasks that we no longer need to do. When machines are doing our analysis, simulation, forecasting and possibly responding for us, the only work left for us to do will be highly skilled. What this means for us is:

We must seek to acquire new skills for which there is a market and which fit with our identity.

Figure 72 presents an overview of Me Inc., which is a kind of personal cockpit. We can use this schema at regular intervals to check whether we have found our ideal "field of business". When doing so, it's critical to listen to our gut instincts as well as what our head tells us. This is the only way to arrive at a correct assessment of the situation and gain some pointers as to how to move forward.

The personal cockpit

Just as in a company, everything starts with a vision that represents a combination of gut instinct and deliberation. You have to work out what your functions are in your private, public and working lives, what abilities and possessions you have and what you can achieve.

The second step begins with a search for target groups for Me Inc. Having analyzed these customers, we become solution providers. The probability of a win-win situation is greater the more we invest of ourselves in the enterprise and the better we exploit our personal potential. It is also useful to make a regular assessment of ourselves by carrying out a SWOT analysis (of our strengths, weaknesses, opportunities and threats) and entering the current status on a 360° chart.

Only then can we find out not just what we are able to do but what we are able to do and is also needed, as well as decide on the things we are ready to take a risk on!

We will return to the SWOT analysis later when we come to the factors that contribute to the success of companies.

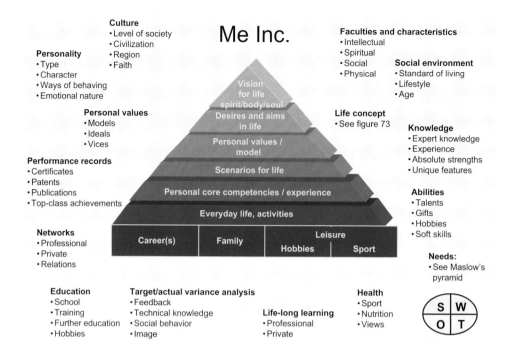

Figure 72   Me Inc.

The figure contains the following labels:

Culture
- Level of society
- Civilization
- Region
- Faith

Personality
- Type
- Character
- Ways of behaving
- Emotional nature

Personal values
- Models
- Ideals
- Vices

Performance records
- Certificates
- Patents
- Publications
- Top-class achievements

Networks
- Professional
- Private
- Relations

Education
- School
- Training
- Further education
- Hobbies

Target/actual variance analysis
- Feedback
- Technical knowledge
- Social behavior
- Image

Life-long learning
- Professional
- Private

Health
- Sport
- Nutrition
- Views

Faculties and characteristics
- Intellectual
- Spiritual
- Social
- Physical

Social environment
- Standard of living
- Lifestyle
- Age

Life concept
- See figure 73

Knowledge
- Expert knowledge
- Experience
- Absolute strengths
- Unique features

Abilities
- Talents
- Gifts
- Hobbies
- Soft skills

Needs:
- See Maslow's pyramid

Pyramid (Me Inc.):
- Vision for life spirit/body/soul
- Desires and aims in life
- Personal values / model
- Scenarios for life
- Personal core competencies / experience
- Everyday life, activities
- Career(s) | Family | Leisure (Hobbies | Sport)

SWOT diagram: S | W / O | T

Soft skills

Soft skills will be among those that continue to distinguish us from machines in the next 25 years. The term is generally used to cover just about everything that does not come under the heading of technical or specialist knowledge. Soft skills include the ability to work in teams, deal with conflict, communicate, motivate yourself, learn and exercise flexibility, creativity and powers of analysis. Social skills such as the ability to act on the basis of a sound knowledge of human nature, be critical, assert yourself, organize, empathize, enthuse and deal well with people from other cultures complete the picture. Rhetorical, presentation, project-management and negotiating skills are among those we have to learn.

An individual with the requisite social skills knows how to communicate and interact appropriately in a given situation, something that is sometimes referred to as emotional intelligence. This is based on the ability to choose the right behavior at the right time from your personal repertoire of responses in order, on the one hand, to meet the requirements of a given situation and, on the other, to achieve your objectives and act in your own interests.

Hard skills

We also have to cope with the challenges presented to us by e-volution, the electronic revolution. To this end, we should make an intensive effort to make ourselves familiar with the new technologies and take advantage of the associated opportunities. Only in this way can we join those who are the driving forces behind new business rather than those who are driven by it. We must also identify innovations, potential and solutions where others do not.

The symbiosis between the employer and Me Inc.

Whereas companies select and reject personnel on the basis of their own version of Darwinism, employees behave in an opportunistic manner by trying to keep themselves attractive for the market – which is, after all, in their own interests.

A career is characterized by the search for the best synergies and potential for both parties: the employer and Me Inc. When we succeed in this search, we establish ourselves at work, strengthen our companies and business locations and help them compete in the global marketplace. Good personal networking is and will always remain the key to success.

Figure 73 shows you some of the many possible elements that go to make up a strategy for your life – a Me Inc. or personal brand. It includes both private and professional aspects.

These and other personal elements are also important to entrepreneurs in two ways:

- They are important for human management (a subject to which we will return below).
- They are important for handling customers, since each of our customers and our customers' customers is likewise a Me Inc. – in other words, an independent individual. More than ever, developers and sales and marketing people must take their bearings from the needs and desires

Everyday life
- Sleeping, eating, drinking
- Thinking, acting, remaining silent, talking
- Leisure time, desires, decisions
- Time allocation, planning, designing
- Projects

Life
- Fundamental views
- Love
- Transcendence
- Philosophy, wisdom, guiding principles
- Vision, goals, pathways to happiness
- Fulfillment

Spirit
- Range of skills
- Learning, memory, system of organization
- Endurance, patience, motivation
- Concentration, creativity, thought
- Reading, absorbing, reproducing
- Health, positivism

Personality
- Knowledge of human nature, tolerance, circumspection, empathy
- Independence, selflessness, ambition, ability to take stress
- Self-assurance, optimism
- Freedom from, freedom to
- Principles, morals

Body
- Health
- Spirit, body, theory, practice
- Sport, sex
- Pain
- Healing

Elements of a Life Concept

Special cases
- Preparation
- Decision-making, stress
- Doubt, anxiety, conflict
- Pain, grief
- Death

Marriage/relationship
- Everyday, happiness, discord
- Consolidation, changing one's ways, future
- Children, upbringing

Career
- Everyday work
- Behavior
- Work: goals – methods
- Company-specific
- Job-specific

Leisure time
- Relaxation, balance
- Hobbies, games
- Activity, passivity
- Travel, going out

Finance
- Money, income
- Property, assets
- Buying, selling
- Giving

Relationships
- Friends, acquaintances, colleagues
- Reaction, action
- Coaching, advising

Strategy for a life   **Figure 73**

of such individuals. It is often not easy to understand the strategies according to which people live their lives, so it pays to invest in customer and application research.

Keeping yourself healthy and fit through sport and good nutrition is essential to a thriving Me Inc. Advances in biology and medicine have made it easier to stay healthy but cannot replace a sensible approach to your health.

People as customers – conclusion

The more of our everyday work that is taken on by machines, the more important it becomes for us to be able to deal with people skillfully.

- We should make more effort to find out what is important to others at any given moment. Only those who take into account the invisible portion of the iceberg and identify the needs and desires of customers at the right time will be successful.

- The person as a customer will continue to appear in the discussions below – either as a genuine customer or as a supplier, subcontractor or employee. Within the framework of a customer-supplier relationship, the customer's purchasing decisions should always be based on what we also think is important.

The entrepreneur's joystick

To draw an analogy with the weather, the radar screens of old would no longer be good enough for today's strategic navigators in the business world. In the rapidly changing weather conditions of today's markets, something more efficient is called for.

Nobody is suggesting strategists should dispense with trusty old tools such as market analyses and portfolio management. However, trends show that they are increasingly getting together with external partners to analyze the core processes within their own companies.

Using scenarios

They are also increasingly simulating business models under different conditions. The judicious use of scenarios permits valid statements to be made about strategic options and their effects on sales and profits. It is useful to think about the information process in the same way we did when discussing the military sphere in an earlier section. It then becomes clearer what is meant by the scenario technique. It's no longer a question of simply putting some data together and showing the results in a nice chart; instead, this is an uncompromising approach to establishing and defending a lead through information. The same rule applies now as has applied for over 3000 years: Only he who knows himself extremely well and his opponents very well will emerge victorious.

It is, of course, very useful to know the rules of the market. Only those who are ready and able to change these rules can take a genuine step forward.

Fitness for the future

Very similar statements can be made about biology and the workings of the natural world. When considering the subject of competitive strength in 1859, Darwin postulated that only the fittest win through in the struggle for survival. On the subject of differentiation, Gause hypothesized in 1934 that it was not possible for two species with the same sources of food to exist alongside each other, while Flik dealt with the subject of anticipation in 1986, stating that organisms cannot survive unless they can learn as fast or faster than the rate of change in their environment.

There is no chance of the rate of development and change slowing down. On the contrary, it can only get faster. To cope with this, we need a radical approach based on an appropriate strategy.

It is said about many companies that they are wanting in this respect. They should change before they have no other choice. While there are always risks associated with a transformation, the risks of doing nothing are much greater. We can rely less than ever on the hope that established rules and laws will continue to apply. Even market growth does not necessarily guarantee the growth of your own business, let alone its profitability. Outdated strategies will consign you to the scrapheap of history, and historical strengths can become future weaknesses.

Let's now turn our attention to the tried and trusted strategic tools that will continue to be used, as well as the new methods that will augment our strategic toolkit.

The way to achieve corporate objectives

Fast-growing, fast-changing companies need to buy or sell other companies, divisions or fields of business and establish a cross-industry network of partners around the world with which they collaborate. In the Internet age, strategy – which marks out the route to achieving a clearly defined corporate goal – is playing an increasingly important role.

Good chief executives or managing boards devise a set of ideas about what the future will be like, as we are doing in this book, and then project the role of their company onto this vision. From this they define the mission and central objectives of the company. Finally, they draw up a strategy, setting out how these objectives are to be achieved. At the operational planning stage, they translate this into programs and campaigns of activities for the various parts of the company. To achieve success, the management then has to keep a sharp eye on day-to-day developments.

The company's ideas about what the future will be like and its vision, mission, strategy and scenarios are essential elements contributing to its long-term success. However, excellent contacts between strategists and all operational parts of the company, customers and analysts are also an important prerequisite. Unless there is adequate business information and intelligence, and unless scenarios are employed that take into account all the various possibilities, the strategy will not be flexible enough and will turn out to be of little use. The same principles apply as in a ball game: Only if you know the playing area, your opponent and yourself, and only if you have the flexibility to play in a number of different ways, do you have a good chance of winning.

From the vision to the processes involved

Your ideas about what the future will be like must be as detailed and coherent as possible so that your vision and mission can be put into this context. To this end, you have to compile information on the environment in which your company operates. You may decide to have this done by external consultants or analysts, for example. Ideally, your vision of the future will take into account society, politics, economics, the environment, customers, competitors and technologies at a given point in time.

Important trends, in particular those that affect your own business, must be properly understood, which means you also need an understanding of how they interact. The identification and analysis of these trends with a view to generating successful business ideas is an essential part of the work of companies and their management. This can only be achieved by continuously collecting and evaluating information far beyond the horizon of day-to-day operations. At the same time, it should not be ignored that discontinuities and paradigm changes can occur in the longer term.

From a vision of the future to a vision for your company

To obtain a better understanding of a vision of the future, it is necessary to draw up trend scenarios. Credible, coherent images and histories must be developed for typical future situations. The better the scenarios, the more that can be derived from them.

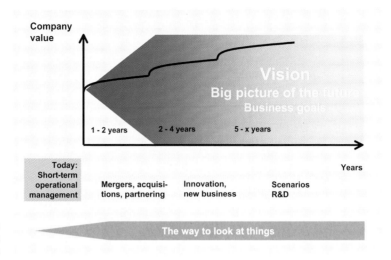

Company value

1 - 2 years   2 - 4 years   5 - x years

Vision
Big picture of the future
Business goals

Years

| Today: Short-term operational management | Mergers, acquisitions, partnering | Innovation, new business | Scenarios R&D |

The way to look at things

Figure 74
A vision creates opportunities

Extreme scenarios are also often used. In this technique, imaginary worlds that are as far apart as possible are generated, as we shall see later, thus maximizing their scope.

A company's vision is its self-portrait for the future. A good vision is made up of an image and the company behind that image, as well as possible solutions for its medium-term or even distant future.

Not unless you have a vision and make inferences about tomorrow on the basis of your assessment of the day after tomorrow (see figure 74) will you really be able to manage the development of your company and its suppliers:

- In the long term you can make decisions on the areas to be looked into with a view to initiating preliminary development.
- In the medium term you can develop innovations and business alternatives.
- In the short term you can, for example, establish partnerships and buy and sell companies or parts of companies.

The more comprehensively and successfully you apply a vision for your business, the more your company increases in value.

Once you have identified the trends and developed a clear vision, you can develop all the strategic elements of corporate management, while taking into account the needs and desires of customers.

This is shown in figure 75.

Mission   The mission should be worked out in much the same way as the vision. This is the business assignment a company sets itself to be implemented with each of its customers. Essentially, it gets right to the heart of a company's purpose.

Model of the company   The model of the company augments the vision and mission with a company-specific code of behavior. This describes the corporate culture and

Future scenarios
▶ Image of future self

Vision

▶ Own business mandate

Mission

▶ Code of behavior – target culture

Guiding principles

▶ Unique features / core competencies
which contribute to customer success

Value proposition

▶ Challenges we set ourselfes

Overall goals

▶ Different scenarios for future
developments

Trend scenarios

▶ Ways of reaching the goals set

Core strategy

▶ Issues and processes which
have to be perfectly mastered

Core competencies

▶ Daily contribution to
goal achievement
▶ Enjoyment at work

Tactics/operations/processes

From the vision to the process   **Figure 75**

the basic principles of how people are to work together effectively in the interests of the company and defines the roles of customers, staff, management, cooperation, innovation and business appraisal.

The value proposition is a single sentence setting forth the key reason why the customer should buy the solutions, products and services of this company rather than those of another.

Value proposition

The primary objectives of the company and its staff are derived from the vision, mission and scenarios. The primary objectives determine the direction the company is to take in the next few years. It is the responsibility of the company's management to decide how challenging, ambitious and motivating these objectives are to be. The primary objectives generally go in one of two directions:

Primary objectives

- They may demand an increase in effectiveness and efficiency (less input for the same output).
- Alternatively, they may demand more innovation (more output for the same input).

Once the objectives are clearly defined, the route to be taken in order to achieve them emerges. This can be marked out and documented as an implementation path to be followed, together with the individual steps involved and the action that needs to be taken. Strategic planning comes into play here, the primary task of which is to define the core strategy.

Core strategy

A clear core strategy is of decisive importance to the entire company. The company as a whole will only function provided the strategy is broken down and applied, as appropriate, to the different parts of the company and provided the various tasks involved are clearly allocated. A useful analogy can be drawn with the human body: We can only give our body the nutrition it requires if our hands put the food into a suitable form for our mouth, the fork transfers the food into our mouth, we chew the food using our jaws and teeth, and so on. In the same way, everyone in the company makes a contribution to its overall success, and they all gain great satisfaction from knowing what they themselves have contributed toward achieving the objective.

Internal communication

The vision of the future and the vision, mission, primary objectives and core strategy of the company must be vigorously communicated throughout the company. Generally, the usual internal company publications are not up to this task. An alternative is to inform all staff personally in a cascading process from the top down. The advantage of this approach is that discussions lead to the information being absorbed better.

If this sequence is not clear to every member of staff, those to whom it is not will inevitably pursue different objectives and take different routes to those required. Consequently, time and energy are wasted during a phase when the company needs to act quickly and accelerate the process of change.

Strategic planning

In the English-speaking countries a disproportionate number of books are published on strategy, marketing and sales compared to other business topics. This is, after all, the real core task of business management. A constantly changing environment requires a new orientation and approach.

The methods described below, which are to be applied in a step-by-step process, will continue to be components of the strategic toolkit for years to come. However, thanks to e-volution, it will be possible to apply them significantly more quickly than before. This strategic tool-box is helpful for people, companies and countries.

Definition of fields of business

The matrix of fields of business shown in figure 76 will continue to be used, although, as market forces become increasingly dynamic, the definitions will not remain stable for as long as they did in the past. The new electronic markets are revolutionizing sales and distribution structures, and increasing globalization is forcing us to look beyond our own national borders and continents.

Figure 76
Definition of fields of business

Discount supermarkets such as Aldi, Lidl and Plus in Europe are already offering many new products from the Far East, for example. For some time now we have been able to fill the same shopping cart with socks, computers and milk. And on the Internet, too, these products are now only a mouse click away from each other.

Benefit matrix

Once you have defined your field of business, you can position it in a benefit matrix (see figure 77). To do this, you have to ask yourself the following questions:

- Is the business subject to economies of scale?
- Does the customer buy primarily on the basis of quality or price?

Not until the answers to these questions are known do the competitive advantages become clear. In the two boxes at the top of the matrix, customers

Volume brings limited benefits	Volume brings major benefits	
Niche business · Custom applications software · Installation · Consulting/services	**Specialized business** · Trucks · Games software · CD/DVD players · Industrial plant	**Customer buys on basis of performance**
Bulk business · Standard paper · Plate glass · Steel · Wood-fiber boards	**Volume business** · Memory chips · Cameras · Computers · Energy-saving lamps	**Customer buys on basis of price**

Figure 77
Benefit matrix

value performance, quality and uniqueness, whereas, in the two boxes at the bottom, their main consideration is cost.

In order to be able to better assess your cost and performance benefits in comparison to the competition, it is important to know your own position in the market. The price/performance matrix (see figure 78) is an important aid to carrying out this self-assessment.

The next step is market analysis. To make an initial assessment of the market, it is helpful to use Porter's Five Forces Model (see figure 79). Today there are additional factors to be taken into account when assessing market attraction:

Market analysis

- The cyclical nature of business
- The dynamics of development
- Changes to segments
- Risks of unforeseeable disasters and dramatic events

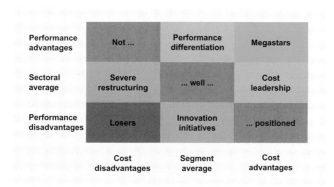

Figure 78
Cost/benefit matrix

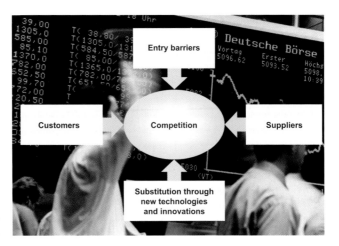

Figure 79
Porter's model for
market analysis

Examples of such unforeseeable events are the nuclear accident at Chernobyl, the fall of the wall between East and West Germany and the destruction of the World Trade Center in New York. In order to take discontinuities like this into account, you should use scenarios in your thinking and planning.

The visible changes both within and outside companies that have occurred as a result of electronic business shed a totally new light on the issues of performance, costs and time as far as the market is concerned. There is now a new buzzword to describe the extent to which a company is prepared for the transition from traditional markets to the new markets of the networked world: e-readiness. One consequence of increasing globalization is that R&D efficiency and effectiveness in acquiring new business have taken on even more significance.

As a consequence of e-procurement with its online invitations to tender, shopping portals and marketplaces, the power of the customer over the supplier is increasing. If you don't like what you are being offered, the next offer is only a click away.

On the other hand, the electronic data highway allows suppliers to appeal to customers they would otherwise have been unable to target. The contact between the customer and supplier is more direct, with fewer disruptive factors. At the same time, the trend in e-procurement is toward standardized products, thus making differentiation difficult. New technologies and greater efficiency open up a larger market, but they also increase competition. Fewer salespeople are required for e-procurement. As a result, variable costs decrease, thus increasing the pressure on prices. One big challenge to be faced by vendors in e-procurement is to preserve an independent approach – whether in terms of the applications they use or their offerings – thus increasing the attractiveness of the various things they are offering, while nevertheless remaining compatible with other systems.

We have to take all these aspects into account in market analysis.

Figure 80 shows the classical portfolio analysis matrix developed by the Boston Consulting Group (BCG). This enables authoritative statements to be made about the balance and future prospects of businesses and is particularly suitable for the evaluation of volume business. The central idea is the dominance of the innovator, who can secure a lead on the learning curve.

Using the BCG matrix it is possible to discuss potential business success in detail. It permits conclusions to be drawn about the balance of a product portfolio, future capability, investment funds, cash flow and strategic options.

Even criteria for filling the most important positions in the company can be derived from this, since different phases of the product life cycle require different character traits and ways of working.

The incentive system with its targets for business development can also be based on it. After all, when it comes to our market share, we simply cannot be ambitious enough. After all, let there be no mistake: a market share of 30% is not great; it means we are losing out on 70%.

The matrix developed by McKinsey shown in figure 81 can also help identify the right strategy. The axes of this matrix are aligned in such a way that they are almost compatible with the BCG portfolio. The color coding is identical to that used in figure 80.

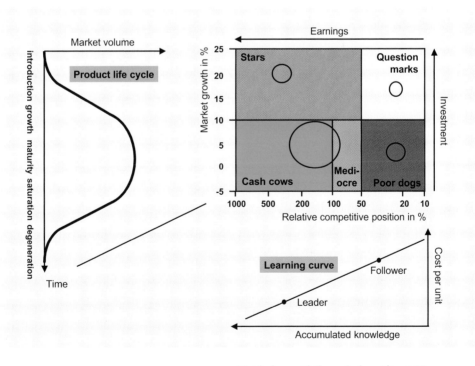

Matrix for portfolio analysis   **Figure 80**

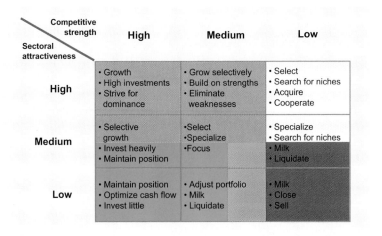

Competitive strength	High	Medium	Low
High	• Growth • High investments • Strive for dominance	• Grow selectively • Build on strengths • Eliminate weaknesses	• Select • Search for niches • Acquire • Cooperate
Medium	• Selective growth • Invest heavily • Maintain position	•Select •Specialize •Focus	• Specialize • Search for niches • Milk • Liquidate
Low	• Maintain position • Optimize cash flow • Invest little	• Adjust portfolio • Milk • Liquidate	• Milk • Close • Sell

Sectoral attractiveness

Figure 81
McKinsey's strategy matrix

Planning the product life cycle

Before we invest, we have to know what the life cycle of our product is likely to be. The recovery of all costs and the achievement of a profit during this period are essential criteria when deciding for or against a product.

The life cycle of a product can be subdivided into a number of phases: introduction, growth, maturity, saturation and decline.

In the introduction phase, the product is new on the market and sales are therefore low. Production and marketing costs, on the other hand, are high, resulting in losses. The market structure is monopolistic. A certain proportion of consumers (innovators and opinion leaders) are open to the new product.

The transition to the growth phase is followed by above-average growth in sales and high profits. Competitors begin to enter the market, and the market structure becomes oligopolistic. "Early adapters" now start to buy the product, as well.

In the maturity phase, sales continue to rise, reaching their highest level at the transition to the saturation phase. Sales and profits then begin to decline, and the market structure becomes polypolistic. Only by means of product differentiation can you attempt to gain an advantage over your competitors. Consumers belonging to the "early majority", who previously hesitated to buy, now become new customers.

Sales begin to fall with the saturation phase. As a result of negative growth rates, profits decline and reach the breakeven point at the end of this phase. The consumers in this phase are referred to as the "late majority". Marketing activities seek only to limit the decline in sales.

In the decline phase, the fall in sales can no longer be checked, and the threat of losses looms unless costs are cut. The product portfolio is streamlined. First-time customers in this phase are known as laggards.

This portrayal of the product life cycle applies in full to products offered at the same time by more than one vendor, such as CD players, or to products that are dependent on fashions. Only parts of the cycle apply to investment goods or mass-produced products. This can be clearly seen in the case of new cars, for example, where the introduction phase generally begins before the product is even launched on the market in order to build up a sense of expectation among consumers.

In addition, there are two important effects that overlay the product life cycle itself, namely the cyclical nature of business and the hype cycle touched on earlier in the book. The cyclical nature of business will be very familiar to pig farmers in Europe, for example, as well as to manufacturers of memory chips.

The consulting company Arthur D. Little goes beyond considering the product life cycle alone when considering a company's competitive position. The key points made are that there is a need for high investment when you have a leading position and are at the beginning of the cycle:

The worse your relative competitive position is and the more advanced the stage of product maturity, the more cautious you should therefore be about making investments.

This will remain essentially the same in the future, except that some product life cycles will proceed at a speed previously seen only for ladies' fashions and pop songs.

In order to develop and launch a successful product onto the market, we have to have a precise idea about what our customers require and how we can help them successfully get it. This knowledge can no longer be the exclusive preserve of the people in sales and marketing departments; it is worth a lot of money and is needed by all departments. The solution is either to send the entire company to the customer – which is both expensive and inefficient – or to introduce a good system of knowledge management.

Customer analysis

For the purpose of strategic planning it is crucial to know both what customers are satisfied with and where they have cause for complaint.

This makes it easier to eliminate weaknesses and identify the company's core competencies. The results of such an analysis – which may affect the definition of fields of business mentioned above – are illustrated in figure 82 by way of example.

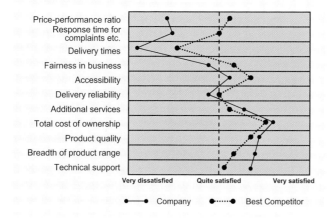

Figure 82
Satisfaction profile, including strengths and weaknesses

A profile like this is adequate for an initial assessment, but not for long-term survival and profits. We will deal with that later when we come to customer research.

Core competencies
and factors
contributing to
success

The concept of core competencies is a program in itself. Every country, every company and every Me Inc. needs them. But core competencies are only of any use in the effort to achieve objectives if they can be converted into factors that contribute to success.

The concept of core competencies is a program in itself. Every country, every company and every Me Inc. needs them. But core competencies are only of any use in the effort to achieve objectives if they can be converted into factors that contribute to success.

A company cannot prevail in the marketplace in the long term with an arbitrary range of products and services. It must therefore establish leads over the competition in terms of costs and/or performance and then set about defending those leads. Figure 83 shows how these can be categorized.

The business-specific success factors ideally provide a basis for competitive advantages that can be defended because they cannot easily be copied by others.

Figure 84 gives an impression of how diverse the factors contributing to a company's success can be.

In business, nothing is more effective than launching very successful and popular products and services on a continuous basis. To be the leader in terms of innovation in a market – or a strong number two – is to be in a very desirable and profitable position in the competition for business. We can reach this position all the easier the more concrete our competitive advantages are and the more our products have unique selling points that are valued by customers.

The company's core competencies must be applied to a large enough number of customers before the business becomes worthwhile. In addition, there is always a question as to whether the company's current core competencies also promise to bring success in the future. Can the competencies be transferred to the new age described earlier in the book? Will new business ideas and business models such as those of an Amazon or an Ebay pose a threat to us or spur us on? In the age of the Internet, hyper-

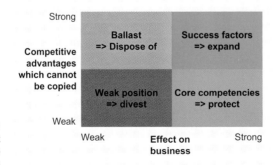

Figure 83
Factors that
contribute to
success

The entrepreneur's joystick

Factors that contribute to success in different areas of a company   **Figure 84**

innovation, time advantages and individualized marketing, the guidelines according to which a company operates must be questioned on a regular basis. At this point it is important to ask about new competencies: What new capabilities are required for electronic, mobile, real-time business?

The SWOT analysis mentioned above aims in a similar direction (see figure 85). To prevent a gap opening up between how you see yourself and how others see you, the viewpoints of as many different departments as possible should be included in the analysis, as well as those of customers and the competition. This will then also give you useful information as to where there is a need for action in terms of new or new kinds of products, e-volution and mobile business. E-volution is essentially the process whereby all activities and content are changed by the new electronic processes.

The proverbial cobbler can no longer stick to his last.

These days, with so many changes taking place seemingly all at once, every company has to open itself up to the possibility of reorientation. Hardly a single business will remain unaffected by the trends and developments described at the beginning of the book. It pays to have the courage to strike out in new directions:

- A Dresden baker of stollen, a German fruit loaf eaten at Christmas, receives orders from as far away as Australia now that he has an Internet presence.

Figure 85
SWOT analysis

Reorientation

- Hairdressers who use scanned photographs to show their customers pictures of themselves with different hairstyles on the computer ensure that they receive plenty of repeat business.
- Other successful examples of new, Internet-based attractions are to be found at www.landsend.com, where you can try on clothes virtually, www.planetfashion.com, where you can look at the window displays in New York shopping streets, www.maxx.de, where there is a mountain bike configurator, or www.volkswagen.de, where you will find a car configurator.

This is all very convenient for the customer (on the home PC) as well as being customer-oriented in a strategic sense.

These examples of personalized offerings illustrate the necessity of reorientation, the opportunities it brings and the dynamic effect of e-volution on all types of business. The companies mentioned are not all large corporations, which always used to dictate the speed at which new technologies were deployed; some of them are agile and enterprising small and medium-sized companies. Internet business is also affordable for the one-man show and thus also for the "Me Inc." individual described in this book. It is thus clear that the changes being wrought by the Internet concern everyone.

Business development

Let's now turn from the static field-of-business matrix or product-market matrix to business development, which takes us into marketing territory. Now that we have integrated, enterprise-wide processes, the integration of marketing is no longer a problem.

But let's first take a look at another representation of positioning, the Ansoff matrix (see figure 86). This is also a product-market matrix, as described above in the section on the definition of fields of business. However, it differs from the matrices of the Boston Consulting Group and McKinsey in that it concerns itself specifically with markets.

When developing new products for new markets, we draw distinctions between horizontal, vertical and lateral diversification.

- In horizontal diversification, products of the same type are added.

	Market development	Market conquest	Diversification
New	Market development	Market conquest	Diversification
Related	Market extension	Market enlargement	Market acquisition
Existing	Market penetration	Product development	Portfolio extension
Markets / **Products**	Current	Improved (horizontal)	New, innovative (lateral)

Figure 86
Extended Ansoff matrix

- In vertical diversification, products from other stages of production in the value-added chain are added.
- Lateral diversification means there is no direct link between the new products and the previous ones.

Lateral diversification is the most risky option. Do you want to conquer new markets with improved products, or do you dare to break into an entirely new business? You should make a point of continually considering all the possible avenues for developing your business and then making plans accordingly. If we do not pursue these opportunities, one of our well-known competitors will do it for us. A new competitor may even take the stage and possibly end up playing a starring role. One excellent example of lateral diversification is the entry of Mannesmann, a steel manufacturer, into the mobile phone business.

When attempting to break into new markets, it is preferable to be driven by customer demand rather than development. You should carry out detailed research to establish whether a new product is likely to be well received by consumers. However, caution is advisable here: A widely scattered portfolio of products does not constitute further development.

One interesting alternative is targeted, joint innovation with customers, which we will examine in the section on innovation.

It is also interesting to compare a list of reasons for buying your new product compiled by customers with a list compiled by your own staff.

But we still haven't addressed the question of how to come up with new products for new markets. Innovation is, of course, and will remain the most important generator of business. Innovative product development can be achieved in-house, by using contract developers, by acquiring licenses (production or sales licenses), by buying development or production companies, by entering into joint ventures or by exchanging information and experience with other companies. Modern means of communication facilitate all this by overcoming geographical distances, saving time and making processes more transparent.

The best basis for scenario planning is an internal company information system that provides valuable data and thus secures a lead in terms of knowledge. Without such an information system, the environment in which the company operates must be explored as extensively as possible with the help of a wide range of experts.

Scenario planning

It is highly probable that it will be necessary to take a global view – as we have already done above. By planning scenarios you can project customer potential and requirements, competitors' strategies and alternative courses of action as well as your own strengths and weaknesses onto the future.

On the basis of a variety of assumptions, a simulated world of future scenarios and their consequences can be created. Master actions that appear to have favorable effects in all scenarios are identified and implemented immediately. Examples of these might be the best possible electronic and mobile, internal and external networking, higher standards of safety or strategic collaboration.

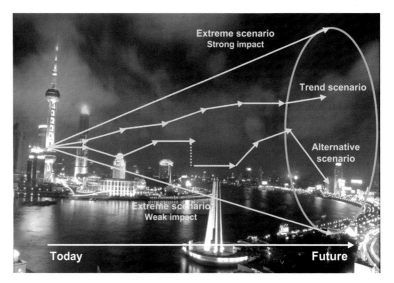

Figure 87
Scenario planning

A core strategy that provides the direction for day-to-day activities can be derived from the various future scenarios.

Scenario planning is still used far too infrequently, but in the future it will be an established element of every planning process. Complex business models will be simulated by running business plans through suitable application software. The kind of linear planning usually preferred up to now is not nearly dynamic enough and does not take account of any disruptive factors. A successful business concept must be designed in such a way that it is also possible to respond quickly to changes. Scenario planning helps you to prepare for a future that is full of surprises because it allows you to follow through several possible courses of development – not simply the most probable one – and train your company for the future using a wide variety of models (see figure 87).

Operational implementation

Good ideas are no good to you unless you actually follow them through and take action. The need for action is particularly acute now, since we live in a time in which all the indications are that product life cycles, the period for which business models remain valid and the length of customer relationships are all going to continue to become shorter.

Information is now gathered from countless sources, and knowledge is drawn from large numbers of people. During operational planning, the strategic plans are broken down, applied at the departmental level and translated into targets for the action that needs to be taken.

Converting the company's vision and central objectives into strategies that are comprehensible to all those involved is thus something that the entire management team needs to do on a continuous basis.

Competent, informed and responsible staff then base their actions on the company's central objectives and strategy. Moreover, they do it with conviction and enthusiasm because they know why they are doing what they are doing.

To make this a reality, the various activities carried out within the framework of operational planning for different areas, fields of business, functions and departments must be stipulated as clearly as possible so that each member of staff understands how he or she can personally contribute to the company's success and how these contributions tie in with other activities. Here, too, an appropriate appeal must be made both to people's emotions and their rationality to ensure that they are both committed and motivated.

Business plans made in accordance with the central objectives stipulate which figures need to be monitored. Deviations from these planning figures are thus detected in good time by an early warning system known as a balanced scorecard (a subject to which we will return later).

Strategic concepts are translated into specific actions within the framework of a program.

Programs

Programs for improving competitiveness are derived from the definition of the field of business and the course marked out there.

Follow-up operational programs to improve the company's position can be drawn up once the factors that contribute to success in the market and the company's core competencies have been identified.

Functional programs optimize the various different tasks of departments, whereas cross-functional programs structure the value-added chain, define sequences of activities and improve processes.

Targeted advertising, roadshows, e-marketing and m-marketing improve the positioning of the company and how it is perceived from the outside.

Programs for increasing sales and optimizing channels, e-sales and marketing and customer programs emphasizing the total cost or value of ownership or the return on investment improve the effectiveness of the company's sales and marketing efforts.

Turning to development, programs for platform design, modularization, standardization, reducing the number of types and implementing 24/7 development are suitable for improving the position of the company relative to the competition. Production segmentation, automation, increased output, reduced supplier numbers, e-purchasing and e-logistics also strengthen the company's position with regard to development.

As far as the service sector is concerned, we will no longer be able to ignore e-services and m-services if we want to avoid being left behind.

Finally, to ensure that we have better staff than the competition in the 21st century, we should make use of programs for e-recruiting and e-learning.

In order to be successful in business, we have to defend and build on our competitive advantages. However, that does not mean that you have to do everything yourself. It is better to focus on your strengths and take the opportunity to work with other companies where appropriate. A company that is strong in R&D, for example, might consider folding its production

Deciding whether to make, buy or form a partnership

operations and concluding an agreement with another company to do its production for it.

When making decisions like this, in addition to hard figures it is essential that you also identify the numerous soft factors that hold a company together. For instance, a production manager will often know his own sales and distribution people better than an outsider ever could, and he will be able to make a very accurate assessment of their sales forecasts based on previous experience. Similarly, if you rely on an external supplier for your production needs, a sudden reduction or increase in the number of units required can lead to considerable problems, particularly if the contract does not specify exactly what is to be done in such situations.

If you are faced with the stark choice of either making something or buying it, you will opt to make it if the strategic importance of the components/ systems is very high and/or their availability is very poor or uncertain.

In short, standard components are generally bought in, whereas key components are produced in-house. Between these extremes there are obviously gradations, as shown in figure 88.

- If you decide to buy, there are a number of different ways of doing it. You might enter into a supplier agreement, grant a company preferred supplier status, conclude a collaboration agreement for joint development, marketing, sales, service or production services or outsource production or business processes in their entirety. If you take the outsourcing alternative, you are effectively ceding part of your own added value to an outside company.

- Another form of collaboration involves the conclusion of an OEM (original equipment manufacturing) agreement, on the basis of which products or entire systems are distributed under another name.

- In a joint venture or a merger (with either a majority or minority holding), cooperation is even closer.

- The closest form of cooperation is a complete takeover.

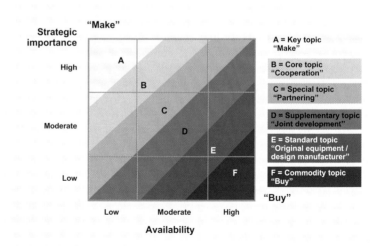

Figure 88
Make or buy

Before you consider a merger or takeover, you should have formulated a clear collaboration or acquisition strategy. The next step is to search for promising companies. Once you have identified the candidates, you have to evaluate and investigate them in detail in a due diligence process. The last element of a successful merger and acquisition (M&A) process involves regularly reviewing your M&A strategy.

A systematic approach should be adopted when searching for partners. The relevant part of your company must provide support during the negotiating process and develop and implement a suitable integration concept. The process of continuously monitoring the market for potential targets for acquisition also helps track down new prospective partners.

You should also consider whether and, if so, which new core competencies can be acquired from a prospective partner.

In order to be able to assess the advantages of a possible merger or acquisition, you have to scrutinize the company's competencies, regional coverage, distribution channels, customers and range of products and services to establish whether they complement or overlap with your own.

It is important to repeatedly ask ourselves the following questions:

- Are we unique and outstanding enough?
- How can we learn from the best in our industry or other industries?
- Where can we go on the offensive, and where do we have to defend ourselves?

Procedure in the market

Paradigm shifts bring with them both dangers and opportunities in abundance. Not for nothing is much of the vocabulary used in this connection borrowed from the military sphere. A company seeking to gain ground might mount a frontal attack, an attack from the flanks or a guerilla attack, while a company defending its position might mount a counteroffensive, make a pre-emptive strike, secure its flanks or take flight. The weapons used are information and disinformation, time advantages, technology leads, cost benefits, the product portfolio, a narrowing of focus, diversification, repositioning, innovation, outsourcing, patent strategy, pricing policy, distribution channel alteration, finance deals, regional strategy, service policy, partnerships, takeovers, sell-offs, restructuring, cost reduction, relocation of production facilities, changes to the value-added depth and downstream or upstream integration.

Regardless of the particular battlefield on which we are engaged, whatever we do, we should make sure the whole company is behind the effort. To this end, we have to optimize the way we work together. And the innovations in the information and communication sector are just what we need to help us do that.

Organizations fit for individuals

Many companies are now networked both internally and externally, and consequently many workflows have changed. New ground rules are reshaping the structure of businesses and the actual content of the business done as well as the workflows involved. Thanks to knowledge management, comprehensive, up-to-date information can now be constantly available wherever you are, and the trend toward online business is leading to real-time management, in which decisions have to be taken within a very short space of time. Moreover, online business models require all of a company's employees to acquire new skills.

Organizations have to redefine themselves.

The ideal employees of the future will be outstanding individuals who identify with the company, commit themselves to achieving business success and get pleasure out of doing it. They therefore need to know themselves, be self-motivated and want to develop. The coaching, management and ongoing training of individuals will thus be of huge importance in the coming years.

Forms of organization

Functional organizations are generally subdivided into development, marketing, sales and distribution and service divisions or departments, which makes it inevitable that there will be problems coordinating their activities (see figure 89). With good management, however, a functional structure can still be very effective, but it will not survive without including processes that involve and integrate the various divisions or departments and without defining how collaboration is to take place at the interfaces between them and at the company's external interfaces to the outside world.

Much the same kind of thing can be said about forms of organization involving business units that are divided up on the basis of different fields of business (see figure 90). These require several marketing and sales departments, which often do not coordinate their activities with customers. In addition, central departments tend to increase disproportionately in size and number, resulting in snowballing costs and reduced profits.

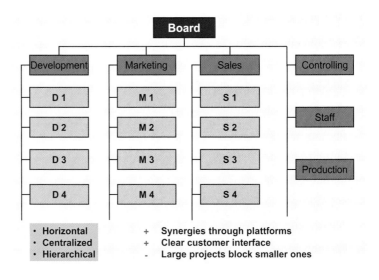

Figure 89
The functional organization

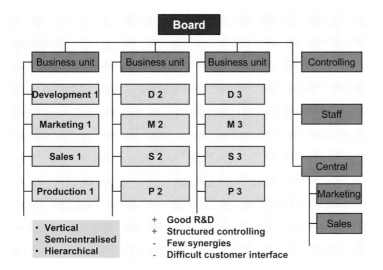

Figure 90
Field of business
organization

Neither of these structures is particularly well suited to collaboration with other companies because the integration of the partners initially causes a considerable amount of disruption and it takes some time before new processes are settled on.

Particularly in times when business conditions are difficult, the pendulum tends to swing in the direction of centralization, but this should not stop us from trying to find better solutions. And there are better solutions.

In process organizations, which are on the rise (see figure 91), the activities of smaller business units and departments can be organized on the basis of processes and their content.

Process organizations

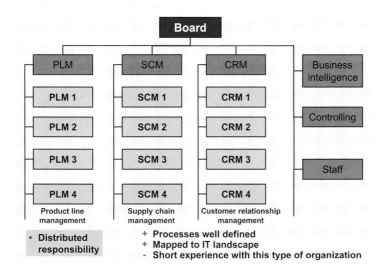

Figure 91
Process organization

The advantages are obvious: The information and communication infrastructure follows the workflows, thus bringing productivity improvements. The changing role of managers in workflow processes, both as suppliers and customers, means there is no longer any room for personal vanity and they have to adapt to the new imperatives. In the event of restructuring, it is not necessary to redefine all tasks and workflows; well established processes can simply be linked to new interfaces.

Biological and computer systems demonstrate that the basic prerequisites for the efficient allocation of tasks are clearly defined, focused workflows and processes, together with compatible interfaces and protocols.

On the one hand, each unit must aim to realize the jointly defined vision and achieve the objectives derived from it. On the other, it has to strive for the best possible price/performance ratio and world-class quality. To this end, we should take our inspiration from nature and think in terms of dynamic processes.

Project organizations If a company cannot achieve this, it is better advised to outsource certain functions or bring in new partners rather than persevere with its existing constellation and go down in a blaze of glory. Companies will thus become virtual project organizations consisting of a large number of independent parts (see figure 92). These, in turn, may consist of a certain number of independent "Me Inc." employees.

While project organizations are common in plant engineering and construction and in the consulting and systems businesses, for example, this does not apply to the same extent to volume businesses. More experience is required here.

Project management

Biotechnology, microelectronics, software technologies and information and communication technologies are shaking up many of our established

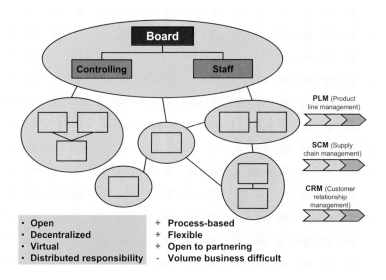

Figure 92
Project organization

- Open
- Decentralized
- Virtual
- Distributed responsibility

+ Process-based
+ Flexible
+ Open to partnering
- Volume business difficult

patterns of thinking. The time from the start of product development to the market launch is getting shorter in every industry you care to look at.

Projects and project teams represent a dynamic form of organization that is well suited to increasing the speed at which companies can respond.

A project consists of a one-off, unique set of requirements to be met within a limited period that is characterized by clearly defined project goals and responsibilities.

Projects are an effective form of organization for non-recurring, complex tasks of a limited duration. In order to manage projects efficiently and effectively, project managers need to know and be able to master certain ground rules relating to the organization and running of projects.

Increasingly often, projects with international involvement and external partners are the chosen form of organization in cases where satisfactory results could not be achieved by one company alone.

Because it permits flexible responses to be made to changing requirements, project management is often superior to other, more inflexible forms of organization.

We should therefore make efforts to find out which new business areas are suitable for projects.

The various aspects of project management are outlined in figure 93.

Organizations structured on the basis of projects and processes place great emphasis on having open interfaces. These allow them to globalize and/or outsource processes. The marketing can be done in Italy, for example, development in Germany, production in China and sales and distribution locally in just the same way as if everything was done in the same place. If external partners are used for all these processes, the company essentially becomes a virtual company. Competitive advantages that cannot easily be reproduced thus acquire increasing significance. Many manufacturers of

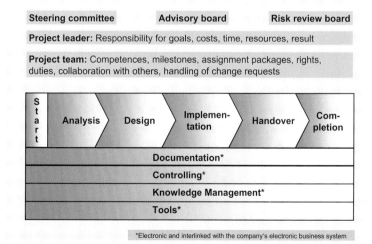

Figure 93
Project
management

Steering committee | Advisory board | Risk review board

Project leader: Responsibility for goals, costs, time, resources, result

Project team: Competences, milestones, assignment packages, rights, duties, collaboration with others, handling of change requests

Start → Analysis → Design → Implementation → Handover → Completion

Documentation*
Controlling*
Knowledge Management*
Tools*

*Electronic and interlinked with the company's electronic business system

consumer goods now actually control only two or three of around twenty steps in the value-added chain, yet they are still successful.

There are a number of different forms of organization that are suitable for running projects:

- A separate organizational unit can be formed for a project. The project manager in this conventional form of organization is a responsible entrepreneur. However, the process of how the team is to be dissolved at the end of the project is often unclear.

- The weakest form of organization for projects involves coordinating them within the line organization without a specially designated, separate team. The people involved remain in their existing posts, from which they are released, as required, to work in the project team. In contrast to a project manager, the coordinator has little responsibility or authority. Consequently, it may be difficult to respond quickly enough to changes and gain priority over other tasks.

- The matrix organization, in which project managers stipulate the requirements they have of the existing line organization in terms of functionality and time, is more rigorous. The line managers then specify resources and define a concept. Uncertainties often arise here in interpersonal dealings. In one particular form of this type of organization, the project manager is also given control of the budget and thus more influence.

- However, forms of project organization are in a process of ongoing development. In pool organization, for example, line responsibilities are largely done away with. Project managers and team members are recruited from these pools in structures with very flat hierarchies. Problems such as employee transfer or dual control – which occur in the matrix form of organization – are thus eliminated. The sluggishness and inflexibility associated with other forms of organization are overcome, and the barriers between departments and partner companies are broken down. However, issues such as the income and career paths of staff have to be re-examined, and the staff in the pool have to face up to the challenge. Their qualifications, commitment and social skills determine whether they are used in a project. The new demands on the staff are that they have to keep proving themselves at regular intervals, and they also have to keep developing, possibly even changing their orientation, as required.

The "Me Inc." individual has thus become a reality inside companies. Pool organization is very well suited to the provision of services such as management consulting, for example.

The project manager is the central contact person, entrepreneur, coordinator, conflict manager and marketing man for the project. Project managers' tasks, authorization, responsibilities and management brief must always be made clear to them.

They are responsible for the successful business implementation of the project entrusted to them. Successful in this context means that performance, the budget and schedule must be within the target range.

Within the limited timeframe of the project, the project manager has to take on a number of different roles. The most important of these is that of the entrepreneur. Direct access to the customer at management level makes it easier to evaluate and solve difficult situations. On account of the many interfaces involved, the project manager also has to fulfill the role of information and knowledge manager, conflict manager and project coordinator. Consequently, the demands on project managers in terms of their ability to assert themselves and demonstrate analytical and social skills are very high. They must be able to adapt their management style to suit different situations, and an effective, efficient and constructive approach is expected from all concerned.

Projects can only be successful if there are clearly defined rules for how the project team is to work together with others. This means good processes and a tolerance-based and accepting management concept in which each person and each organizational unit shows respect for others and can expect the same in return, thus forming the foundation for working relationships based on trust.

Many companies are still managed in an almost military manner. Orders are issued and followed and the work done is checked in a command structure that demands a high degree of respect. This is an established model in wartime, but military dictatorships are highly unstable in the long term and often lead to competitive disadvantages. However, democratic arrangements where everyone has their say but there is little sense of direction are also ineffective. These extremes clearly indicate that – just as in politics – management and coaching are crucial to the success of a company and will remain so.

When a drug is used for medical purposes, its success depends on its active agent and the dosage, and much the same kind of cause and effect relationship applies to the biology of the company.

The necessity of having a tighter, more coaching-oriented style of management on the one hand, and of granting freedoms to entrepreneurs in the company on the other, will continue to provide fertile ground for much debate in the future, as companies seek to attain the best possible balance. Effective controlling and transparency will be achieved by means of IT. Companies will increasingly comprise smaller permanent teams with business relationships to partners, suppliers, subcontractors and outsourcers.

In most industries, the trend is already toward companies that consist of small, responsible, agile core teams. If a bigger team is required, subcontractors can be used. Agency workers, contract workers or the self-employed can work for the company for limited periods, depending on the volume of orders the company receives. In this way, companies remain agile and can respond quickly. They should, however, ensure that they do not allow themselves to lose their core competencies.

It must be ensured that core knowledge about products, processes and industrial property rights is transferred to the company from such suppliers.

Partnering and collaboration

If a company shapes itself around defined, networked processes, its organizational structure will be less hierarchical and more team-oriented, as we have seen. If this strategy is extended beyond the boundaries of the company, it will result in partnering and collaboration agreements with other companies. Ariane, the European rocket used primarily to launch satellites, is a good example of collaboration. What causes companies to join forces? The aim is generally either to secure economies of scale or to have control of several stages of the value-added chain. Broadening the customer base is more often the motivation than the wish to add technology competency.

A number of different factors have to come into play for successful collaboration. Figure 94 shows a selection of these.

In the next few years we can expect processes to be subject to disaggregation throughout the world. Companies will concentrate on the factors that contribute to their success and their core competencies and outsource everything else – which is why the outsourcing of IT, business processes, facility management and personnel management, for example, is on the increase. Companies are concentrating on the essentials, and secondary functions are being handled more cost-effectively than ever before.

The advantages of partnerships over mergers are that they can be set up relatively quickly, do not require a great deal of investment and do not lead to spectacular debts or depreciation. On the contrary, if a partnership is successful, sales, profits and stock prices rise more rapidly than they would have done if the partners had gone it alone. A partnership is thus an easy route to take that leaves many options open for the future. Figure 95 illustrates the advantages, taking collaboration with suppliers as an example.

Figure 94
Factors contributing to successful collaboration

The entrepreneur's joystick

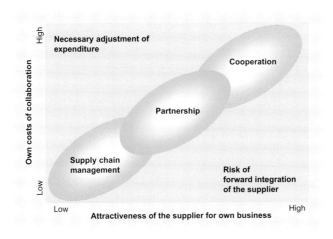

Figure 95
Advantages of
partnerships

Let's assume we have found the best form of organization and have put in place efficient, dynamic processes. Can anything go wrong now? It certainly can! A bad boss could still mess everything up. The main question is whether the company's strategies and values are adhered to in everyday business. It is up to the management to ensure they are.

Management and coaching

If we are to take on a management role and play it well, we must know ourselves, accept our weaknesses as well as our strengths, be open to feedback and be willing to keep learning for as long as we live. The expectations that managers have to live up to have changed significantly in the last few decades:

Does what is feasible	→ achieves what is achievable
Gets results by wielding power	→ gets results through force of personality
Asks how and when	→ asks what and why
Administers	→ renews
Relies on checking up on people	→ inspires trust
Takes a short-term view of the situation	→ takes a long-term perspective
Is stuck in the here and now	→ looks at what is on the horizon
Accepts the status quo	→ questions the status quo
Is geared to structures	→ is geared to people
Orders	→ communicates
Copies	→ innovates
Does things right	→ does the right things
Generates pressure	→ generates ambition
Sticks to established procedure	→ feels his way into new approaches
Is industrious	→ is committed

Evolution from the traditional manager to today's modern manager

Is hesitant about trying out something new	→	has the courage of his convictions
Restructures	→	transforms
Checks up on people	→	gives people support
Has a good knowledge of the system	→	has a good knowledge of people
Demands respect	→	wins hearts and minds
Appears well trained	→	appears genuine
Believes in power structures	→	relies on charisma
Relies on people higher up the chain of command	→	believes in himself
Has limited tolerance	→	is forgiving

It pays to adopt an ethical approach, and it is important that managers manage actively and get things done quickly. They should start with themselves, by exercising self-discipline and constantly increasing the targets they set themselves. What is required is a careful yet strong, consistent, coherent and realistic approach that wins over employees' hearts and minds. Good managers must be able to handle and read emotions; they need to know how to draw the poison out of negative emotions and transform them into positive ones. In this way, they encourage all members of staff to contribute their energy and skills to the common cause and continue to develop themselves. To a good manager, each person is important and deserves to be trusted, listened to carefully and respected. And the majority must not be prevented by a few individuals from purposefully following this path.

It is essential that managers take advantage of the achievements of the information age. Figures, data and facts are easier to access then ever before, and being prepared means maintaining a broad overview while not being afraid to bore for details when the situation requires it. Management information systems and databases permit simulations and measurements to be carried out, but only if you keep track of the important parameters on your scorecard, for example, will you be able to evaluate the results obtained.

The manager of the future

Like Moses, managers today must take their people to a new land. It is simply not enough just to carry on as before, because technological progress and the democratization of society will continue to have dramatic effects on organizations and how people work together. Teleworkers and "Me Inc." employees require new, more sensitive management mechanisms than those established over the last century.

It is up to each individual to clearly identify the direction things are taking and how they can best bring all their strengths to bear to take us where we are going. It must also be clear in advance how success is to be measured. Of course, nobody is infallible. Good managers should offer their employees support and training to prevent mistakes happening in the future. The challenge is to channel the energy of "Me Inc." employees into the required direction in order to achieve a common purpose through synergy.

As managers, we need to learn how to effectively use new communication technologies such as e-mail, video mail, video conferences, online chatting, SMS texting and instant messaging in order to fulfill our management role. All of these technologies have the potential to break down hierarchical power relationships and promote a constant, productive exchange of thoughts and ideas. To get the most out of both our emotional and our rational sides, we need managers who are genuine, honest, credible, inspiring, professional, wise, open, willing to learn, pragmatic, entrepreneurial, empathetic, mature, communicative, authoritative, resilient, experienced and honorable and who thus set an example of what they expect from others.

Another reason why management is being redefined is that companies will increasingly consist of small, core teams of full-time employees, with more and more work done externally by partners, other companies, part-time employees or "Me Inc." one-man or one-woman operations. Personnel departments might have their payroll accounting done externally, marketing departments the new advertising campaign, development departments the design of the case for a new device, and the chief information officer (CIO) the operation of the information and communication infrastructure. **Management of third parties**

The result is the same every time: Constantly changing partners who do not necessarily optimize how they do what they do in accordance with our corporate objectives have to be managed in a different way, which may be stipulated by contract. External people and companies also need to be motivated and feel integrated. At the same time, the price and quality of the work done must be monitored, as must the time taken to do it. Finally, the overall costs of the collaboration must be measured against the benefits derived from it.

New managers also have to look at new ways of organizing working time. As the values of staff change and the trend toward individualization continues, people are making new demands of the working environment and want to organize their time in new ways. Provided it is financially viable, people are increasingly interested in freelancing, working from home, temporary work, part-time time work, flexitime or simply in taking time out. This development is often referred to as the attempt to find a work-life balance. The challenge is to achieve the company's objectives within a loose framework of international relationships, while maintaining process stability. **Redefining working hours**

In sport, a good coach is expected to have comprehensive, interdisciplinary knowledge in order to get the best out of top athletes. In addition to physical training, the coach is expected to be able to convey the essential techniques, tactics and theories required, as well as knowledge about nutrition and mental training. To enable them to achieve the best possible performance, athletes' mental and physical capabilities also have to be improved in a balanced way. The coach's team is thus augmented by external advisers such as doctors, biomechanics and physiotherapists. Figure 96 makes these connections clear. **Coaching skills**

The coaching process just described for sport can also be applied in a business context, with the manager as the coach and a support team consisting

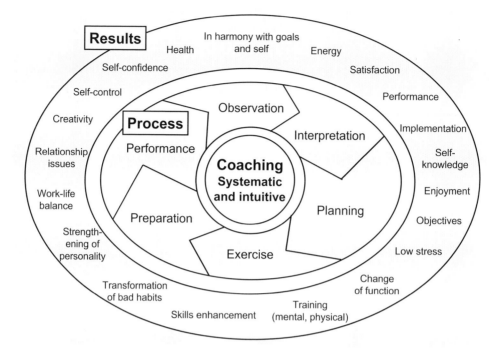

Figure 96   Coaching

of the personnel department, further training instructors, the company doctor and possibly others. Unfortunately, however, this approach has not yet been adopted widely enough outside the field of sport.

This is regrettable, since the coaching of entrepreneurial individuals could release previously unimagined potential from which companies could benefit directly.

If you are able to use your core skills at work and at the same time do what you like doing, you will have no difficulty delivering top performance and will enjoy receiving positive feedback.

Companies in which staff can give of themselves fully are more successful than those where no process of identification with the company takes place. Coaches concern themselves with encouraging people to develop in useful directions, and the development of employees' knowledge, capabilities and personalities is fully in line with the company's objectives. Employees are thus encouraged to become entrepreneurial and can be thought of as "intrapreneurs" within the company. New technologies also facilitate online coaching by eliminating delayed feedback and allowing people to continue their training or development even when on business trips.

These new forms of coaching must be adapted to today's young people, who have grown up in the age of Nintendo and are now growing into the age of mobile living.

They are sophisticated, straightforward, constantly online and thus constantly available to provide a quick impression or piece of information.

Management means not losing sight of objectives, while building up the skills and capabilities required by the company. As described in the section on strategy, the challenge is to secure lasting competitive advantages that are recognized as such by customers. This involves deploying technologies quickly wherever they bring advantages, using knowledge management proactively, making strategic use of knowledge and constantly creating additional value for customers. At the same time, coaching often takes individuals out of the comfort zone, but this is normal and something that is familiar to anyone who has been involved in competitive sport. No progress can be made without a real effort.

The coaching manager remains the preferred contact person for customers, the team and individuals and is responsible for ensuring objectives are achieved, tasks are completed and schedules and budgets are adhered to. The variety of the roles such a manager is expected to fulfill is on the increase: entrepreneur, advisor, teacher, pacesetter, mentor, consultant, motivator and relationship manager, to name but a few. At the same time, the manager must keep a constant focus on processes and how to improve them.

Processes

Our bodies, the plants in our gardens and the computers in our offices are characterized by well-ordered processes, and the same should apply to our companies as well. However, inflexible and complex processes often lead to friction, resulting in the loss of time and money.

Given that corporate departments are filled with specialists working in specific areas and that business processes generally involve several such departments, it is clear that only well-defined, well-implemented processes can guarantee smooth operation. It is useful to think of processes as the tracks along which projects and day-to-day operations run, as shown in figure 97.

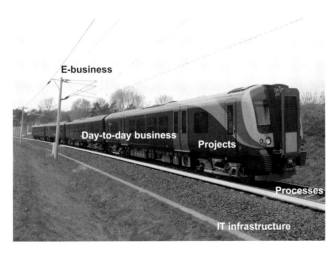

Figure 97
Processes as tracks

Chief information officers are faced with the challenge of implementing world-class processes that will take their electronic, mobile, real-time companies into the future. Their task is to provide these processes with a seamless, universal information and communication infrastructure and to standardize the process interfaces.

Standardized interfaces are particularly important because processes frequently have to be adapted to cope with the increasing rate of change. The interfaces can be compared with the railroad switches not shown in figure 96. They allow changes to be made quickly without the need to lay new track, with all the disruption that involves. Outsourcing is also facilitated by clear process interfaces. Make no mistake: Value chains are going to need to be continuously readjusted as a result of globalization. We therefore have to prepare ourselves and our IT systems now for the dynamic value chains of the future.

Figure 98 illustrates how traditional business processes are developing into the new corporate processes of the electronic age. The product development process has become product life-cycle management (PLM), the logistical process has turned into supply chain management (SCM), and the sales and marketing process now goes by the name of customer relationship management (CRM). A management information system (MIS) may be used to display scorecards and cockpits. Further processes are accounting and controlling, which take traditional business accounting to

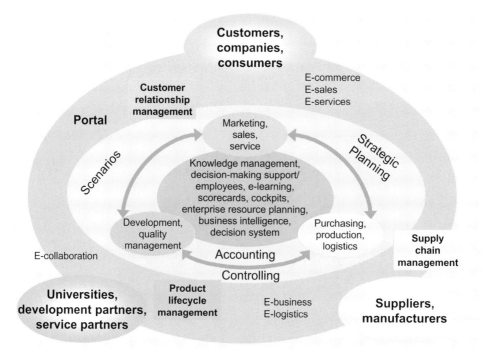

Figure 98   Electronic processes

new levels, strategic planning and personnel management, which is now often referred to as human resources management.

As the years go by, the names of the processes may change – but they are still there and their fundamental logic remains the same.

All of these processes generate large volumes of data, which is then stored automatically. Whereas product life-cycle management produces product- and project-specific information, the knowledge management process provides check lists, contracts, best practice guidelines, project debriefings, records of people's skills and qualifications, training schemes and so on. Business intelligence, on the other hand, contributes business ratios, analyses, reports, forecasts and process performance data, whereas accounting and controlling IT provide key business data and status information from the early warning system to the cockpit.

Today, different programs are used in each of these areas, but unfortunately they communicate with each other no better than the people they serve. This will all have to change – and quickly. All these processes will be interlinked via standard interfaces, databases will permit access only to those with authorization, and intelligent programs will establish connections, compress data and provide assistance with decisions, forecasts and scenarios.

Today's process landscape is still far from uniform, often consisting of cumbersome, incompatible, stand-alone solutions. Furthermore, efforts to improve efficiency are impeded by complex software structures and custom solutions throughout the process chain. There is a considerable need for action here at all levels. The level of computer networking may now be high, but in no way does that necessarily translate into efficient process and project support for staff.

It therefore pays to make a point of launching regular fitness programs. Using a fishbone chart (see figure 99) or similar method, it is possible to trace and remove the causes of productivity deficits.

Regular monitoring of processes is particularly important at a time like the present, when there is an increasing amount of information in circulation

Process controlling

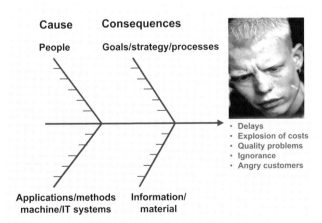

Figure 99
Fishbone chart

and this needs to be intelligently interlinked. It is always the weakest link that determines the performance of the entire process chain, and its effect may be much more dramatic than you might at first assume. The output of a process chain is obtained by multiplying the outputs and qualities of the various processes involved in it. For example, if efficiency in supply chain management is 80%, in enterprise resource planning 30%, in product life-cycle management 45% and in customer relationship management 70%, overall efficiency is 8%.

Creating business plans for new products and simulations of new business still entails a high, one-off outlay today. That will have to change. As a result of evolutionary business improvements, restructuring in the conventional sense will become unnecessary. What often happens now is that change is delayed for as long as it possibly can be, which means that everything then has to be questioned, analyzed and rearranged in one fell swoop. An early warning system that indicates problems as they arise, rigorously implemented networks and a coaching style of management with integrated fitness programs could finally put an end to the repeated restructuring that seems to have become almost inevitable.

Knowledge management

The saying "knowledge is power" may be something of a truism, but it has greater validity now than ever before. The more we know about our competitors and the less they know about us, the more successful our company will be. The company's intelligent information system, sometimes referred to as the knowledge management system, provides us with the information we need on which to base a selection of the correct tactics.

You would think it would go without saying that you need to understand and be in control of your business. Unfortunately, the failures of too many companies both large and small have shown us that this is far from the truth. By the time the great crisis is looming on the horizon, ad hoc analyses and restructuring are of only limited use. However, disaster can usually be averted by means of an integrated online process that brings together all the relevant data about the market, the competition and the company. By using balanced scorecards and trend scenarios and by assessing different alternatives to provide orientation, management has a better chance of arriving at the right decisions.

Twenty years or so ago, there was a popular saying doing the rounds in many companies that is worth remembering: "If the company only knew what the company knows." Knowledge management could prove to be what is needed to cut the Gordian knot. It may no longer be the most fashionable term, but sooner or later it will have to be revived. If it is accepted in modern management culture that you can make the same mistake once, but once only, the same principle should apply to the whole company.

Knowledge management is faced with an enormous challenge if it is to prevent several people – or even one person – from making the same mistake repeatedly.

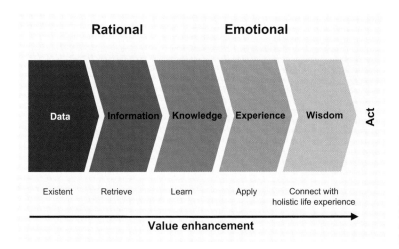

Rational   **Emotional**

| Data | Information | Knowledge | Experience | Wisdom | Act |
| Existent | Retrieve | Learn | Apply | Connect with holistic life experience | |

Value enhancement

Figure 100
Enhancing the
decision-making
process

In industries such as microelectronics, biotechnology or pharmaceuticals, in particular, the company's knowledge may account for a huge part of its worth. Although they do not yet appear in balance sheets, knowledge and wisdom can make an enormous difference to the value of a company (see figure 100). Intangible assets generally appear in a company's balance sheet as a small sub-item under fixed assets. These include licenses, industrial property rights, patents and so on – assets that give a company a competitive advantage or allow it to receive income from other companies. The rest of the knowledge bound up in the company is totally disregarded. Just how extensive that is can be seen in figure 101, which brings in new aspects and shows the greater part of the huge spectrum of knowledge held by a company.

The value of knowledge to a company

Although we are now in the information age, the subject of knowledge management receives far too little professional attention. The stand-alone solutions and departmental egos that hinder progress today will hopefully be gone tomorrow, but much research and development work also still needs to be done into the subject. The fact that we talk of knowledge bases, knowledge communities, knowledge marketplaces, knowledge processes, knowledge structures, knowledge organization, knowledge strategies, knowledge quality and so on cannot hide the fact that progress is slow.

It is therefore useful to focus increasingly on providing everyone with the information they require as quickly as possible and enabling them to access the knowledge of others. In short:

The company's knowledge needs to be protected against those outside the company but made universally available to those inside it.

Sometimes, however, what we end up with is the opposite. In internal networks we often still come across hurdles such as media discontinuity, heterogeneous operating systems or software versions and department-specific access rights. All of this stands in the way of the implementation of a digital nervous system. In living creatures, such phenomena lead to paralysis.

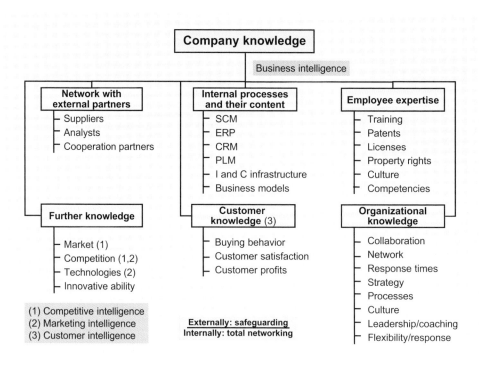

Figure 101   A company's knowledge

Competitive
intelligence In volume markets only the global number one and two do well, so they have to press home any advantage they have in terms of information and turn it into marketable products. The rise in industrial espionage indicates that companies are well aware of the value of knowledge management, and there are also legal approaches to the problem. The function of competitive intelligence is to obtain knowledge about market trends and the positioning and market access of competitors. There is also potential in benchmarking or comparing a company's performance against its competitors or the industry leaders. At the same time, it is essential to learn as much as possible about your customers – thus gaining customer intelligence – and to make this knowledge accessible to everyone in the company.

Knowledge means not just power but also money, and an increasing number of companies are making money from the sale of knowledge. In the simplest case, they charge for access to their databases and archives.

Automated electronic services providing knowledge are a new source of revenue.

The challenge is to tap all the relevant sources of knowledge. Once you have plundered all these sources for information, the information obtained is just a dead asset unless it is used to form the basis for decision-making and unless the knowledge acquired is exploited to take advantage of business opportunities. The following kinds of sources are available to us:

- Internet/intranet
- Customers/dealers/business partners
- Newspapers/magazines
- Staff in your own company
- Consultants/analysts
- Interviews/visits
- Conferences/meetings/fairs
- Customer events
- Customer surveys
- Suppliers
- Banks
- Organizations/associations
- Benchmarking
- Competitors
- Staff of other companies
- Databases

Sources of knowledge

It is worth emphasizing again that knowledge is worth nothing unless it is put to use. The information and communication industry has much to learn here. The missing ingredients in many cases are automatic data preparation and a focus on the really important data. Unless there is some kind of filtering in place, information systems often produce a huge volume of data in response to almost any query. Reliable and intelligent applications with user-friendly interfaces are therefore required to process and prepare this data. Business people need to take a leaf out of the book of journalists, who have always known that better information logically leads to a competitive advantage.

Another central aspect of knowledge management is the exchange of knowledge. In the interest of providing everyone with a comprehensive, all-encompassing understanding of the business they are involved in, it is often very helpful if people from different departments or specialist areas come together at regular intervals and report on their work. Important personal contacts can also be established in this way, thus improving interpersonal networking within the company. And the company also saves itself the costs of bringing in external instructors.

Exchanging knowledge

Learning organizations

Knowledge and learning will be key issues in the future, and in order to remain on the ball, a company needs to continuously learn and improve. For companies involved in volume segments, cost leadership is an essential prerequisite for business success.

However, cost leadership can only be attained through high volumes. This is based on the empirical finding that real total unit costs can be reduced by around 25 – 30% if the production volume is doubled. This applies both to the accumulated volume over time and the current production capacity. There are minor deviations from this rule as a result of fixed costs when new production machines or additional production lines are introduced, for example.

Volume and learning effects contribute to the reduction of unit costs:

- Volume effects include purchasing advantages, larger production machines, fewer personnel per production unit and higher machine capacity utilization. Similar effects are obtained with a higher level of production automation, lower setup costs when products are changed, specialized and optimized production lines, a lower proportion of the budget accounted for by development and overhead costs and declining fixed costs.

- Learning effects are obtained from a continuous program of improvement to increase quality and output, reduce costs and improve processes, as well as from an intensive examination of aspects of mass production.

Even market leaders can never be sure of not being bettered by their competitors. By optimizing volumes and costs you can set the right course, but it is always possible that new competitors will appear and shift the goalposts.

This applies in the technology sector, in particular, where specialized devices may tomorrow be superseded by standardized components, as is currently happening to video and audio recorders, which are being squeezed out by PCs. Alternatively, a new, more effective channel to the customer may open up and change the ground rules. New business models are emerging in e-business, in particular, and threatening established businesses.

Effectiveness and efficiency can also be improved as a result of learning effects and well-targeted measures in research and development, sales and marketing and accounting. It is important to preserve the company's knowledge in the event of its reorientation or realignment.

The more intelligent electronic systems become, the more important it is that man and machine are closely linked. The organization can then realize much more of their potential.

Finance and controlling

Business administrators tend to want to put a value on everything and think in terms of ratios. And by examining operational processes, financial flows and the prevailing rules and regulations it is perfectly possible to do this. Here we are going to restrict ourselves to examining only the most commonly used and meaningful business management ratios. Figure 102 shows the most important ratios used in controlling.

EBITDA and EVA   In most annual reports the operating result is presented in the form of EBITDA (earnings before interest, taxes, depreciation and amortization) and EVA (economic value added), which is derived from it. Both of these relate to profitability – in other words, the bottom line.

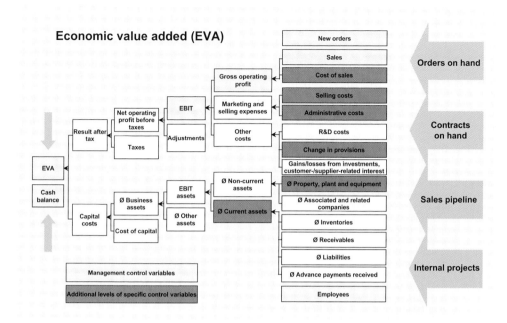

EVA, in particular, can be used to measure real business success. Let's assume a startup company begins with 2 million euros of borrowed initial capital at an interest rate of 15%. If the profit in the first year is 500,000 euros, 300,000 euros of interest has to be deducted from this to obtain an economic value added of 200,000 euros.

The market value is also affected by non-monetary factors. Being non-monetary it is, of course, hard to put a figure on them. Knowledge and the ability to take the lead in a rapidly growing market, however, are two such factors that are increasingly also being taken into account by analysts when assessing the value of a stock. These non-monetary factors play an important role in the balanced scorecard, which we will now take a closer look at.

Non-monetary factors

Balanced scorecard

In searching for a model that allows a company to be assessed and controlled, it is essential to strike a balance between strategic statements and key financial data. It is also important to focus on the future as well as the past. Figure 103 illustrates the factors involved in this balancing act.

On the balanced scorecard there are four areas that have to be taken into account in a vision and strategy:

- Finances
- Customers and market
- Organization and partners
- Innovation and learning

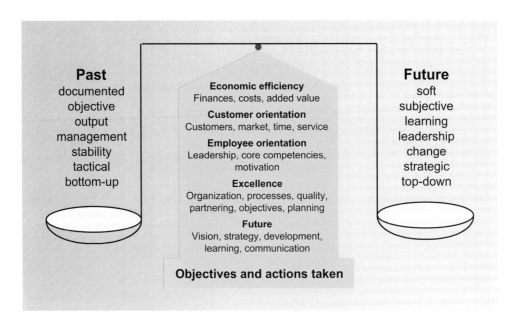

Past
documented
objective
output
management
stability
tactical
bottom-up

Economic efficiency
Finances, costs, added value

Customer orientation
Customers, market, time, service

Employee orientation
Leadership, core competencies,
motivation

Excellence
Organization, processes, quality,
partnering, objectives, planning

Future
Vision, strategy, development,
learning, communication

Objectives and actions taken

Future
soft
subjective
learning
leadership
change
strategic
top-down

Figure 103   The balancing act between the past and the future

Each of these areas contains measurable factors that have a decisive influence on earning capacity. The factors can be standardized by means of benchmarking, and the rate of improvement can thus be measured as well. Attention must be directed to core competencies and critical processes as well as the best of the competition and the latest threats from new technology.

However, balanced scorecards are only effective when they are disseminated throughout the organization in a cascading flow of information. These processes have to go bottom-up and top-down.

The mission of a corporate division, for example, is broken down into objectives for departments, teams and individuals. It is critical that everybody involved knows the company's entire "DNA" or blueprint. Only then can they identify with its objectives and work to optimum effect on their part of the process. Such an approach might be referred to as "bio-logical".

If you carry out separate analyses for finances, strategy, benchmarks, processes and so on, you do not take into account that changes in one area have consequences for all the other areas. Effective planning has to take all the different areas into account.

Balanced scorecards close the strategic loop and indicate whether the direction, core competencies and driving factors are in need of adjustment. We should always be aware that customers, employees and markets are input-figures. Financial data are the resulting output-figures.

If a company is to be managed successfully, a number of basic prerequisites have to be in place: clear corporate structures, excellent, modular processes and a universal and clearly structured information and communication infrastructure.

In an efficient system of reporting, the process of obtaining the figures must not be complicated, time-consuming or subject to manipulation in any way.

The system should be automatic, scalable and flexible so as to cope with changes to the business structure as a result of new partnerships, for example. Output in the form of reports distributed to the various interest groups involved – staff, stockholders, analysts and so on – must be automatic. To this end, the various IT systems involved must either be uniform or linked by means of standard interfaces.

A good system of business reporting can adapt to new circumstances. If there are sudden changes in the market, for example – the effects of which can only be really serious in the absence of good scenario planning – new ratios often come to the fore. Adding new forms of reporting in times of crisis is a tacit acceptance of the weakness of the old ones, and attempting to change ratios on the hoof essentially amounts to treating the symptoms rather than dealing with the causes. The reporting systems of the future will avoid this and bring new clarity.

Controlling will thus become fit for the future, by which time, if not before, it will be clear that its essential purpose is to improve performance in the future rather than monitor performance in the past. As in the case of real-time business, there is still much to do here.

Just like modular, biological processes, a system of up-to-the-minute reporting that relies on the digital nerve fibers of the information and communication infrastructure needs a control center in the "brain". If useful results are to be produced, it is critical that important drivers and ratios of the factors that contribute to success are indicated in this control center.

In the balanced scorecard method, all current ratios are usually shown on a cockpit control panel (see figure 104). This provides a comprehensive overview that allows countermeasures to be taken immediately as soon as any of the ratios goes – or threatens to go – off course.

The idea behind this is that, if all the various processes involved are running well, success is inevitable. Thus, the strategy-scorecard-cockpit control loop ensures the availability of a constantly up-to-date, real-time description of the company's situation.

Let's take the competencies indicated in the cockpit and examine this issue separately. After all, if we are to secure and maintain competitive advantages, we will need the right core competencies. In order to assess our current position, we need to compare the targets set when the strategy was formulated with the actual situation indicated by the scorecard. Figure 105 provides an example.

The competency axes shown could, of course, be labeled quite differently, depending on the requirements of the individual company. For managers and their staff it is important to keep all the business-specific factors in

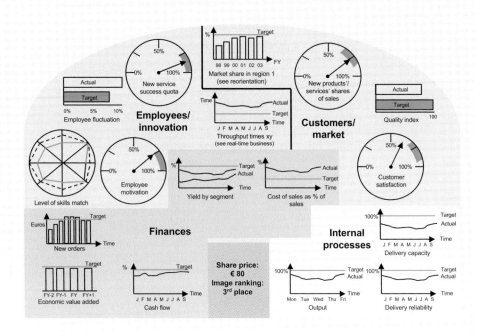

Figure 104   Balanced scorecard: an example of a cockpit

view: headwinds, productivity levers, agreed business objectives and other factors from the balanced scorecard. The sum of the discrepancies between the actual situation and the targets indicates wasted or insufficient energy in areas that are important to the company.

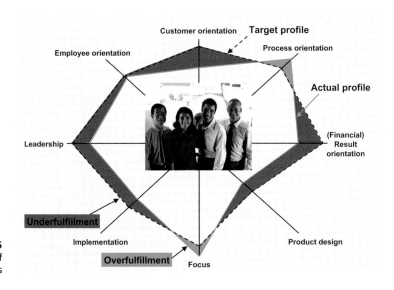

Figure 105
Profile of
competencies

On the basis of this overall view and the specific requirements of their own tasks, each of the "Me Inc." individuals in the company can work out the further training they need. To put it simply, the profile of competencies of each individual should match the company's target profile. However, the following should always be borne in mind:

Changes to the company's objectives have a direct effect on the orientation of the people or "Me Inc." individuals who work for it.

Strategy and controlling must not remain the preserve of only a small group of the initiated. And the variable portions of employees' incomes should be linked to the fulfillment of requirements and acquisition of the necessary competencies.

By going through different scenarios in advance, a company ensures it is able to respond more quickly to events and benefit from improved forecasting, thus enabling the management to see which competencies will be required – which brings us back to the neural networks mentioned earlier. Regardless of how the world changes and the headwinds that are blowing, the better the company's program of training, the sooner it will be able to count itself among the winners.

Sizing

When there is a need to adapt the organization to changing markets, re-structuring and sizing are the tools of choice for major changes, whereas business plans are ideal for fine-tuning – and this is not likely to change in the future. We will therefore be examining both below.

The business world is increasingly fast-moving, and companies have to respond rapidly to changing circumstances. Like an athlete, a company needs flexibility and freedom of movement. And a successful athlete needs to build up muscle rather than just put on weight.

In business it is best to strengthen your company by sizing it dynamically and quickly in good time to suit the market. This approach can save the company from having to engage in dramatic restructuring with all the at-tendant heartache.

So what is the best way to proceed? It is best to approach sizing in the same way as anything else: by drawing conclusions about today from what we know about tomorrow. In this planning process, all conceivable future eventualities are taken into account and expressed in numerical terms, and their effects on today's business are assessed. Figure 106 outlines this principle. We should always be thinking and calculating in terms of scenarios, so no distinctions are drawn between headwinds – whether planned or unplanned – and increases in productivity. At the end of the day, it really does not matter whether or not something that happens was planned for; the important thing is that the correct response is made to it.

Many headwinds have their basis in market trends and can thus be predicted, whereas one-off occurrences such as wars, terrorist attacks, epidemics and natural disasters are not taken into account in many standard planning processes. It therefore makes sense to put in place a variety of means of providing early warnings of imminent crises. As with a fire drill, when

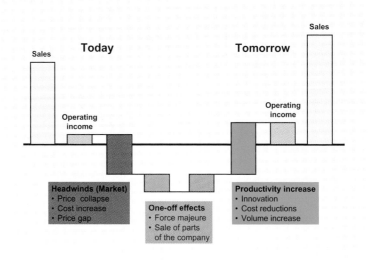

Figure 106
Planning for future
profits

a certain alarm value is exceeded there must be a detailed plan of action available. If panic and chaos are to be avoided, openness and communication are imperative.

Risks and opportunities have to be included in equal measure in your calculations. There should be no place for blind optimism or, indeed, pessimism.

There are many ways to increase productivity in the short term. The table on the next side provides a number of examples. Best-in-class companies do not wait until there is a crisis before using them; they employ them when times are still good.

Order-to-cash and purchase-to-pay times must be optimized. Skillful operators can make healthy profits by having shorter payment periods with their customers than they have with their suppliers.

Reducing inventory levels and outstanding debts can also make a contribution toward productivity, and tied-up capital is a perennial issue. Improving the asset positions is a key topic of EVA. Capital deployed must be profitable, or stockholders may switch to other more secure forms of investment.

Companies must take a long-term view and make provisions for the future. A management team that expects to stay with the company will be more likely to do this because they will anticipate receiving the credit for any success.

Interim management solutions and excessive rotation should therefore be used with caution.

These may breathe new life into the company, but they may also bring a wind of change in the wrong direction – possibly with long-term effects.

	Increase output	Reduce input
Sales	Increase sales Improve prices Review the portfolio of customers Recover debts	Reduce administrative costs Make more use of automated tools Increase e-commerce Improve forecasting
Strategy	Optimize the business portfolio Engage in partnering Optimize channels Charge for services Strengthen unique selling points	Disinvest Outsource Use indirect channels Relocate Buy rather than make
Marketing	Improve the portfolio Put a higher value on services Review regional strategy Use target pricing Sharpen focus Improve design/appeal more to the emotions Promote new development	Adapt the mix to improve its effectiveness Conduct e-marketing Improve positioning Integrate customers earlier Decide whether to make or buy Optimize the portal Discontinue products
Development	Cut development times Improve quality Innovate Improve serviceability	Introduce a platform concept Design to cost Introduce modularity Introduce electronic remote diagnostics
Others	Innovate Link processes Review contracts Rethink licenses	Exercise purchasing power Improve processes Reduce IT costs Reduce the size of the head office Reduce inventory Increase inventory turnover Review investments Optimize payment periods

The business plan

It is often not that easy to calculate the profitability of individual products and services. Even if there are enough cost centers, it is difficult to allocate costs to specific products and services.

It is scarcely any easier to decide whether or not a business plan adds up. There is a real art to working out whether the assumptions made are too positive or too conservative. For example, once a startup company has been through a hype cycle, it is faced with the same kind of simple yet vital questions facing any established company: Are we earning more than we are spending, and will we have enough cash to avoid being unable to pay – even for a short period? Profits and cash flow are important – but they are not everything.

Much of what we have examined in the previous sections is also important for business plans:

The business idea
The business idea must solve a customer problem in a unique way, ideally involving a patent.

The next step is to focus on customers, the market, core competencies and operational implementation.

Figure 107 shows the factors involved in the development of a business idea.

The implementation concept
The business idea can be implemented as a project (see the section on project management) subdivided into work packages, with progress marked out by milestones. Here, too, it is advisable to think in scenarios and always have a "plan B" in reserve.

Finance
Once the business and its alternatives have assumed concrete form, the next step is to think about how it will be financed during its various phases, as shown in figure 108. Some of the finance for the startup may come from government programs or seed venture capital. Later, decisions have to be taken as to whether to use capital from banks or venture capital companies. Not until the business is stable and growing strongly is going public an option.

New forms of finance can be expected to emerge in the coming years.

Partnering
Partnering is a further important option that should be considered as part of a future strategy for new business. Businesses can be very vulnerable

Figure 107   Development of a business idea

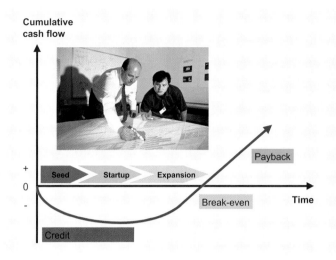

Cumulative cash flow

Seed | Startup | Expansion

Payback

Break-even

Time

Credit

+

0

-

Figure 108
Financial
considerations

in the initial stages, and it may help them to collaborate on development, marketing, sales and services with partners or even other divisions within the same company.

The entrepreneur's joystick – conclusion

- Although, as a result of globalization and the Internet, the pace of business is increasing all the time, it is essential to remain calm and keep a clear head.
- You have to keep focused on your own company's objectives.
- More than ever, it is necessary to secure your core competencies in times of change and, at the same time, to keep open other routes to achieving your objectives in the form of alternative scenarios. This applies both to large corporations and "Me Inc." individuals.
- To this end, the entire team must be put in the picture and know how they can contribute to the company's success – each in his or her own way. They can only do this when their competencies and personal objectives match up with those of the company.
- Controllers will need to be very creative in the future. They will have to identify the key factors and ratios and simulate their development under different circumstances. In addition to hard facts and figures, there are also numerous soft factors involved, which often provide early indications of a need to take action.

Process e-volution in companies

Our offices are filling up with more and more computers, and there seem to be more and more cables running through them, disappearing into boxes with flashing lights that often have to be accommodated in what used to be cleaning closets. Yet these are only some of the external symptoms that make it clear how quickly change is taking place. Nothing will remain as it was.

Marketing

Externally, marketing departments are becoming increasingly active, attempting to attract the attention of customers and prospects in order to convince them of the merits of the company's products and solutions and ultimately win them over.

Within the organization, the marketing department aims to ensure that customer-oriented decisions are taken and unique products and services are developed.

There are various approaches to integrating marketing into the organization. In the American model, the marketing department is strong and has a broad spectrum of activities, taking on responsibility for the strategic planning process, strategic marketing, the supply chain process, including purchasing and logistics marketing, and ultimately customer relationship management. However, there are also organizations in which marketing activities and all these associated responsibilities are distributed among different units. Thanks to information and communication technology, it will soon go without saying that all the parties involved will have access to shared databases.

The main objective of marketing is to emphasize the competitive advantages of the company in the form of unique selling points – positive attributes that differentiate it and its offerings from the competition. At the same time, we should put ourselves in our customers' shoes and make their concerns ours in order to understand how we can improve their profitability or increase the benefit of the product for them.

Market research

Market research can be thought of as radar for companies. The information obtained from it is used to make decisions on business field definition, customer segmentation, product definition and channels of distribution. Whereas strategists require fundamental market data – such as information about the overall market, the size of the market that can be reached and market shares – market research breaks this information down further, identifying customer groups with different purchasing behavior that have to be addressed in different ways.

Market research companies – and increasingly the Internet, as well – are used to obtain the information required. The data obtained then needs to be filtered and presented.

Customers' purchasing habits and interests can be analyzed extremely well on the basis of their clicks on the Internet. Now that we can get precise information on customers' preferences electronically, we will increasingly be in the position of making them offers that are tailored to suit their particular interests and requirements. The future belongs to this kind of one-to-one marketing. Storing and analyzing information on customers in order to personalize what is offered to them is sometimes referred to as "Amazonizing". Whereas the challenge used to lie in finding important customer data in the first place, it now consists in filtering the relevant data from countless sources and turning it into marketing knowledge.

One-to-one marketing

In the future, marketing professionals will have to maintain even closer links to their colleagues working in corporate strategy, development and sales. At a time when market cycles and paradigms are subject to rapid change, departmental boundaries and process interfaces must not form barriers. Stored information has no value in itself unless it is made available to people who can then use it. Thus, the challenge here is to implement excellent knowledge management (see figure 109).

Marketing knowledge management

In primary research, data is obtained directly from the customer or on the basis of a company's own observations. In the future the link to the customer will increasingly be electronic: through e-mails and Internet surveys, searches, profiling, panels, forums, chat rooms, portals, focus groups, click analyses, customer reviews and product assessments. In future, direct surveys will be possible on customers' PCs and on the basis of statistics from Internet servers.

Primary research

When intelligent labels can be applied to products, it will be possible to obtain a wealth of very detailed information in this way: Where do the products go and how does the customer use them?

Secondary research is carried out by analysts, banks, governments, associations and organizations and makes information available on a macro level, taking in politics, society, the economy and technology. Like primary

Secondary research

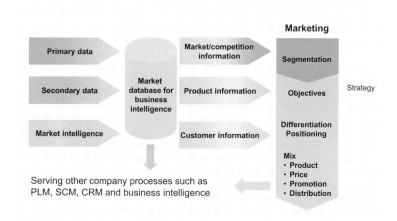

Figure 109
Marketing
Knowledge
Management

research, secondary research is increasingly being carried out electronically, and because making it available electronically is relatively cheap, some of this information is available free of charge.

Electronic information is generally more up-to-date, comprehensive and cheaper to obtain than other forms of information. There are often additional costs to be taken into account because the data obtained is not compatible with a company's own databases and has to be converted. However, this pool of data is then just a mouse click away for all involved.

Customer research Some marketeers still do not seem to have understood that the customer is actually a human being. Instead, they have been working on the assumption that people make logical purchasing decisions. Although they then emotionalize the results of their research and turn them into advertising messages, they do not really know what they are doing.

New market research no longer concerns itself with the tip of the emotional/rational iceberg but with the mass below the waterline. Since the trend toward individualization means that categorizing customers into target groups is of little use, and since fashions and trends are changing increasingly in our society, customers need to be characterized more strongly on the basis of their emotions. The old sales and marketing rule to put yourself in the customer's place is now at last being implemented more effectively:

- In addition to the effects on a customer's five senses, pulse, perspiration, behavior and attention are being measured electronically.
- In-depth psychological interviews mine for associations and images.
- Subjects are questioned about themselves and the people they hold in esteem in order to learn how their purchasing decisions might be influenced.
- Findings from the fields of neurology, brain research and medicine and from the study of literature, music and art are used.
- The latest methods of analysis and computer techniques are at last helping researchers to understand why people really buy a particular product.

As the struggle for the budgets of customers intensifies, which it will continue to do as time goes on, this new form of customer and market research will develop into the company's spearhead.

Customer segmentation

Before you begin researching, you need to work out exactly what it is you want to know. In order to be able to address markets economically and effectively, you can investigate a variety of criteria. Figure 110 shows an example of customer segmentation.

The various segments should be sufficiently large, distinguishable, accessible and, for controlling purposes, measurable. On the basis of these criteria, categories of customer can be defined. But you can never stand still, because products change in character over time. Take the mobile phone, for example, which has turned from a business tool into a fashionable lifestyle product to which entirely different market conditions apply.

Industry-oriented B2B		Customer segmentation		Consumer-oriented B2C
Macro-segmentation • Sector • Size • Company characteristics • Deployment/use	**Geo-graphical** • Regions • Countries • Cities	**Demo-graphic** • Gender • Age • Family status	**Socio-economic** • Social class • Income • Profession • Quantity purchased • Purchasing frequency	**Psycho-graphic** • Personality • Lifestyle • Values • Attitude
Micro-segmentation • Buying strategy • Selection methods • Decision-making process				**Behavior-related** • Buying opportunity • Buying behavior • Occasion-related • Usage-related • Approach

Customer segmentation   **Figure 110**

The Internet makes the workings of the market transparent and gives all participants the same opportunity to obtain information. Consequently, it is important to retain focus when offering a product on the market and addressing customers, because customers generally believe specialists have the most differentiated offerings.

Differentiation

There is a well-known saying in marketing: "Be different or die." Yet just being different is not enough, otherwise why would so many innovative young companies go out of business? "Be better and different" would be a more appropriate approach.

Before proceeding down this road, it is worth taking a look at the abundance of differentiation options shown in figure 111.

Central to a company's efforts to differentiate itself from the competition are, of course, its image and brand and the emotional charge behind them.

The reliability, stability and global presence of an adaptable, professional company that has been in existence for decades inspire more confidence than the forceful claims of a newcomer could ever do.

Purchasing	Product	Additional benefit	Employees	Service

Purchasing
- Terms & conditions
- Payment period
- Target controlling
- Customer satisfaction
- Response times
- Total value of ownership
- Quantity scales
- Guarantees
- Contract terms
- Forecasting
- Auctions
- Tenders
- Delivery terms
- Benchmarking
- Market screening

via new electronic media

Product
- Portfolio
- Program depth
- Program breadth
- Quality
- Warranty/fairness
- Ergonomics
- Operability
- Performance
- Total cost of ownership
- Reliability
- Documentation
- Support
- Design
- Updates
- Simulation
- Virtual reality

Communication
- Sales promotion
- Advertising
- Press
- Community

Additional benefit
- Financing
- Barter transactions
- Operation
- Investment protect
- Migration pathway
- Personalization
- Live references

Price
- Price reduction (rebates, discounts, bonus points)
- Payment terms
- Credit
- Operating costs
- Price list

Employees
- Competence
- Reliability
- Response
- Commitment
- E-mail/chat
- Online hotline

Image
- Sponsoring
- Events
- Branding
- Online marketing
- Portal
- Community
- Public relations

Differentiation

Service
- Consulting
- Configuration
- Setup
- Maintenance
- Repair
- Download service
- Online services
- Forecasting
- Process
- Predictive service

Distribution
- Warehousing
- Trade
- Account management
- Direct servicing
- Specialized trade
- Regional coverage
- Logistics
- Online ordering
- One2one relationship
- Process
- Personalization
- E-commerce

Figure 111   Differentiation

Marketing mix

The various marketing instruments need to be employed in the optimum mix for each target group. Figure 112 provides an overview of the new key areas in marketing, which we will be examining more closely below.

Figure 112
Marketing
instruments

All these areas are shown as being interlinked, which represents the ideal. It is these links together with customer feedback and any information that can be gleaned about the competition – in particular, information on customers' requirements and the extent to which they are met – that essentially forms the foundation on which marketing measures are built. To ensure continuous improvement, the responses of customers to changes in the marketing measures taken have to be monitored. As elsewhere, it is clear here that there is a need for intense cooperation with those involved in sales and distribution.

A product consists not just of the sum of its physical, chemical and technical properties but also of the value ascribed to it by the buyer, which is made up of elements such as basic benefit, additional benefit, convenience, image and the contribution made by the product to the consumer's quality of life and lifestyle. In this context, products may be capital goods, consumer goods, services or even ideas.

Product policy involves developing roadmaps for optimized new products and optimizing the existing product portfolio to align it with the corporate and marketing objectives, while at the same time taking due account of the sales prospects and the costs involved. Don't fear self-cannibalizing approaches!

The most important product policy decisions have to do with ongoing technical development and product design, differentiation and discontinuation. This is not something that can be left to the solitary development engineer. All new elements and innovations should be integrated in a larger context, starting with the company's vision, from which its objectives are derived and on the basis of which its strategy is formed. Clearly formulated information must be available on the market and competition, the relevant technology trends and the company's core competencies and key selling points.

When we know where we want to be, what we are capable of and what we stand for, we will be better able to focus on our strengths.

We have already dealt with the needs and desires of consumers in the section entitled "People as customers". Now we are going to turn our attention to business customers. If we want to make the correct decisions about products in a business-to-business environment, it is helpful to ask ourselves the kind of questions shown in figure 113.

Product development consists of the phases examined below in the section on innovation.

Decisions about product discontinuation – as opposed to further developing a product – are generally based on marketing controlling data such as the contribution margin, the profit or the current phase of the product life cycle.

With the help of modern information technology it is possible to update and reposition all electronic, non-physical products:

- By means of simulation, certain attributes of chemical products, for example, can be presented to the customer for an initial assessment before they are sold.

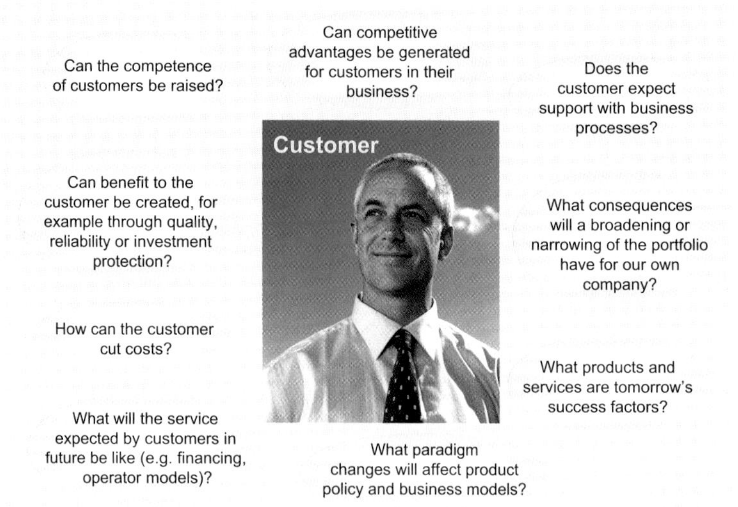

Can competitive
advantages be generated
for customers in their
business?

Can the competence
of customers be raised?

Does the
customer expect
support with business
processes?

Customer

Can benefit to the
customer be created, for
example through quality,
reliability or investment
protection?

What consequences
will a broadening or
narrowing of the portfolio
have for our own
company?

How can the customer
cut costs?

What products and
services are tomorrow's
success factors?

Figure 113
Questions to be
asked before
making decisions
on products

What will the service
expected by customers in
future be like (e.g. financing,
operator models)?

What paradigm
changes will affect product
policy and business models?

- On the Internet, products and services can be regrouped, aggregated or disaggregated (separated).
- Virtual reality also improves the customer's understanding of a product's attributes.

All these new processes and services allow closer bonds to be formed with the customer.

Another issue to be addressed in product policy is the extent to which software should be used for routine activities in connection with the products, for example the automatic generation of responses to price inquiries, product configurations, software upgrades and means of payment.

The entire value chain can be examined with a view to exploiting the potential of automation.

Pricing policy | As a marketing instrument, pricing has the great advantage that it can be used immediately and selectively. Pricing policy decisions are subject to a range of influences and constraints imposed by demand, the competition, costs and legal factors.

Price elasticity relates to the extent to which customers respond to price changes. Demand is said to be inelastic when sales volumes remain relatively constant in spite of price changes, whereas when demand is elastic, the volumes sold vary considerably in response to price changes.

The closer the link between the producer and customer, the sooner the customer's responses to price changes are felt. Companies that sell on the Internet, for example, get useful sales statistics in real time and can thus tell very quickly whether or not price changes have been effective.

And just to recapitulate: The greater the benefit to the customer, the better the competitive advantage and the more marked the unique selling points, the less pressure there is to reduce prices.

The lower limit for a price is the price that has to be achieved in order to recover the company's costs. The information required for this is supplied by the accounting department. In practice, a break-even analysis indicates the sales volume at which costs are covered by sales.

To be successful, however, you have to do more than just get your sums right. This is not the way to come up with winning products.

The competition-oriented price is based, as you might expect, on competitors' prices. If there is a price leader, this company will owe its position to the fact that its competitors are either forced to adapt their prices to its own or that they choose to.

Having said that, it is rare that you are forced to adhere to the price of the market leader. Whether you decide to price your products above or below the price of the market leader is a question of strategy. However:

Simply to base your pricing on the prices of the competition constitutes an unenterprising, "me-too" kind of strategy.

If the price is essentially determined by the customer, the price is said to be demand-oriented. The customer makes an assessment of how reasonable the price is and of the price/performance ratio by comparing the price with the benefit brought by the product. A price based on the benefit to the customer offers the company a considerable amount of leeway.

The right pricing strategy depends on the specific market situation.

Pricing strategies

High prices can be achieved with high-quality, unique products or products that are of exceptional benefit to customers or have a positive image – which of course generally means high profits as well. If competitors launch comparable products, prices can be gradually or even dramatically reduced to preserve or expand market share.

It is also possible to charge different customers different prices in order to exploit the full potential of the market. In order to achieve this, however, the market has to be split up into segments with different price elasticity and easily distinguishable groups of customers.

It is only possible to have different prices for different customers if the market is not transparent, something which is increasingly unlikely in the mobile information age.

Some pricing strategies are losing their significance in the information age, while other forms of pricing are just emerging. The global market is becoming increasingly transparent, and it is possible to gain a huge amount of information using a search engine. As the number of mobile devices increases, so will the number of consumers who check other vendors' prices before deciding to buy a particular product. In addition, customers will increasingly be able to call on intelligent software agents that will trawl the Internet for products on the basis of specified criteria.

In reverse auctioning, companies or private individuals can invite offers from companies to provide them with products or services. Interested vendors submit their offers in the auction and try to undercut each other in order to win the contract. At the end of the auction, the initiator can decide which offer to accept.

Reverse auctioning

In this way, a private individual could find a builder for a house renovation project, for example, or a company could find another company to carry out a mailing campaign for it.

The scope for creativity is unlimited, and the potential of this new form of business is by no means exhausted.

However, we are still only at the beginning. The use of electronic media in radically new business models has really hardly got off the ground yet.

E-commerce From the vendor's viewpoint, e-commerce offers the possibility of achieving large-scale increases in volume by means of small price changes, since an offer can often reach many more customers via the Internet than by means of conventional media such as advertising supplements in newspapers or display window advertising.

However, there are a number of costs associated with this that it would be unwise to neglect:

- First, there are delivery costs, which can make up a not inconsiderable portion of the overall costs of low-price goods.
- The costs of customer acquisition on the Internet run into the double-digit euro or US dollar range for each new customer.
- If intermediaries are used, they demand a commission of between 5% and 15%.

All these factors have to be taken into account in the business plan. It should also be remembered that you can lose online customers just as quickly as you can gain them; customers show significantly less loyalty when they can change their supplier at the click of a mouse. Given that there is no personal contact and there are no longer any geographical constraints on the Internet, this is only logical. However, customer bonding can be improved by means of incentives such as personalization, bonus points or discounts.

Terms and It is also important to decide on the discounts, sales credit and terms of
conditions delivery and payment to be offered.

A discount is a price reduction offered to customers for a particular product or in order to achieve a particular psychological effect. The legislation governing discounts may vary from country to country.

The most important types of discount include:

- Trade or functional discounts granted by manufacturers to those in the trade
- Volume discounts and bonuses
- Discounts for a limited period when a product is launched, for example

Other established instruments used for the purpose of customer bonding include:

- Cash discounts for immediate payment
- Interest-free loans and finance deals
- Discounts in the form of old products taken in part payment
- Discounts in the form of bonuses as of certain volumes

Recently, the following types of scheme have become increasingly important:

- Loyalty discounts with bonus points, customer cards or customer accounts
- Coupons, free gifts and vouchers

It is a small step from Lufthansa miles to Web miles. The principle is the same: You collect your Web miles by clicking your way through a Web portal or shop and placing an order there.

Another way of encouraging customers or prospective customers to buy is to grant loans with favorable terms to enable them to buy specific, expensive products.

Terms of delivery and payment are stipulated in the purchase agreement specifying the nature and volume of the products or services sold. In some industries, uniform terms and conditions are used by all vendors. On the Internet in the global marketplace things are not quite so simple. International and national legislation and provisions increasingly have to be taken into account.

In the classical form of distribution, products go from the manufacturer to intermediaries such as wholesalers and then on to dealers or retailers before they reach the consumer.

Distribution policy

Decisions about channels and forms of distribution depend on the type, nature and size of the products or services, the market and customer segment, the competitive situation, the size of the company and the costs and revenue involved.

Fast, reliable, cost-effective channels of distribution are essential to the success of a product and customer satisfaction.

All the most important business data ends up in the marketing department, where sales and revenue figures from distribution and product marketing are then forecast. Thus, the success of distribution can easily be compared with the forecasts made because the marketing department is responsible for both.

There is a choice to make between direct and indirect channels of distribution, which may be real or electronic.

Channels of distribution

Direct sales from the manufacturer to the consumer (business-to-consumer, B2C) cut out the retailer. This is the preferred form of distribution for capital goods and products where there is a need for explanation. In this case the channels of distribution are sales executives, key account managers or sales branches. However, external channels with close ties to the company such as agents, dealers or franchise partners may also be used.

In indirect sales, other companies are used for distribution: wholesalers, retailers or multi-level distribution companies. We will return to these in the section on customer loyalty.

Procurement policy

The product marketing people draw up and negotiate procurement contracts for products and services. They monitor the market and analyze the terms and conditions of competitors and partners. In conjunction with the sales and development departments, the marketing people come up with target costs that customers are expected to be prepared to pay. They are also constantly on the lookout for attractive new products and partners, and they use SWOT analyses to evaluate existing and potential partnerships. Taking into account logistical aspects, service and technology, they optimize the portfolio, and they check the total cost of ownership of the most important hardware and software products and services that the company uses. They also work with preferred suppliers to establish win-win alliances. Delivery time, quantity, quality and price are the key parameters. Together with preferred suppliers they analyze the total value and total costs of the relationship with a view to taking it to a higher level.

Combining their technical, marketing and legal skills, purchasers and marketeers join forces to conduct contract negotiations and achieve top terms and conditions. The challenge is to find the best combination and optimum deployment of the various tools in each negotiation.

Purchasing on the Internet saves time and money through faster order processing and an online connection to the supplier, while automation through a link to the inventory data improves delivery quality. In addition, a seamless process without media discontinuity reduces errors. As we have seen, invitations to tender on the Internet are the new model for purchasing. Further savings can be made by forming alliances with other customers in electronic marketplaces and ordering in bulk.

Product life-cycle management

Figure 114 illustrates once more the different phases of the product life cycle and their significance to revenue and profit. As processes increasingly become electronic, the aim of product life-cycle management today is to bring together the different processes of the various departments involved and thus rationalize them. In development, for example, this includes processes such as computer-aided design, engineering and manufacturing (CAD, CAE and CAM). Simulations and representations of virtual reality in two to four dimensions have become really quite common, facilitating decision-making and allowing decision-makers to take due account of customers' responses.

Product life-cycle management optimizes the magical development triangle of costs, time and quality. At a time when innovation and product life cycles are getting shorter, it becomes critical to raise the level of productivity. Time to market and profitability are crucial in this context.

Digitization of all processes is only possible when business intelligence, product life-cycle management, supply chain management, enterprise resource planning and customer relationship management are linked from end to end without any loss of flexibility.

Communication policy

Before we turn to the challenges of information and telecommunication technologies in marketing, let's briefly go over the use of marketing communication in the product life cycle (see figure 115).

Marketing communication aims to ensure a high rate of repeat buying. If a product is known to 50% of all potential customers, bought by 50% of

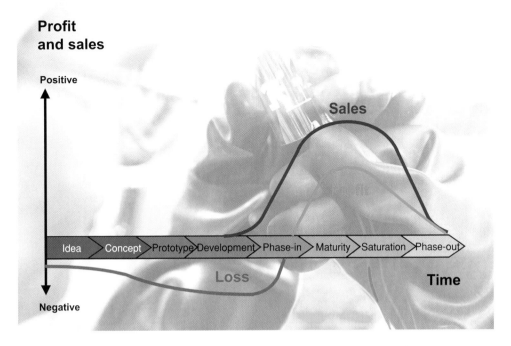

Product life cycle　　**Figure 114**

those who know it and bought again by 50% of those who bought it first time around because they are so satisfied with it, this means that only 12.5% of prospective customers turn into repeat buyers. The purpose of marketing communication is to retain or increase this market share.

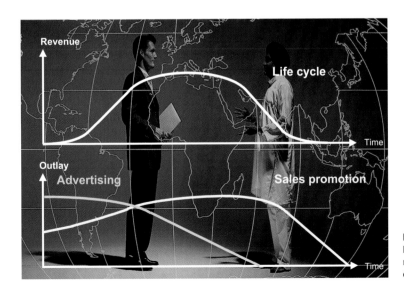

Figure 115
Life cycle and marketing communication

Advertising may focus on products, product ranges, services or even an entire company or organization. Advertising for consumer goods, capital goods and services aims to position the brand, a process known as branding. Company advertising puts the focus on the company and contributes to its image. Marketing objectives may be financial (to increase sales, for example) or non-financial (to improve the image, for example).

Each piece of advertising that fails to connect with the target group entails a loss of money and is known as waste coverage. However, it is never quite clear what percentage of the money spent on advertising has been spent ineffectively. The target group and the advertising objective for each advertising campaign therefore have to be defined very precisely. The trend is clearly toward one-to-one marketing, in which target groups and customer segments are narrowed down to individual people and companies.

The advertising message to be conveyed to the target group must also be precisely defined. The means used to convey it include language, color, pictures, videos and music. Interactive advertising using ploys such as PC games, phone call quizzes and raffles are also an option. The advertising message is conveyed in a manner designed to appeal to the target group's emotional and/or rational side (see the section on the emotional versus the rational). The criteria used to judge its effectiveness include originality, topicality, coherence and credibility. The precise use of language is still very important here: A single word can say more than a thousand pictures. Particularly in the turbulent multimedia times that are now upon us, it is important for the customer to know what a company actually sells. Examples such as Coca-Cola, Sony, BMW and Harley-Davidson illustrate how customers stay with strong brands. A Harley-Davidson is not just any motorcycle.

Depending on our position in the product life cycle, we use advertising to introduce a product, increase or reinforce its market share, remind consumers of its existence or manage its decline. In addition to advertising on their own, companies may very well engage in joint marketing and advertise their products together with other companies, which can prove very effective. In a pull strategy, manufacturers' advertising is aimed at consumers and is designed to stimulate demand that exerts a kind of suction on the product. Push advertising today is generally advertising by the retail trade, concerning itself with prices, terms and conditions and only a few important product features.

Once the advertising objectives and target group are defined, the advertising strategy is then drawn up, the advertisements are created, the media and their distribution are selected, and the advertising period is set. The advertising campaign is generally tested before it is launched, and its effectiveness is monitored constantly so that any necessary adjustments can be made. Finally, the effects of the advertising are evaluated. This can be done increasingly accurately and cost-effectively by electronic means, whereas the costs of doing it in the classical media are rising steadily.

The advertising budget is usually based on the company's revenue and profit from the industry – but also depends on the advertising objectives and the cost of suitable advertising measures. The advertising budget is generally a few percentage points of the revenue. This obviously favors companies with higher sales volumes, since if they invest the same percentage of their revenue in advertising as smaller companies they can finance much bigger campaigns.

The importance of traditional media such as print, TV and radio is dwindling as the new media begin to take over. In the years from 1996 to 2000 alone, the use of electronic advertising increased by a factor of 40. Experts expect the volume of interactive advertising on the Internet to triple by the year 2010.

Mobile devices have not yet really been discovered for the purpose of advertising, in spite of being our constant companions and online for long periods. It is now possible to send multimedia messages via broadband mobile networks, and companies can also target customers by means of network operators' local services, making it possible to inform customers about what may interest them in their current location on the basis of their previous purchasing behavior and interests. Figure 116 offers an evaluation of traditional and new media.

The desired effect is, of course, for the recipients of the advertising to exhibit the "correct" behavior and buy the product. Lewis's AIDA rule (attention, interest, desire, action) describes how this happens. But let's be honest:

In the age of e-commerce, the AIDA formula no longer tells the full story. The aim is to keep customers over the long term, which can only succeed

Advertising medium / Charac- teristics	Traditional media ←				→ Emerging media		
	News- paper	Mail	Radio	Television	Web/fixed	Web/mobile	Robots/ agents
Coverage	Local	Regional	Local	Regional	Global	Global	Global
Target groups	Good	Very good	Good	Good	Excellent *	Excellent *	Excellent *
Reviewable	Satis- factory	Very good	Satis- factory	Satis- factory	Excellent	Excellent	Excellent
Interactive	Hardly at all	Moderate	Good	Hardly at all	Excellent	Excellent	Excellent
Multimedia	No	Good (CD)	Audio	Video	Multimedia	Multimedia	Multimedia
Personaliz- able	No	Moderate	No	No	Excellent	Excellent	Excellent
Location- dependent	Good	Good	Good	Good	Satis- factory	Excellent	Excellent
Exercising costs	Mode- rate	Moderate	Low	Moderate	Moderate	Moderate	Moderate

* Provided the target group has access to the network (fixed or mobile)

Attributes of different advertising media　**Figure 116**

if they are satisfied with what we are offering them. So we need to add an "S" for satisfaction.

Unless you want to just throw your money away, you need to constantly monitor the effectiveness of your advertising. Advertising success may be measured in terms of increased sales or by counting the number of customers who refer to the advertisement when placing an order. Factors that cannot be expressed in financial terms, such as perception, assimilation or behavior, can be investigated in tests carried out before and after the advertising and by using psychological market research techniques. Here, too, the new technologies are on the rise: for IT-assisted media resonance analysis or database-assisted contact and mailing list management, for example.

The more personal and direct the appeal to the customer, the more successful the advertising is.

Direct advertising
In direct advertising, a direct appeal is made to a specific target group. In the past this was always done by means of advertising letters, catalogs, brochures, price lists or samples in conjunction with order forms and telephone calls. CDs, DVDs, e-mails and SMS and MMS messages are opening up new possibilities. The scope will be increased as further progress is made in agent and robot technology.

The effect of direct advertising can be measured precisely, and there is little waste coverage. However, it is developing into a problem for customers.

Advertising mail – or spam in the case of e-mails – is taking up an ever increasing proportion of the mail we receive. Customers are increasingly setting up more than one e-mail address: a public account where all the advertising mail arrives and a private address known only to their friends.

It is therefore important not to shower consumers with information they do not want. This generally only leads to the opposite of the desired effect.

A much more promising avenue are personal customer portals, where customers' individual preferences and product wish lists are stored, thus permitting only relevant advertising information to get through. In this case, consumers give the advertising their full attention, and both they and the advertisers are kept happy.

Sales promotion
Unlike classical advertising, sales promotion begins at the point of sale. Sales promotion is a push strategy, encompassing all the measures used to promote sales at the point of sale and to provide information to sales assistants and consumers. It thus represents something of a bridge between advertising and sales.

Already there are many shops that bombard us with advertising films on video recorders, and technology is likely to play an increasing role here. A screen on our shopping cart, for example, could guide us around and provide us with information. Let's just hope that our agents will be able to help us here and tell all these media to give us only what we are interested in or leave us in peace.

The success of sales staff depends very much on the training they receive about new products, the market and the position of the company. Training

This training is backed up by demonstration material such as catalogs, brochures, samples, sales manuals, videos, business TV, preference lists, test reports and information on customers and the competition. In recent years, an increasing number of CDs, DVDs and interactive websites have come along as well, the latter permitting information to be downloaded anywhere in the world whenever it is needed.

Information and training at the point of sale is provided by displays, decorations and advertising media such as posters, videos and new media. Sales promotion aids like this – often also referred to as merchandisers – are a great help to sales staff. Dealers or retailers can be offered more in-depth information over an extranet that gives them direct access to the supplier. This is generally integrated in the portal.

Public relations or PR aims to improve the whole image of a company and how it is perceived. PR is thus aimed at those inside the company as well as those outside. Public relations

External PR helps the company to systematically develop and continuously maintain the public's awareness of and confidence in the company, as well as to shape and improve the company's image. External target groups are all those individuals or organizations that are of interest to the company, such as customers, suppliers, associations, interest groups, investors, stockholders, analysts, media and government, whereas the internal target groups are staff, any staff organizations and the company's management. Business TV films and recordings of press events complete the picture.

Public relations measures cannot simply be applied indiscriminately; they need to be planned and carried out with specific target groups in mind.

Press work is aimed directly at the media and its representatives and typically consists of printed information, press releases and press conferences. The aim is to represent the company in the editorial content of newsletters, newspapers, magazines, radio and television programs and information providers on the Internet. These days there are many different aspects to good, modern press work, and it requires great expertise and sensitivity. The emotional aspect is just as important here as the rational aspect – for the reasons already mentioned.

The difficulty of doing good press work should not be underestimated. If you do not have the right staff for the job or simply cannot spare the staff, you should use the services of an appropriate outside company.

PR campaigns are aimed at specific target groups and may take the form of open days, sponsorship or support for cultural and social events. With appropriate coverage in the media, a certain image is developed.

Public relations work should be seen as a long-term communication instrument and be coordinated with the other marketing instruments. If you are involved in the kind of business that is viewed critically by some or that involves potentially dangerous technical processes, you should take preventive action in advance rather than just react in a crisis. What is said after an incident or accident is extremely critical and may decide on the future of the company.

There is a great deal of secondary and tertiary information to be found about a company on the Internet, and this is a good way to monitor the company's image, decide on subsequent PR measures and counteract misinformation.

Branding
Brands represent a promise made to those inside the company as well as those outside it. Recognized by customers, competitors and analysts, they are linked with the company and bring certain associations to mind. Brands are very valuable and require a holistic brand strategy. Figure 117 illustrates what a brand depends on.

The best-known brands are those we come across in everyday life, such as Microsoft, Siemens, Coca-Cola and so on. The vision and business practices of the company must always harmonize with the brand, in both an emotional and a rational sense, and careful consideration is required before it is taken in a new direction.

Sponsorship
Sponsorship is the provision of money, resources and/or services to individuals or organizations by a company, for which the company receives something in return that serves its purposes (even it is only that its name is mentioned). Public awareness of it is increased, and its links to its target groups are developed and maintained.

Sponsorship of sport is the best-known form of sponsorship. Companies make funds – but also other resources – available to sports events, clubs and teams as well as to individual sports people. Sometimes there are huge sums of money involved, as in Formula One racing, for example. In return, the sponsor's name may appear on equipment and clothing and in other prominent positions.

Figure 117
Brand

New, increasingly weird and wonderful forms of competition and extreme sports are increasing the scope for sponsorship. In these cases, the target group is particularly well defined.

There are also other forms of sponsorship, such as cultural, social or environmental sponsorship. It very much depends on what is fashionable, has a widespread impact and is likely to enhance the company's image.

Contest sponsorship on the Web is another new form of sponsorship, in which attention is captured by attractive content and advertising.

Computer games can also be sponsored and distributed as gifts. There are games, for example, where you can shoot everything except the advertising – unless you want minus points!

Product placement entails placing products and services in cinema or television films. The advantages of this are the extent of the coverage obtained, the relaxed atmosphere provided by the entertainment context – unlike in classical advertising – and the fact that the product's image will benefit from being in this context.

Product placement

The focus is not on the product here, but the audience soon recognizes that James Bond's car comes from a prestigious German car maker. Given the internationalization of the markets that is taking place, the significance of product placement for consumer goods is increasing.

Electronic marketing

The Internet age is transforming both the content of marketing and the processes involved in it. Electronic marketing offers a wealth of new opportunities that it is essential to take – unless, of course, you want to hand the initiative to the competition.

In the future, companies will not be able to survive without being on the Internet. Any company that is not, simply will not exist for the customer. It will be e-business or no business.

The online media provide new scope for differentiation. The Internet will continue to migrate to mobile devices and everyday objects and will thus reach consumers and businesses in a wide variety of ways.

Portals

We cannot ask ourselves often enough what other products, services or content we should be offering online in order to appeal to customers.

The Internet is thus developing into a channel for distribution, information, communication and customer relationships, all in one. Customers can access a company's portal 24 hours a day, 365 days a year, and portals can be personalized to suit individuals' requirements, preferences and interests.

There are considerable differences in the quality of the portals, with not all of them being what they should be: user-friendly, intuitive, attractive and packed with services and functionality.

In many cases, companies are still not making enough use of online services. Yet it is well worth investing energy to provide demonstrations of products and services, demo downloads or live installations of reference customers, for example. And all of these applications are just waiting to be implemented.

To position your company well, you need to offer more than just bald facts; above all, you need to appeal to the emotions. A company's positioning essentially amounts to what customers think of it. Interviews with opinion leaders can indicate a need for action.

Maintaining the company's website is the job of the Web master, who co-ordinates all the subject matter and prepares it for the website in order to address the different target groups involved: customers, staff, analysts and journalists.

- For staff it is important that the company's vision, mission and objectives are portrayed.
- Customers are more interested in the portfolio of products and services and the online shop.
- Analysts and journalists, on the other hand, want business facts and figures.

To exploit the full potential of the new medium, the portal must be of exceptional quality and, above all, kept constantly up to date (see figure 118). Both emotional and rational aspects are involved here as well, of course.

As a fast, direct channel of communication, electronic marketing intensifies the contact with the customer through an enhanced range of services, a closer customer-supplier relationship, scope for direct interaction and

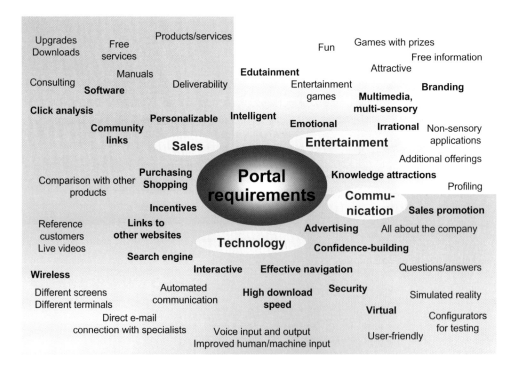

Figure 118 Requirements to be met by portals

greater customer satisfaction. In addition, innovative multimedia marketing (games on mobile phones, for example) brings competitive advantages. As far as customer contact is concerned, it is particularly important to be able to switch from automatic online support to expert human support and back, as and when the need arises.

Branding also plays a significant role on the Internet. The portals of big-name companies with good reputations are extremely busy, whereas unreliable manufacturers and service providers are avoided. The influence of Internet forums and chat rooms should not be underestimated in this context. Word soon spreads about good or bad performance.

Electronic marketing generates new target groups, market segments and channels of distribution. It increases the level of awareness about the company, its attractiveness and what it offers. At the same time, it also promotes the development of new Internet-specific products and services and new context- and customer-related forms of advertising.

One very important advantage of electronic marketing is that it allows processes to be optimized. End-to-end marketing processes can be designed that are integrated with other business processes without any media discontinuity.

Electronic marketing also offers ways to cut costs by improving marketing efficiency and reducing waste coverage and the costs of printing. In addition, the FAQ (frequently asked questions) section on the website reduces the number of phone calls the company has to field, which allows it to save on personnel costs. Overall, fixed costs are reduced because less warehouse space and fewer permanent staff are required.

However, e-marketing does not always ensure reduced costs:

If traditional channels are (or have to be) used to the same extent as before, marketing may end up being significantly more expensive than before, and that has to be compensated in the form of additional online business.

The behavior of website visitors can be tracked down to the second, thus permitting the success of electronic marketing campaigns to be measured. Precise customer profiling can be carried out on the basis of users' surfing, clicking and responses. These profiles include the customer's purchasing history and information on their purchasing behavior, clicking, the information they have requested and their requirements, as well as comments, payment preferences and purchasing habits.

By analyzing this data, it is possible to obtain the information required in order to come up with products and services to appeal to a specific customer. This marks the beginning of the transition from customer group marketing to one-to-one marketing.

It is quite conceivable that our personal agent, having been fed with our preferences, likes and interests, will in effect become a private home page for us. By making the appropriate queries, electronic direct marketing can now find out what customers are interested in. Subsequently it will be possible to make personalized offers based on these interests.

The attention of customers can be attracted even more if extended and complementary offers are made to them. It therefore makes sense to col-

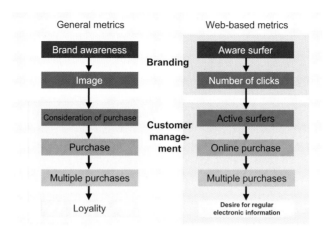

Figure 119
Marketing chains

laborate with other companies. Portals reflecting this collaboration that are frequently used by target customers are an important asset here.

Marketing efficiency

For most functions in companies there are clear criteria for measuring performance – for example, revenue per employee involved in sales and distribution or volume of error-free software code per time unit in the development department. In marketing, on the other hand, there is no way of being sure whether money has been spent to optimum effect or whether it has been wasted.

However, there are some starting points that provide a useful basis for measuring success. Figure 119 outlines general and Web-based metrics in marketing chains, following the process through to repeat purchases.

The efficiency of marketing measures can be represented in two ways:

- The number of portal clicks divided by the number of active surfers produces a value for contact efficiency.
- The number of active surfers divided by the number of online purchasers produces a value for conversion efficiency.

One conceivable marketing strategy would be to optimize the different efficiency ratios for as little outlay as possible and significantly improve them in comparison to the competition.

This is a sure way of increasing customer loyalty. For example, brand awareness of 90% multiplied by an image of 70%, a ratio for considering a purchase of 8%, a purchasing ratio of 9%, a repeat purchase ratio of 40% and loyalty of 50% results in 0.09% loyal customers.

Customer loyalty

In many companies today, sales and distribution is a separate unit within a field of business or corporate division. The interfaces to marketing functions are generally fluid. Customer, market and product information should be represented three-dimensionally or "holographically" in both

Process e-volution in companies

sales and distribution and marketing. In other words, it must be possible to issue queries on the basis of each of the three coordinates – customers, market and product – and any combination of the three. However, business intelligence systems that offer this kind of representation are only useful when business processes are well designed and the individuals involved can talk to each other.

At first glance, people in marketing have a very different way of looking at things from people in sales and distribution. The marketing people steer the company toward offering what the customer wants, whereas sales and distribution people try to make the customer want whatever the company has to offer.

In spite of their different approaches, it is clear to both, however, that, before making a decision to buy a product, customers will ask what they have to pay for it and what advantages and benefits it will bring them. In order to be able to make a correct assessment of the customer here, a detailed understanding of the customer is required, going far beyond just pricing and product specification.

Knowing the customer

As is so often the case in business life, the following simple rule applies when examining customer requirements: Analyze the situation, develop a strategy, and then implement it. This is illustrated in figure 120.

The customer is king and, as such, needs to be thoroughly understood and well served. If you succeed in doing this, you increase the customer's willingness to purchase and remain loyal.

If you want to know what a customer wants, you have to find out what that company's strategy is, encompassing everything from the vision down to the processes involved.

You then have to decide whether the customer really is a prospective customer for you. Only then do you ask how you can help the customer add value – by reducing costs and increasing profits.

Customers that bring the company a profit should be securely bonded to the company over the long term.

Figure 120
The route to the customer

Total value of ownership

A valuable relationship with a customer can only be achieved by working together with that customer. Figure 121 combines traditional and modern approaches in an overall view.

The value of a relationship increases if you can address the customer's needs better than others can. The question to ask is how you can set yourself apart from your competitors. One answer to this is as follows:

It is still possible to distinguish yourself from the competition in electronic customer support because this is a field that is still largely under development.

The same rule applies here as in racing. The one with his nose in front wins – even if it takes a photo finish.

The emotional versus the rational

It is not difficult to work out rational purchasing criteria with the customer. Working out the "true" purchasing criteria, on the other hand, is a different thing entirely. The iceberg model illustrates the complex process involved in a customer's decision to purchase (see figure 122).

If you want to acquire a new customer, it is useful to begin by gathering as much information on the customer as possible, and the Internet is a big help here. By analyzing the four personality profiles in the lower part of the iceberg, it is possible to obtain good hypotheses, core statements and procedures. The astonishing thing here is not just that the decision to purchase is strongly influenced by the emotions but that most of the factors relevant to the decision remain under the surface. Thus, we should not

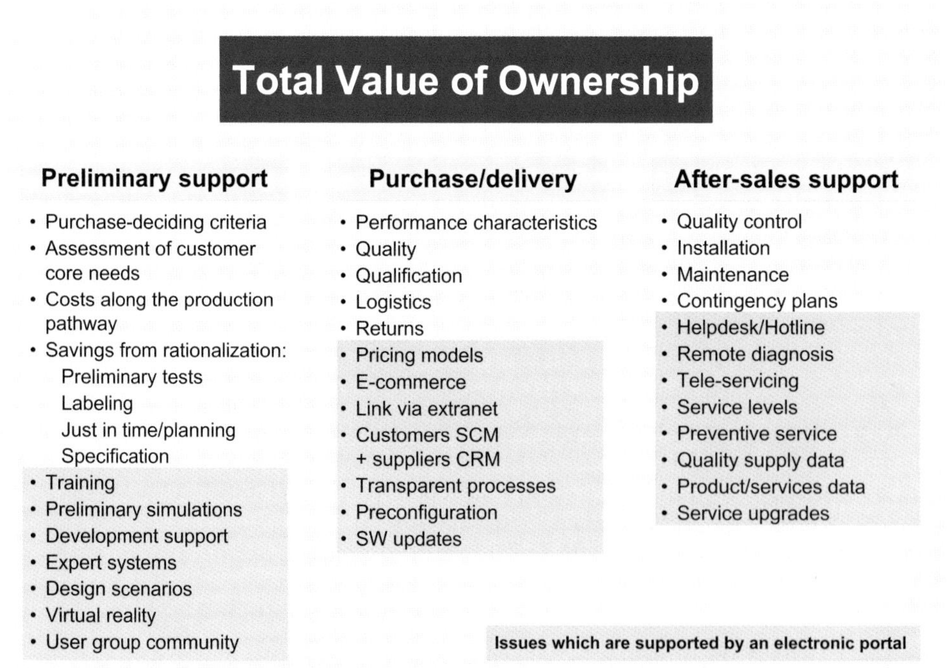

Total Value of Ownership
Preliminary support
• Purchase-deciding criteria
• Assessment of customer core needs
• Costs along the production pathway
• Savings from rationalization:
Preliminary tests
Labeling
Just in time/planning
Specification
• Training
• Preliminary simulations
• Development support
• Expert systems
• Design scenarios
• Virtual reality
• User group community
Purchase/delivery
• Performance characteristics
• Quality
• Qualification
• Logistics
• Returns
• Pricing models
• E-commerce
• Link via extranet
• Customers SCM + suppliers CRM
• Transparent processes
• Preconfiguration
• SW updates
After-sales support
• Quality control
• Installation
• Maintenance
• Contingency plans
• Helpdesk/Hotline
• Remote diagnosis
• Tele-servicing
• Service levels
• Preventive service
• Quality supply data
• Product/services data
• Service upgrades
Issues which are supported by an electronic portal

Figure 121 Total value of ownership

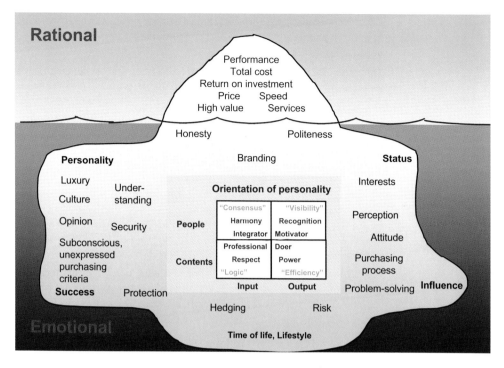

The iceberg model: emotional and rational purchasing criteria **Figure 122**

be surprised if decision-making processes take an unexpected turn when there may be factors and strategic principles that are not revealed to us.

The factors beneath the surface that influence a purchasing decision have to do with culture, social status, personality, circumstances and other emotional elements.

In order to take all of this into account, the sales person needs to be a committed, well-rounded individual who takes a holistic approach. This is a million miles away from selling pure and simple. Analyses and studies have repeatedly shown that there is a strong correlation between the attitude of sales staff and the company's revenue and profits.

The world of the customer's experience

There is a great deal of information in circulation about our company over which we have hardly any direct influence. Analysts, for example, publish their opinions against the background of their current concerns. However, what is discussed about our products in specialist publications and Internet communities has to be taken much more seriously. Try entering the name of your company or one of your products in a search engine, and see what it comes up with. You may be surprised by what others are saying about your company and products.

Figure 123 portrays the world of the customer's experience, including all the information and communication channels involved. More and more of these channels are now electronic. Although electronic systems and proc-

Figure 123
The world of
the customer's
experience

Personal contact
Delivery & performance
Call center
Information, assistance, advertising, sales, service
Competence center
Post
Telephone
Mobile phone
Fax
E-mail

Customer

Portal experience
Consultation experience
Transaction experience
Product experience
SCM
Service experience
Contracts
Quality and reliability
Press
Reviews
Problems, queries, interests
Customer ratings
Community
Advertising
Internet access   Image   E-payment   Payment
via electronic media

esses in themselves are not a solution, merely an aid, it is clear that, as far as communication with the customer is concerned, the importance of these electronic aids to the success of your own strategy cannot be underestimated. They play a decisive role in shaping the world of the customer's experience. However, it always takes a great deal of time and effort to get everything running smoothly, automatically and to the satisfaction of both sides.

Customer support

Key account managers and sales executives need to be not just excellent negotiators but also ambassadors who represent both the interests of the customer and their own company. In order to be able to do this successfully, they need to know both parties inside out and to be able to perform a balancing act between the different interests involved, being careful not to demand too much from either side, while at the same time always challenging them. They need to know the customer's company in all its many facets, going far beyond knowledge of its corporate hierarchy and the projects it is involved in. Moreover, they must be valued by the customer as expert partners. After all, they play a key role in working with the customer along the decision-making chain – incorporating objectives, strategy and the value chain – as the customer moves toward a decision to buy. This cooperative approach offers much scope for taking decisions that benefit both parties. A voyage of discovery like this becomes even more interesting when your customer's customers are also included in the equation.

Figure 124, which portrays a holistic sales system, makes it clear that the customer and supplier have to come together at every level in order to put joint projects on the right track.

The customer's challenges and unresolved problems have to fit with your own company's core competencies if both parties are to derive benefits and pleasure from the relationship.

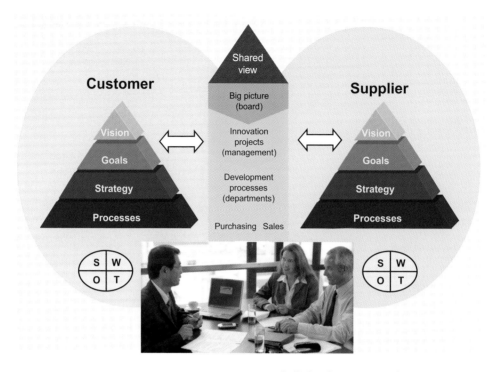

A holistic sales system   **Figure 124**

The key to this is that both parties should benefit, resulting in a win-win situation for all those involved.

The chain rule can also be applied to the working relationship between sales executives and the customer. All the different links of the chain have to work well and effectively in order to achieve a satisfactory end result. This is illustrated well by a quick calculation: If your product range matches 60% of the market's requirements, and 40% of your sales executives have a 20% sale completion rate, this results in a market share of only 5%.

The effectiveness and efficiency of sales activities should be constantly reviewed to ensure success. The result is shown in figure 125.

Sales activities still center around intensive price negotiations – which can also be a sign of not having enough competitive advantages or unique selling points and not offering sufficient benefit to the customer.

The price negotiated can have a dramatic effect on profit. The tornado chart in figure 126 shows the effect on the operating result of a 10% change in price compared to the same change in total manufacturing costs or development, marketing and sales and distribution costs. In this example, the operating result would normally be 2 million euros.

These figures allow only one conclusion to be drawn:

Whatever is won or lost in price negotiations cannot be achieved or compensated by similar adjustments to any other single factor within the

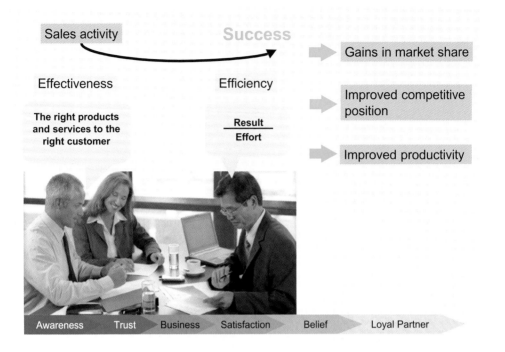

Figure 125 Successful sales and distribution activities

company. The only way to compensate is to obtain better prices from suppliers.

It is therefore necessary to use all available modern means of providing customers with value. This value must be recognized as such by customers and make them feel they have won. The more they feel they have won, the less occasion they have to put pressure on the price. As product life cycles become shorter, it becomes more important for the product to achieve rapid success. That means there is no margin for error in sales.

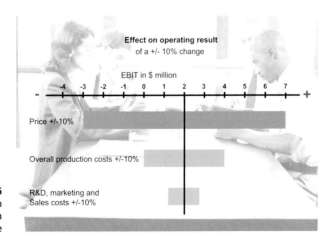

Figure 126
Tornado chart: an example based on practical experience

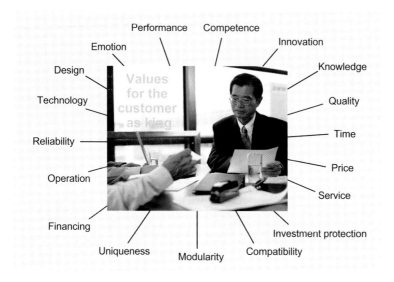

Performance Competence
Emotion
Innovation
Design
Knowledge
Technology
Values
for the
customer
as king
Quality
Reliability
Time
Operation
Price
Service
Financing
Investment protection
Uniqueness Modularity Compatibility

Figure 127
Positives required
by the customer

Figure 127 lists a number of positives that are close to customers' hearts. Others could, of course, be added, depending on the company and industry involved. The better we tackle and fulfill each individual customer's particular mix of requirements, the less relevant the price becomes.

Knowledge represents a further competitive advantage, yet knowledge marketing is still relatively undeveloped. Thus far, many services have been provided free as part of product or system business. However, just as former presidents get much more for their appearances than simply an appreciative smile, the knowledge of our staff is often a valuable information resource to customers, something they would be prepared to pay for. Our knowledge should be treated and marketed as a product. Publishing books on specialist subjects is not the right way to go about this on account of the expense involved and the limited revenue to be gained, but used as an additional means of acquisition this can bring great benefit in terms of image enhancement (see the contacts on the imprint page).

Knowledge
as a competitive
advantage

- Have we given our customers everything they wanted, and have we given it to them in the way they wanted it?
- How satisfied are they?
- Have we given our customers everything they wanted, and have we given it to them in the way they wanted it?
- How satisfied are they?

Customer
satisfaction
analysis

This should be investigated regularly by means of customer satisfaction analyses. Particularly in the case of valuable customers, it is important to probe deeper and explore what is going on under the surface. Satisfaction, bonding and loyalty are all interrelated and need to be constantly addressed and maintained. We should carry out analyses annually to obtain a detailed impression of what our customers are thinking:

- Is what we are offering meeting requirements?
- Do our customers understand our unique selling points?

- Is our attitude the right one for the business?
- How is our brand and company viewed?

The company's top management have a burning interest in the answers to these questions, as do all those involved in marketing and sales. Business intelligence provides this information in an overall context including information on competitors, reports of sales visits and analyses of orders won and lost. Nothing is sadder and more expensive than losing a good customer.

Regularly reviewing the win-win situation At regular intervals the customer and supplier should take a detailed look at their partnership. As illustrated above, from the supplier's point of view customer segmentation is necessary in order to come up with profitable offerings in the first place. The sales staff can provide support here by carrying out appropriate analyses. Which customers boost market share and are profitable, loyal drivers of innovation, and which are not? How might the business change as a result of changes in the industry and the market?

It is no secret that companies with a better customer mix are more successful. Loyal, profitable customers should be retained at all costs. Airlines and hotels have schemes for regular customers, whereby they receive preferential treatment and a host of extras.

Channels to the customer In many industries there has always been a great variety of channels to the customer, and this variety has been increased by the new electronic media. Companies therefore need to keep revisiting the question of what the most effective and efficient channel to the customer is.

Each channel has to be evaluated from the viewpoint of both the customer and the supplier. Factors such as life cycle and product structure – regardless of whether this is simple or in need of explanation – influence this decision. This is illustrated in figure 128.

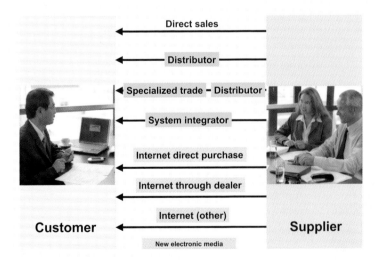

Figure 128
Channels to the customer

Different industries have different ways of addressing the customer. Distributors and wholesalers do little more than distribute and in the past have added little value, but integrators are different, which gives them a competitive advantage. It would be wrong to think that your sales activities should end at the wholesaler. It is perfectly possible for a company to send its own marketing people and sales executives to the customer, who is then supplied via indirect channels. Figure 129 indicates the functions fulfilled by distributors and integrators.

The correct channel to the customer must be selected after considering the relevant benefits, features, cost advantages and the competition.

Large numbers of companies have now discovered electronic channels to the customer.

Pure Internet companies like Amazon.com have emerged with new business models and introduced new paradigms. By personalizing what they offer, these companies have returned to the old, practically extinct corner shop philosophy of maintaining a dialog with the customer (although, given the size of online vendors' product ranges, that is where the similarity ends). Customers are offered suggestions for new products on the basis of what others have bought in the past: "Other customers who bought such and such a product also bought product X." And there are also product reviews and recommendations: "John Brown has already tried this product out and this is what he thinks of it."

The Internet company Autoscout24.de personalizes car buying. It is basically a used car dealer that allows you to specify your personal criteria for a vehicle search. After you specify where you live, the type of vehicle, the accessories you are looking for and so on, the search engine searches within a specified area for used cars that meet these criteria. This is one of the first generation of search agents referred to in the first part of the book.

Figure 129
Distributors/
integrators

Car manufacturers have also discovered companies like this and are using them as a distribution channel for their one-year-old cars. They thus promote their own product portfolio and increase the level of awareness of their brand.

Electronic sales

In order to remain up to date, the use of market statistics has been largely avoided in this book, but it is worth making a small exception at this point. Commercial use of the Internet began in 1995, and after only 8 years, electronic sales amounts to billions of euros each year. Even in difficult times, e-business sales have doubled annually. A small example from the world of flora and fauna might help our imaginations a little here:

Under favorable conditions, water lilies can double in number every day. Let's assume that 1.5% of a pond's surface is covered by water lilies on day one.

How long will it take before the entire pond is covered with water lilies? The answer is: after only one week ($1.5\% \times 2^6 = 96\%$).

It is worth reminding ourselves that the share of world trade accounted for by electronic business in the year 2001 was also only 1.5% (see figure 130). Even in the year 2002, when the dot.com boom collapsed, electronic business doubled. Given the potential for rationalization, growth in e-business is expected to continue at the same rate, particularly between companies.

There are still a number of hurdles to be cleared before business can be conducted entirely on the Internet. Legislation and regulations currently vary from country to country, whereas electronic processes span the globe, and there is also a lack of uniformity when it comes to tax issues. Overall, there is still a fair amount of work to be done to ensure a smooth electronic sales process on the Internet, as shown in figure 131.

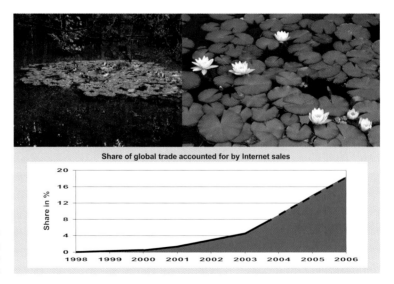

Figure 130
E-business is growing at the rate of water lilies

Share of global trade accounted for by Internet sales

Process e-volution in companies

Figure 131
Sales over the
Internet

A further stumbling block to electronic sales today is security for transactions and payment. Thus far, banks have not played much of a role in payment transactions – as trust centers, for example. And for smaller amounts such as those involved when data is downloaded, there is still no practicable solution. Yet particularly in the content-based media sector, the success of electronic sales channels depends very much on precisely these kinds of transactions. Instead of a record company earning a small amount each time a song is downloaded, for example, the black market is flourishing in this area. To put it another way:

E-payment

Systems permitting convenient, secure payment – of amounts large or small – are the key both to successful sales over the Internet and to tackling the black market.

The first signs of success can already be seen: Apple's efforts to charge a dollar for each song legally downloaded have gone very well so far. And Microsoft and other software vendors are successfully accepting electronic payment for downloaded program upgrades. Electronic sales works well for digital products, above all, because these can be obtained on the Internet directly and downloaded. You no longer have to wait to have the product delivered.

Charging for content and knowledge on the Internet requires a degree of creativity. The business model that is used in the future to market knowledge and content will depend on the value of the content, the frequency of the demand and the speed of access. There are already suitable models available, such as pay per use, prices depending on the data volume or the depth of the data provided and service subscriptions – to name just a few.

Selecting the right price model for knowledge on the Internet will require skill and intuition as well as luck. There are bound to be many companies whose initial price models will not meet users' expectations and will misjudge their willingness to pay.

Selling on the Internet reduces costs. Whereas a customer visit might cost at least a three-digit euro figure and a telephone call a two-digit figure, the costs of a sale through the company's Internet portal can be measured in single digits, amounting to around 1% of the cost of a sales visit and 10% of the cost of a personal phone call. It is no wonder that companies are making such strenuous efforts to change how they make contact with customers!

The situation is similar in banking, where the costs of Internet banking are only 1% of the costs of banking in a branch. The customer-oriented computer vendor Dell, for instance, has put more and more of its processes on the Internet and introduced a build-to-order principle to keep costs low and flexibility high – thus providing an excellent example of how electronic and mobile business will generate new sales potential in the future.

Customer relationship management (CRM)

Two thirds of the cases where companies lose customers can be put down to poor service. Customer relationship management (CRM) helps to improve relationships with customers by bringing marketing, sales and service processes under a single roof. All these processes are oriented toward customer acquisition and bonding.

The different parts of the information puzzle from the various processes involved have to be put together to provide an overall picture of the customer, which is ultimately what determines the quality of business intelligence.

If this works properly, customers receive the product or service portfolio in the form that is most suitable to them. The CRM pyramid illustrates the interrelationships involved (see figure 132).

CRM is thus a suitable tool for forming a close relationship with the customer and binding the customer to your company. This, too, brings us a step further along the path toward becoming a learning company.

Ideally, innovation and research, supply chain management, enterprise resource planning and business intelligence work together like cogs in well-oiled machinery.

Each employee receives the same information about customers and the market – in real time. The aim of CRM is thus more about synchronization than the interpretation of processes. Information and communication technologies facilitate this process by automating sequences of activities and analyses and subsequently producing suggestions about how to proceed.

One-to-one marketing should be complemented by one-to-one sales. In business with the consumer, in particular, e- and m-marketing, sales and service are important means of setting your company apart from the competition. To this end:

- Comprehensive information on the customer, including all the emotional and rational aspects involved, must be constantly available.
- It must be possible to call up the history of the relationship with the customer and the customer's objectives, needs and desires at all times.

The CRM pyramid   **Figure 132**

- You must never overshoot the mark, either in terms of the frequency and intensity with which you address the customer or in the way you set out to acquire the customer or use the customer's data.

Customers place orders not because they are transparent to you but because they are satisfied.

Innovation

There are two ways for a company to secure profitable growth. The first is to increase effectiveness and efficiency with the aim of becoming the benchmark in a line of business. Quality circles and a program of continuous improvement are required in order to achieve this. This approach suggests itself for specialist companies – production companies that only supply other companies, for example.

The second route to profitable growth is through innovation.

Innovation is the process of turning a new idea into a marketable solution.

The result of innovation can be a product, a service or a business model. Companies have made extensive gains in market share through more or less chance innovations in the past. Generally, however, they are not able to retain this market share, because as soon as customers' desires change and new types of business emerge as a result of paradigm changes, these companies find themselves unable to cope due to their lack of planned, structured innovation processes. This has been the fate of a large number of smaller software companies, in particular, which often orient themselves toward the needs of a larger customer with an innovative product, possibly their only product. Those who do not want to make do with short-lived success should bear the following in mind:

If a company wants not only to be successful but to remain so, it must be able to implement well-targeted innovations both frequently and when the time is right.

Let's take a look at the product life cycle again. As figure 133 clearly shows, the really high margins are earned on the left-hand side of the chart as a result of innovation.

Only companies that attain product leadership secure a profitable market for themselves.

Consequently, we should be constantly asking ourselves how many products we have on the left-hand side of the product life-cycle chart.

Innovation is the correct response to pressure on prices as a result of global competition. Innovation secures jobs, companies and business locations. The question thus arises as to whether innovation can be planned. And, somewhat surprisingly, the answer is "yes", as indicated by the examination of the innovation process below.

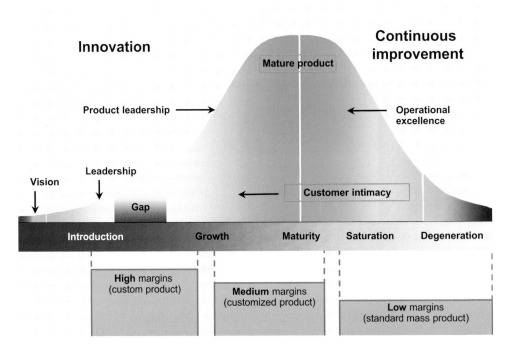

Figure 133   Product life cycle

The innovation process

As a rule of thumb, you need around two thousand ideas for every one that becomes a successful business.

This rule of thumb applies in all industries. There are various procedures and methods that can be used to generate ideas, such as brainstorming, brainwriting, syntactic association and mental provocation – to name only a few. Each company must find its own approach, one that is appropriate for its corporate culture. In this context, appropriate can – perhaps even must – also mean provocative!

Making inferences about tomorrow on the basis of what you know about the day after is a good way to arrive at new ways of looking at things – which is why it was the approach chosen for this book. You start at a point in time perhaps ten to twenty years into the future and imagine how things will be by then (see figure 134).

- How will the customers of our customers be living, and what will they be doing?
- What problems will there be to solve, what challenges to meet?

At this stage, imagination and vision are often more important than knowledge. The question to ask then is whether you have already gone down this path too often or whether the staff need to have their vision kick-started.

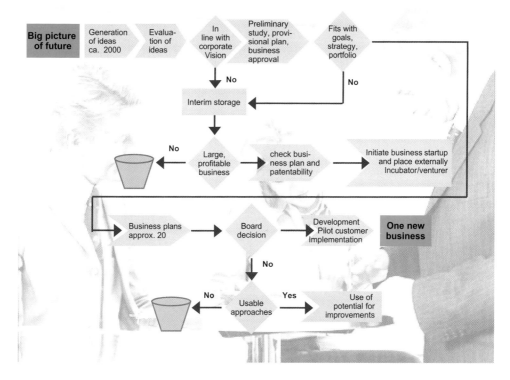

How the innovation process works   **Figure 134**

In either case, it may help to bring in a good futurologist or even a science fiction author.

Innovation teams

An even better option is to sit down with the customer and discuss the future in a structured approach, as described in the sections entitled "The way to achieve corporate objectives" and "Customer loyalty". Thinking about or agreeing on joint development projects with leading customers in key account teams, focus groups, meetings of colleagues or user groups means developing a business together right from the beginning. The more heterogeneous these groups are, the more effective they are. Observers of trends, technology scouts, sales professionals, strategic marketing people and heads of development from both sides can come up with great ideas when they sit down together.

The innovation team should be chosen carefully and be capable of working together to achieve really excellent results.

A sponsor – in this case, a manager with sufficient freedom of action and decision-making authority – must make the required resources available and clear the way for the team. It is important that the team contains at least one person with an entrepreneurial attitude who is willing to take risks and question and change the status quo. The most important factors involved in the innovation process are shown in figure 135.

The company as a force for innovation

The whole company must be geared toward generating innovations. This then becomes the driving force that takes the company forward, attracts the best staff and keeps investors happy. The section entitled "Project management" outlines how this is implemented at the operational level.

It is essential to keep communicating with key customers at the development stage. After all, they are the ones that will decide whether or not innovations are a success – whether the benefits, competitive advantages and unique selling points are really sufficiently marked. Digital development can make a contribution toward better communication with customers.

Figure 135
The most important factors in the innovation process

Figure 136
Virtual planning

Digital development

The more computing power there is available, the greater the freedom enjoyed by developers. Physical models can be replaced by simulations. This also applies to the media industry or medical technology, for example, where entire films can be made on the computer. The better the interrelationships involved in physics, chemistry, biology, mechanical engineering and electrical engineering are understood and implemented in software, the more realistic are the virtual pictures that can be generated on the computer. Darwinist programs vary the parameters involved in the search for the optimum.

User interfaces, products, production lines and high-rise buildings can be portrayed virtually in three dimensions, rotated and entered (see figure 136). Practically anything dreamed up by our imaginations or generated by artificial intelligence can be represented in this way.

Platform concepts

If innovation can be described as the engine driving business forward, the platform concept is the lubricant that ensures that new developments are integrated smoothly with what exists already. Car manufacturers, mechanical engineering companies, PC manufacturers, manufacturers of branded products in the textile industry, manufacturers of consumer goods and software companies are redoubling their efforts to reuse proven elements on the modular principle. Time and costs are being saved and flexibility increased as a result of modularization, standardization and compliance with new global (industry) standards.

Personalization and product specialization take place as close as possible to the end of the production chain. This allows companies to set themselves apart from the competition and give their brand certain recognizable attributes (see figure 137).

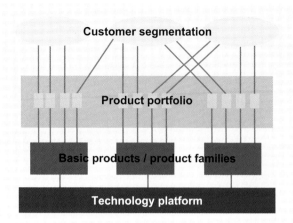

Figure 137
Platform concept

If a company's platform concept is future-oriented in outlook, outdated hardware and software modules can be easily replaced in spite of Moore's law.

Further positive aspects are security of investment for the customer and development flexibility for new applications and services. Designing the platform concept is one of the main tasks of the chief technology officer (CTO).

Applications

As described in the chapters "Journey through time and guide to trends" and "The different spheres of our lives", data computation, storage and transfer will not present any problems, and many new applications will become possible.

What we need now are new applications that fit the needs of our customers and our company's competencies. By talking to our customers and examining their visions for the future we can, of course, make it much easier for ourselves to find these new applications. Often the very simple, people-oriented solutions are the biggest successes.

We can only observe with astonishment the triumphant progress of applications that initially appear to be of no use whatsoever, such as SMS texting. After all, if you are picking up a phone you can just as easily leave a message on an answering machine.

Application research
Application research is thus a good way of developing new ideas. We can also make use of the market research discussed earlier in innovation projects. Moreover, it is worth testing new applications and products that have already been developed in the application laboratory to see how they rate:

- Is the design good?
- Is the product's handling intuitive for people from different cultures?

Trends, technologies, roadmaps and the company's own competencies can indicate the direction for new applications and the right moment to launch them on the market.

For example, it is not worth investing too much in interactive, computer-based voice communication until the technology is mature enough for it to be widely used.

Services

There is scarcely a service anywhere that does not make use of electronic information and communication. In addition, many new services are emerging that have only been made possible by the trends described at the beginning of the book. As devices and systems become more sophisticated, it gets easier to maintain them electronically, in advance and taking the overall context into account.

Much of the potential in product-related services lies in the networking and automation of processes. The less people have to do with it, the better.

Much the same applies to portals and call, contact, convenience and core centers. As we have seen, human support should be integrated seamlessly in the interplay of automated processes.

The processes of industrial customers and the challenges presented by their customers in turn offer much potential for new applications. It may also be possible for services to be grouped together or increased in value. Improvements in productivity, the ability to supply and reliability are always welcome, and these can be achieved by bringing information together and putting it in new contexts. There is also much scope for innovation in the use of knowledge-based applications to improve the skills of customers' staff. It is important to introduce electronic, real-time and mobile processes and transactions along the entire chain from consulting through designing, building, maintenance and operation.

There is much potential for new, people-related services in the fields of protection, security, knowledge, searching for information and consulting, as well as throughout the entire Maslow pyramid.

A key field for such services will be proactive support following people's personal preferences, predilections and desires in a wide variety of environments – representing a huge task for personal agents and robots.

Business models

As we have seen, processes and value chains are changing as a result of e-volution. The analysis and rearrangement of the value chain, which may involve crossing the boundaries between industries, can result in new approaches to business. We are already buying PCs and telephones from discount supermarkets, and perhaps tomorrow we will be buying groceries from telecommunication providers. Entirely technology-based approaches, such as private invitations to tender and auctions, are also emerging. More can be expected from this quarter, particularly since much revenue could be generated through advertising and communication links with higher charges. Many a quiz show now covers parts of its costs by charging for phone calls and keeping callers in waiting loops.

Wherever there are customers with unfulfilled or concealed needs and desires, there is potential for new applications, services or business models.

Production

We have all seen pictures of automated production facilities populated by robots, without a human in sight, but anyone who thinks there is no potential for further improvement there is deceiving himself. Robots specialize either in volume production or small batch production. Better sensors, increased computer capacities and more flexible software control systems are improving performance capability all the time. As far as production is concerned, it is, of course, also important to define objectives, a strategy, segments, core competencies, production depth and processes. The decisive factors for successful production are short setup times, high output and quality. Control software optimizes material flows and machine capacity utilization and adapts them to suit different requirements.

Stricter legislation designed to protect the environment and more stringent requirements to recycle products are having profound effects on production: Older modules are increasingly being reused in new products. Systems and machines therefore have to be easy to take apart, and the materials used must be marked precisely so that they can subsequently be recycled, as outlined earlier in the book.

Both customers and stricter legislation and guidelines are making new demands on products in terms of longer warranty periods and thus longer lifetimes. This development impacts on production processes and techniques. Figure 138 illustrates the variety of the demands to be met by production in the future.

There is a classical learning curve effect at work in production, which reduces production costs (see figure 139) and results in market leaders generally also being cost leaders – as discussed in the section entitled "Learning organizations".

The winners of the future may well be the companies that use the best simulation and optimization tools and whose learning curve per unit is thus steepest.

Learning systems   Further progress in production can be expected when production modules can organize themselves and evolutionary programs can automatically change production parameters and learn from the consequences. It is not just production but also the further development of production that will be automated, thus heralding a new generation of production processes.

Customers' requirements for personalization are transforming production processes: Mass production is being superseded by the automated, flexible mass individualization of products. At the same time, the life cycles of virtually all products are getting shorter, whether we are talking about capital goods or toys. Over the last 50 years, the life cycles of many product lines

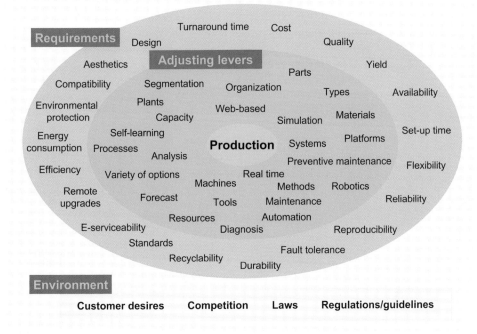

Production requirements and adjusting levers   **Figure 138**

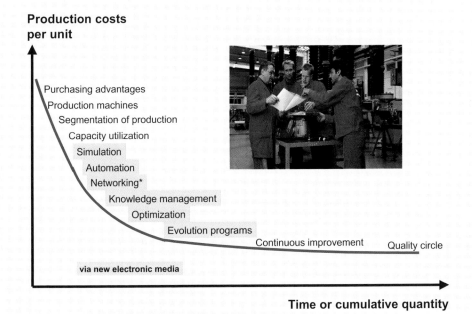

The learning curve effect in production   **Figure 139**

have been cut to as little as a fifth of what they were. Moreover, faster innovation cycles and globalization are accelerating this process.

If this development is to continue, we will need autonomous systems such as robots to work together with other systems and synchronize their activities. Not only will they have to configure, monitor and optimize themselves, they will also have to be capable of learning. To this end, electronic diagnostics will have to be implemented for the processes and methods involved, as well as for product attributes. Machines that can communicate with each other and exchange experiences will also be required, as will methods of simulation and prediction.

All these innovations in the production process rely on improved sensors and actuators, as well as on progress being made with computers and intelligent software – in the form of neural networks, for example. New materials and physical processes complete the array of innovations that will be required in order to move forward into new dimensions of effectiveness in manufacturing.

The digital factory
The same rule applies to the new production processes as applies to all other business processes: There has to be an end to stand-alone solutions. Production and automation processes have to be linked to other processes in the company: in particular, to systems for production planning and control, controlling, warehouse management, the supply of power and other resources and facilities management. To these can be added everything from automated ordering processes to maintenance processes with foresight or quality and status monitoring processes that – thanks to a proliferation of new sensors and new control electronics – initiate electronic processes. Developers, planners, suppliers and production staff will all be using the same data – a trend that has already clearly emerged in industrial automation (sometimes referred to as Totally Integrated Automation (TIA), for example).

The subsequent requirements of the production stage and the components that will be involved in production should be defined as early as the development stage using computer-aided tools. Three-dimensional simulation models provide a virtual representation of the structure and all the processes of the emerging factory. Whereas the rigorous application of digital trials and simulation is still something for the future, computer integrated manufacturing is with us already. Nowadays it is hard to find a machine or a robot that is not controlled by a computer. Nevertheless, we are still a long way from networking them to optimum effect within an integrated overall framework. However, challenges such as shorter setup times, more compact modules for the more flexible production of small number of units and personalized products can now be tackled.

Let's remind ourselves again of the trends outlined in the first part of the book:

The process of miniaturization taking place in mechanical engineering, electronics and chemistry is proceeding unabated. In chemistry, in particular, it is not such a long way from a system or laboratory on a chip to a factory on a chip.

Logistics

The most advanced production methods are of no use if supplies do not arrive on schedule or the product manufactured does not reach the customer on time. The key elements of logistics are storage, packing for transportation, the means of transportation and the means of communication. The smooth processing of orders can even involve automatic delivery initiation by the merchandise management system and the filling of customers' shelves.

Electronic processes open up huge potential for rationalization and improvement in logistics. End-to-end concepts representing the entire value chain electronically are gaining ground rapidly. And as far as physical logistics service providers are concerned, a small number of specialist companies with global operations are taking a really professional approach to their business and to networking that is putting them in a dominant position.

Purchasing, logistics and production processes are now often grouped together and referred to as supply chain management. Supply chain management enables optimized processes to be implemented through global networking, with the inevitable consequence that the entire process becomes automated. If empty vending machines and shelves can automatically report their requirements to the warehouse and the delivery vehicle, for example, no human intervention is required in the ordering process. An end-to-end process like this reduces the number of errors made and brings time and cost savings.

Supply chain management

All that is required of the person responsible for the success of the business is to provide the vending machines and shelves with the parameters they need in order to place orders.

Speed, reliability, punctuality, environmental sensitivity, coherent processes and transparent costs are what every logistics company aspires to. Professional logistics companies use both direct and indirect channels of distribution and carry out short-, medium- and long-term quantity planning, taking into account all their own stocks as well as those of suppliers, distributors, resellers and customers. They provide the direct and indirect channels with reliable information on value flows and current delivery times. They also endeavor to optimize their portfolio constantly on the basis of customers' wishes, sales requirements and costs. If the company is clever, it will group together comparable aspects of different product or system groups within the framework of joint solutions. It can also offer other services such as warehousing, picking and packing or system testing.

To what extent is the Internet changing familiar processes and solutions in logistics? The first thing to say is that life is being made difficult for all kinds of physical intermediaries. Standardized purchasing software is facilitating direct B2B and B2C sales and reducing transaction costs in a process sometimes referred to as disintermediation. The computer vendor Dell is a shining example of excellent direct selling to both businesses and consumers.

Logistics and the Internet

But intermediaries are not going to be eliminated entirely just yet. Online intermediaries such as Yahoo and Evita are gaining ground on account of their low overheads. Purchasing agents fulfill a similar role.

It is thus possible to make out that there is a trend emerging toward virtual rather than real intermediaries.

In the case of digital products, the Internet itself is the distribution channel. As things stand, issues such as bandwidth, transaction security, copy protection and freedom from viruses are still presenting problems. The bandwidth problem will be solved relatively quickly, whereas, given the human element involved in the case of security and freedom from viruses, these issues are likely to be with us for some time. In fact, there is always likely to be a struggle between hackers trying to exploit gaps in security and software vendors making intense efforts to combat them.

From where we stand today, we can say that the Internet facilitates new process sequences and the emergence of specialists for very specific, focused parts of the value chain. Whereas last century companies tended to be involved in a significant part of the value chain, and companies producing finished products may even have manufactured their own screws, now there are an increasing number of "players" in the value chain whose activities complement each other. The extent to which this kind of collaboration will turn out to be beneficial to all involved is not yet clear.

Whatever else happens, however, it is clear that the logistical process is about to be revolutionized by the intelligent identification of merchandise.

Just as with the patients' ID cards that are to be introduced in health services, it will be possible to store information such as product attributes, manufacturing dates and expiration dates directly on the merchandise itself and query it by means of wireless communication. Merchandise systems will thus finally become transparent, independently of humans. It will be possible to take decisions in real time, and there will no longer be a need to take inventory manually. All the relevant information will be displayed at a keystroke. In both business and private households it will be possible to fully automate the storage and ordering of non-durable goods. Radical changes can be expected here. As a result of electronic labeling, both businesses and consumers may increasingly allow suppliers to manage their inventory for them.

Software agents can now act as intermediaries between companies and customers and optimize the flow of goods in direct interaction. Web-based trading on the basis of transparent market conditions means improved delivery quality at an appropriate price level.

Supply chain management is thus the logical extension of interlinked processes within a company to include processes outside the company.

This pushes the door wide open for cost-efficient ad hoc networks for implementing win-win situations for limited periods. Virtual companies will thus emerge only to fade away again. The prerequisite for this is a ubiquitous next-generation Internet that can provide access to all the relevant information in good time and with a high degree of security.

Process e-volution in companies

Process e-volution in companies – conclusion

The most important outcome to be hoped for from further technological development is that the future brought by integrated information and communication technology should make life simpler for us working people. We are not expecting the command center of a science fiction spaceship, but it would be nice to have some of its features. The key data from the business process, certainly, should be available at a keystroke just as quickly as in Star Trek. Other points worth emphasizing are:

- Business processes will not just be electronic; some of them will also run completely differently to how they have so far.
- The time for stand-alone processes has passed; all processes will have to be interlinked.
- Whether you are talking about marketing, sales, development, production or logistics, everyday life in the future will be characterized by new forms of working together, aided by automation.
- The aim of process e-volution – in addition to streamlining processes and speeding them up – is to simplify sequences of activities for us.
- We can be hopeful that we will have more time for the really essential things. We ourselves will still have to do the right thing and do it well. Everything else will be increasingly automated.

Conclusion

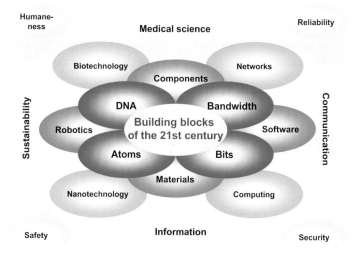

Figure 140
Building blocks of
the 21st century

The key areas of technology that will have most influence on developments in the 21st century are shown again in figure 140.

There is scope for innovation in each of the various building blocks as well as in combining their individual elements. "Me Inc." individuals, companies or governments that want to play at the highest level should put in as much training as possible with these different building blocks. Conscientious training has a direct influence on how well the team plays. But training alone will not be enough unless all the team members know the tactics for the next game. Figure 141 illustrates the overall approach required.

Prosperity and further development are the tip of a pyramid that will collapse unless all four of its sides are built up evenly.

• In the future we will be faced with changes and challenges in all the different spheres of our lives. As a result of the explosive growth in the networking of both people and machines, the speed of progress will increase further. Huge numbers of sensors (cameras, measuring devices and so on) and actuators (robots, machines and so on) will be connected up to the Internet, our global nervous system. It will thus become an artificial system running parallel to reality and analogously to a biological system.

• People and the companies in which they work will not be able to survive unless they adjust to the new laws governing the market environment and learn to help shape them. In addition to an essentially Darwinist strategy for survival, we will also need attributes like courage, openness and sensitivity if we are to master the future. The better that mature and established information and communication technologies do their job in the background, the more we can use our human skills to tackle the really important things. It is up to us to decide what those are. Technology cannot develop emotional values, create nice people and successful companies, make new products and systems or offer first-class service. Only people can do that. Customers and employees are more likely to

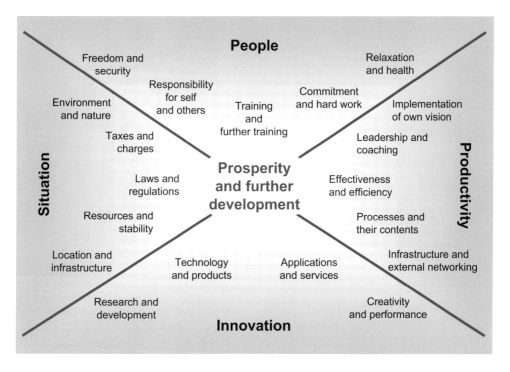

People – situation – innovation – productivity   **Figure 141**

buy what their hearts tell them than their heads and are thus more susceptible to values and visions than performance data and test reports. Supposedly outdated values such as genuineness, credibility, a sense of responsibility and wisdom are flourishing again. It will be just as important to be psychologically attractive as to be biologically intact, technologically optimized, economically profitable and ecologically sustainable.

- Companies that do not invest in process e-volution, productivity or paradigm-free innovations will soon be closing their doors for the last time. If they do only one of these things, they may just survive, but only those companies that properly face up to all three challenges will be among the winners in the future. Only they will be able to create value and new jobs, and only they will be able to make an ongoing contribution to building the foundations for prosperity and further development for mankind in the future, which is – and will remain – the essence of a responsible approach to business.

Appendix

Table indicating the sizes denoted by prefixes

Prefix	Prefix symbol	Power of ten	Example indicating size (in meters)
Zeta	Z	10^{21}	The length of the Milky Way
Exa	E	10^{18}	So far away that the sun seems as small as any other star (around 100 light years)
Peta	P	10^{15}	A hundred times the diameter of our solar system
Tera	T	10^{12}	Approximately the distance to Saturn
Giga	G	10^{9}	Three times the distance from Earth to the moon
Mega	M	10^{6}	Approximately the length of Germany from north to south
Kilo	k	10^{3}	The distance to the next village
		10^{0}	Anything that is 1 meter long, wide or high
Milli	m	10^{-3}	The diameter of a pin head
Micro	μ	10^{-6}	The thickness of a woman's hair
Nano	n	10^{-9}	The width of a DNA molecule
Pico	p	10^{-12}	An atom with an electron or electrons around it
Femto	f	10^{-15}	The nucleus of an atom (proton or neutron)
Atto	a	10^{-18}	An electron or quark

Sources of the pictures and graphics in the figures

Information, communication and media technology timeline:
Media History Project (mediahst@umn.edu), by e-mail on 02/26/2003 from Irving Fang

Figure	source, creator/provided by
1	Looking back at tomorrow: Siemens, Georg Berner
1	Group photograph: Siemens, Lika Meissner
1	Photographs of the spheres in which we live: Siemens, Lika Meissner
2	Growth of the world's population: Siemens, Georg Berner
2	Photograph of Hong Kong: Siemens, Judith Egelhof
3	Employment trends: Siemens, after Kondratieff, Georg Berner
3	Four photographs: Siemens, Judith Egelhof
4	Kondratieff cycles: Nefiodow@gmd.de (The Sixth Kondratieff), by e-mail on 02/27/2003
5	Hype cycle: Bob Hafner, Ian Keene, Gartner Group, by e-mail on 07/29/2003 from Lydia Howe
5	Photograph: Siemens, Judith Egelhof
6	Development of computer performance in relation to costs: Siemens, after Hans Moravek, by e-mail on 02/21/2003
6	Modern computer: Fujitsu Siemens Computers, by e-mail on July 28 from Alexandra Wagner, Chromedia GmbH
6	Abacus: Siemens, Judith Egelhof
6	Man: Siemens, Lika Meissner
6	Chimpanzee: Tobias Berner
6	Mouse: Tobias Berner
6	Lizard: Tobias Berner
6	Spider: Tobias Berner
6	Earthworm: Tobias Berner
6	Bacterium: Siemens, Georg Berner
6	Hand holding pen: Siemens, Judith Egelhof
7	Moore's law: Siemens, Georg Berner
7	Mobile phone with MP3 player: Siemens, Judith Egelhof
7	PDA: Siemens, Lika Meissner
7	DRAM: Infineon Technologies, Gudrun Klingenstein, by e-mail on 08/06/2003
7	Processor: Infineon Technologies, Gudrun Klingenstein, by e-mail on 08/06/2003
8	Prices for 1 Mbit of DRAM: Siemens, Manfred Weick
8	House: Tobias Berner
8	Old Mercedes: Tobias Berner
8	Television: Tobias Berner
8	Bicycle: Tobias Berner
8	Shirt and tie: Tobias Berner
8	Pizza: Tobias Berner
8	Stamp: Tobias Berner
8	Screw: Tobias Berner
8	Chewing gum: Tobias Berner
8	Jelly Baby: Tobias Berner
8	Sheet of paper: Tobias Berner
8	Post-it: Tobias Berner
8	Paper clip: Tobias Berner
9	Carbon nanotubes – the replacement for copper conductors: Siemens, Judith Egelhof

Sources of the pictures and graphics in the figures

Bibliography

Aaker, David A.: *Strategic Market Management.* John Wiley & Sons, New York. 2003

Andrews, David H./Johnson, Kenneth R.: *Revolutionizing IT.* John Wiley & Sons, New York. 2002

Arthur D. Little (Hrsg.): *Management in vernetzten Unternehmen.* Gabler, Wiesbaden. 1996

Arthur D. Little (Hrsg.): *Management der F&E-Strategie.* Gabler, Wiesbaden. 1993

Ashby, Franklin C./Pell, Arthur R.: *Embracing Excellence.* PRENTICE HALL, Englewood. 2001

Baack, Clemens/Eberspächer, Jörg (Hrsg.): *Das Internet von morgen.* Hüthig, Heidelberg. 1999

Bachler, Georg: *Spitzenleistung.* Ueberreuter, Wien. 2003

Bachrach, Bill: *Values-based selling.* Aim High Publishing, San Diego. 2002

Balling, Richard: *Kooperation.* Peter Lang, Frankfurt/Main. 1997

Beck, Peter.: *Unternehmensbewertung bei Akquisitionen.* Gabler, Wiesbaden. 1996

Behrens, D. (Hrsg.): *Wasserstofftechnologie.* Schön & Wetzel, Frankfurt/Main. 1986

Beyer, Lothar et al.: *Vom E-Business zur E-Society.* Hampp, München. 2003

Birkenbihl, Vera F.: *Psycho-Logisch richtig verhandeln.* mvg, München. 2003

Bliemel, Friedhelm/Kotler, Philip: *Marketing-Management.* Schäffer-Poeschel, Stuttgart. 2001

Bockris, John O. M./Justi, Eduard W.: *Wasserstoff – die Energie für alle Zeiten.* Udo Pfriemer. 1980

Börnecke, Dirk (Hrsg.): *Basiswissen für Führungskräfte.* Publicis, Erlangen. 2003

Bossidy, Larry et al.: *Execution.* Crown Business, New York. 2002

Brache, Alan P.: *How Organizations Work.* John Wiley & Sons, New York. 2002

Brown, J. A. C.: *Techniques of Persuasion.* Penguin Books, New York. 1977

Button, Maurice/Bolton, Sarah (Hrsg.): *A Practitioner's Guide To The alternative Investment Market Rules.* City & Financial, Old Woking. 1999

Button, Maurice/Bolton, Sarah (Hrsg.): *A Practitioner's Guide To The City Code on Takeovers and Mergers.* City & Financial, Old Woking. 2000

Calvin, Robert J.: *Sales Management.* McGraw-Hill, New York. 2001

Coates, Joseph F. et al.: *2025. Scenarios of U. S. and Global Society Reshaped by Science and Technology.* OakHill Press, Greensboro. 1997

Collins, James C./Porras, Jerry: *Visionary Companies.* Artemis & Winkler, München. 1995

Collins, Jim: *Good to Great.* HarperCollins, New York. 2001

Computer Science and Telecommunications Board: *Realizing the Information Future.* National Academy, Washington. 1994

Computer Science and Telecommunications Board: *The Unpredictable Certainty.* National Academy, Washington. 1996

Conner, Daryl R.: *Leading at the Edge of Chaos.* John Wiley & Sons, New York. 1998

Conrad, Pamela J.: *Berufs- und Privatleben im Griff.* Ueberreuter, Wien. 1996

Cornish, Edward (Hrsg.): *Exploring Your Future.* World Future Society. 2000

Covey, Stephen R.: *The Seven Habits Of Highly Effective People.* Simon & Schuster, London. 1999

Covey, Stephen R. et al.: *First Things First.* Simon & Schuster, London. 2001

Covey, Stephen R. et al.: *Der Weg zum Wesentlichen.* Campus, Frankfurt/Main. 2003

Crawford, Fred/Mathews, Ryan: *The Myth of Excellence.* Crown Business, New York. 2001

Crichton, Michael. *Beute.* Karl Blessing, München. 2002

Cunningham, Peter/Fröschl, Friedrich: *Electronic Business Revolution.* Springer. 1999

D'Aveni, Richard A.: *Hyperwettbewerb.* Campus, Frankfurt/Main. 1995

Davidow, William H.: *Marketing High Technology.* Free Press, New York. 1986

Davis, Kevin: *Getting Into Your Customer's Head.* Times Books, New York. 1996

Davis, Scott M.: *Brand Asset Management.* John Wiley & Sons, New York. 2000

Deckert, Klaus (Hrsg.): *Geschäftsprozesse optimieren.* ECON, Düsseldorf. 1997

Deiters, Wolfgang/Lienemann, Carsten (Hrsg.): *Report Informationslogistik.* Symposion, Düsseldorf. 2001

Dowling, Michael et al.: *eLearning in Unternehmen.* Springer, Berlin. 2003

Eberspächer, Jörg: *Die Zukunft der Printmedien.* Springer, Berlin. 2002

Eberspächer, Jörg/Hertz, Udo: *Leben in der e-Society.* Springer, Berlin. 2002

Eberspächer, Jörg/Thielmann, Heinz: *Challenges to the Information Society of the 21th Century.* Tagungsband. 2001

Eberspächer, Jörg/Ziemer, Albrecht: *Digitale Medien und Konvergenz.* Hüthig, Heidelberg. 2001

Eglau, Hans Otto, et al.: *Durchstarten zur Spitze.* Campus, Frankfurt/Main. 2000

Fahey, Liam/Randall, Robert M.: *Learning from the Future – Competitive Foresight Scenarios.* John Wiley & Sons, New York. 1998

Fraunhofer-Institut für Systemtechnik und Innovationsforschung (ISI) BMBF (Hrsg.). *DELPHI '98 Umfrage. Studie zur globalen Entwicklung von Wissenschaft und Technik.* Karlsruhe. 1998

Francis, Philip H.: *Product Creation.* Free Press, New York. 2000

Freedman, Mike/Tregoe, Benjamin B.: *The Art and Discipline of Strategic Leadership.* McGraw-Hill, New York. 2003

Friedman, Lawrence G./Furey, Timothy R.: *The Channel Advantage.* Butterworth-Heinemann, Woburn. 1999

Gates, Bill: *Business @ Speed of Thought.* Warner, New York. 1999

Gershenfeld, Neil: *Wenn die Dinge denken lernen.* Econ, München. 1999

Gerson Richard: *Der Marketingplan.* Ueberreuter, Wien. 1992

Goleman, Daniel et al.: *Primal Leadership.* Harvard Business School, Watertown. 2002

Gora, Walter/Mann, Erika (Hrsg.): *Handbuch Electronic Commerce.* Springer, Berlin. 2001

Gouillart, Francis J./Kelly, James N.: *Business Transformation.* Ueberreuter, Wien. 1999

Gretz, Wolfgang: *Erfolgreiches Controlling durch Kennziffernanalyse.* Tylorix, Stuttgart. 1996

Griffin, Jill/Lowenstein, Michael W.: *Customer Winback.* John Wiley & Sons, New York. 2001

Grossman, Jack H.: *Managing with Wisdom.* Pelican Publishing, Gretna. 1996

Gündling Christian: *Maximale Kundenorientierung.* Schäffer-Poeschel, Stuttgart. 1996

Gutzman, Alexis D.: *The E-Commerce Arsenal.* AMACOM, New York. 2001

Haarbeck, Siegfried (Hrsg.): *Deutschland 2010.* Deutscher Wirtschaftsdienst, Köln. 2000

Habeck, Max M. et al.: *After the Merger.* PRENTICE HALL, Englewood. 2000

Hackl, Heinz (Hrsg.): *Praxis des Selbstmanagements.* Publicis, Erlangen. 1994

Hahn, Dietger/Taylor, Bernard (Hrsg.): *Strategische Unternehmungsplanung – Strategische Unternehmungsführung.* Physica, Heidelberg. 1992

Hamel, Gary: *Leading the Revolution.* Harvard Business School, Watertown. 2000

Hamel, Gary/Prahalad C. K.: *Wettlauf um die Zukunft.* Ueberreuter, Wien. 1995

Hammer, Michael: *The Agenda.* Crown Business, New York. 2001

Harry, Mikel/Schroeder, Richard: *Six Sigma.* Random House, New York. 2000

Hauk, Bernd (Hrsg.): *Wie Unternehmen erfolgreich reorganisieren.* Frankfurter Allgemeine Buch. 1998

Hax, Arnoldo C./Majluf Nicolas S.: *Strategic Management: An Interactive Perspective.* PRENTICE HALL, Englewood. 1984

Heidack, Clemens (Hrsg.): *HighTech – HighRisk.* Hampp, München. 2000

Hilty, Lorenz et al.: *Das Vorsorgeprinzip in der Informationsgesellschaft/www.ta-swiss.ch.* 2003

Hofmeister, Roman: *Der Business Plan.* Ueberreuter, Wien. 1999

Hope, Jeremy/Hope, Tony: *Competing in the Third Wave.* Harvard Business School, Watertown. 1997

Institute for the Future: *Ten-Year Forecast* (jährliche Druckschrift des Corporate Associates Program). Institute for the Future. jährlich

Johnson, Michael D./Gustafsson, Anders: *Improving Customer Satisfaction, Loyalty and Profit.* John Wiley & Sons, New York. 2000

Johnson, Spencer: *Who Moved My Cheese?* G. P. Putnam's Sons, New York. 2000

Jonash, Ronald S./Sommerlatte, Tom: *The Innovation Premium.* Perseus, Cambridge. 1999

Jung, Volker/Warnecke, Hans-Jürgen (Hrsg.): *Handbuch für die Telekommunikation.* Springer, Berlin. 2002

Kaku, Michio: *ZukunftsVisionen.* Lichtenberg, München. 1998

Kaku, Michio: *Hyperspace.* Oxford University. 1994

Kaplan, Robert S./Norton, David P.: *The Balanced Scorecard.* Harvard Business School, Watertown. 1996

Kaplan, Robert S./Norton, David P.: *The Strategy-Focused Organization.* Harvard Business School, Watertown. 2001

Kleinfeld, Klaus: *Führungsgrundsätze,* unveröffentlicht

Kleinfeld, Klaus: *Corporate Identity und strategische Unternehmensführung.* Akademischer Verlag, München. 1994

Klodt, Henning et al.: *Die neue Ökonomie: Erscheinungsformen, Ursachen und Auswirkungen.* Springer, Berlin. 2003

Koch, Wolfgang/Wegmann, Jürgen: *Praktiker-Handbuch Due Dilligence.* Schäffer-Poeschel, Stuttgart. 2001

Kotler, Philip, et al.: *Grundlagen des Marketing.* PRENTICE HALL, Englewood. 1999

Kralicek, Peter: *Kennzahlen für Geschäftsführer.* Ueberreuter, Wien. 2001

Kröger, Fritz et al.: *Wachsen wie die Sieger.* Gabler, Wiesbaden. 1999

Kubr, Thomas et al.: *Planen, gründen, wachsen.* Ueberreuter, Wien. 2002

Lamprecht, Rudi: *Zukunft mobile Kommunikation.* Frankfurter Allgemeine Buch. 2001

Laszlo, Ervin: *Das dritte Jahrtausend.* Suhrkamp, Frankfurt/Main. 1998

Leibold, Marius et al.: *Strategic Management in the Knowledge Economy.* John Wiley & Sons, New York. 2002

Lettau, Hans-Georg: *Strategisch verkaufen.* Ueberreuter, Wien. 1996

Lewicki, Roy et al.: *Verhandeln mit Strategie.* Midas Management, St. Gallen. 1998

Lewis, Herschell/Lewis, Robert D.: *Selling on the Net.* NTC, Chicago. 1997

Lewis, Jordan D.: *Strategische Allianzen.* Campus, Frankfurt/Main. 1991

Magyar, Kasimir M.: *Marketingweisheiten und Marketingbosheiten.* Moderne Industrie, Landsberg. 1991

Mattes, Andy/Emmerson, Bob: *21st Century Communications.* Capstone, Oxford. 2003

Mayer, Elmar (Hrsg.)/Freidank, Carl C.: *Controlling-Konzepte.* Gabler, Wiesbaden. 2003

McKenna, Regis: *Real Time.* Harvard Business School, Watertown. 1997

McRae, Hamish: *The World in 2020.* Harvard Business School, Watertown. 1994

Meyer, Peter: *Creating and Dominating New Markets.* AMACOM, New York. 2002

Mićić, Pero: *Der Zukunfts Manager.* Haufe, Freiburg. 2000

Mitroff, Ian I./Anagnos, Gus: *Managing Crises Before They Happen.* AMACOM, New York. 2001

Montgomery, Cynthia A./Porter, Michael E. (Hrsg.): *Strategie.* Moderne Industrie, Landsberg. 1996

Moore, Geoffrey A.: *Inside the Tornado.* HarperCollins, New York. 1999

Moore, Randy A.: *The Science of High-Performance Supplier Management.* AMACOM, New York. 2002

Müller, Mokka: *Das vierte Feld.* Mentopolis, Köln. 1999

Murphy, Michael: *Der Quantenmensch, Ein Blick in die Entfaltung des menschlichen Potentials im 21. Jahrhundert.* Integral, Wessobrunn. 1992

Nefiodow, Leo A.: *Der fünfte Kondratieff.* Gabler, Wiesbaden. 1990

Nefiodow, Leo A.: *Der sechste Kondratieff.* Rhein-Sieg, Sankt Augustin. 2001

Odenthal, Stefan et al.: *Strategische Partnerschaften – Mehr Erfolg mit dem neuen Partnering-Ansatz.* Gabler, Wiesbaden. 2002

OECD: *Science, Technology and Industry Outlook.* OECD, Paris. 2000

OECD: *Technologien des 21. Jahrhunderts.* OECD, New York. 2000

OECD: *Die Welt im Jahr 2020.* OECD, Paris. 1998

OECD: *A new Economy.* OECD, Paris. 2000

OECD: *Energy: The Next Fifty Years.* OECD, Paris. 1999

OECD: *Die Weltwirtschaft von morgen.* OECD, Paris. 1999

OECD: *21st Century.* OECD, Paris. 1998

Oetinger, Bolko von: *Das Boston Consulting Strategie-Buch.* ECON, Düsseldorf. 2003

Ohmae, Kenichi: *Mind of the Strategist.* McGraw-Hill, New York. 1982

O'Reilly III, Charles A./Pfeffer, Jeffrey: *Hidden Value.* Harvard Business School, Watertown. 2000

Ossola-Haring, Claudia (Hrsg.) et al.: *Die 499 besten Checklisten für Ihr Unternehmen.* Moderne Industrie, Landsberg. 1997

Paine, Lynn S.: *Value Shift.* McGraw-Hill, New York. 2002

Pearson, Ian (Hrsg.): *The Atlas of the Future.* Routledge, London. 1998

Peppers, Don/Rogers, Martha: *The One to One Future.* Bantam Doubleday Dell, New York. 1997

Peters, Thomas J./Waterman, Robert H.: *Auf der Suche nach Spitzenleistungen.* Moderne Industrie, Landsberg. 2003

Picot, Arnold (Hrsg.): *Marktplatz Internet.* Hüthig, Heidelberg. 1999

Picot, Arnold/Doeblin, Stefan (Hrsg.): *eCompanies gründen, wachsen, ernten.* Springer. 2000

Picot, Arnold/Doeblin, Stefan (Hrsg.): *Telekommunikation und Kapitalmarkt.* Gabler, Wiesbaden. 2002

Pierer, Heinrich von/Oetinger, Bolko von: *Wie kommt das Neue in die Welt?* Hanser, München. 1997

Pierer, Heinrich von et al.: *Zwischen Profit und Moral.* Hanser, München. 2003

Porter, Michael E.: *Wettbewerbsvorteile.* Campus, Frankfurt/Main. 1992

Porter, Michael E.: *Competitive Strategy.* Free Press, New York. 1980

Porter, Michael E.: *Wettbewerbsstrategie.* Campus, Frankfurt/Main. 1990

Rackham, Neil/Vincentis, John de: *Rethinking the Sales Force.* McGraw-Hill, New York. 1999

Raphel, Murray/Raphel, Neil: *Up the Loyalty Ladder.* HarperCollins, New York. 1995

Reibnitz, Ute von: *Szenario-Technik.* Gabler, Wiesbaden. 1992

Ries, Al/Trout, Jack: *The 22 Immutable Laws of Marketing.* HarperCollins, New York. 1994

Roger, Jean-Yves et al.: *Business and Work in the Information Society: New Technologies and Applications.* IOS, Amsterdam. 1999

Rohner, Kurt: *Cyber Marketing.* Orell Füssli, Zürich. 1996

Rommel, Günter et al.: *Einfach überlegen.* Schäffer-Poeschel, Stuttgart. 1993

Rückle, Horst: *Körpersprache für Manager.* Moderne Industrie, Landsberg. 1998

Savage, Charles M.: *Fifth Generation Management.* vdf Hochschulverlag, Zürich. 1997

Schaible, Jörg/Hönig, Armin: *High-Tech-Marketing in der Praxis.* Vahlen, München. 1996

Schaumburg, Harald (Hrsg.): *Internationale Joint Ventures.* Schäffer-Poeschel, Stuttgart. 1999

Schiava, Manfred della: *Praktische Entwicklung des Marketingplanes.* Ueberreuter, Wien. 1996

Schwartz, Peter: *The Art of the Long View.* Bantam Doubleday Dell, New York. 1991

Schwarzecker, Josef/Spandl, Friedrich: *Kennzahlen-Krisenmanagement. Mit Stufenplan zur Sanierung.* Ueberreuter, Wien. 1993

Seitz, Konrad: *Wettlauf ins 21. Jahrhundert.* Siedler, Berlin. 1998

Servatius, Hans-Gerd: *Reengineering-Programme umsetzen.* Schäffer-Poeschel, Stuttgart. 1994

Siegle, Gert/Thielmann, Heinz (Hrsg.): *Mobil mit digitalen Diensten.* Hüthig, Bonn. 2003

Siemens AG: *Pictures of the Future* (Hrsg. Ulrich Eberl, Dietmar Theis), ISSN 1618-548X, www.siemens.de/pof, www.siemens.com/pof

Simon, Hermann: *Die heimlichen Gewinner.* Campus, Frankfurt/Main. 1996

Slywotzky, Adrian J./Morrison, David J.: *Die Gewinnzone.* Moderne Industrie, Landsberg. 1998

Slywotzky, Adrian J. et al.: *Profit Patterns.* Times Books, New York. 1999

Slywotzky, Adrian J. et al.: *How Digital is Your Business?* Crown Business, New York. 2000

Soundview Editor Staff (Hrsg.): *Skills for Success.* Soundview, Bristol. 1989

Speidel, Joachim (Hrsg.): *Zugangsnetze im Wettbewerb.* Hüthig, Heidelberg. 2000

Staples, Walter D.: *Think like a Winner.* Pelican Publishing, Gretna. 1995

Steinmüller, Angela/Steinmüller, Karlheinz: *Visionen 1900 2000 2100, Eine Chronik der Zukunft.* Rogner & Bernhard Verlag Hamburg. 1999

Steinmüller, Angela/Steinmüller, Karlheinz: *Ungezähmte Zukunft.* Gerling Akademie, München. 2003

Stern, Joel M./Shiely, John S.: *The EVA Challenge.* John Wiley & Sons, New York. 2001

Strebel, Paul: *Trajectory Management.* John Wiley & Sons, Chichester. 2003

Tagungsband Münchner Kreis: *Vision 21.* Marketing und Wirtschaft, München. 2000

Tagungsband Münchner Kreis: *2014 – Die Zukunft von Information, Kommunikation und Medien.* Marketing und Wirtschaft, München. 1999

Tellis, Gerard J./Golder, Peter N: *Will and Vision.* McGraw-Hill, New York. 2002

Thomas, Philip R.: *Competitiveness Through Total Cycle Time.* McGraw-Hill, New York. 1990

Tipler, Frank J.: *Die Physik der Unsterblichkeit.* Piper, München. 2001

Tirez, Dirk: *A Practitioner's Guide To The EASDAQ Rules.* City & Financial, Old Woking. 2000

Treacy, Michael/Wiersema, Fred: *Marktführerschaft.* Campus, Frankfurt/Main. 1995

Trout, Jack/Rivkin, Steve: *The New Positioning.* McGraw-Hill, New York. 1996

Trout, Jack/Rivkin, Steve: *Differentiate or Die.* John Wiley & Sons, New York. 2000

Tze, Sun: *Die dreizehn Gebote der Kriegskunst.* Rogner & Bernhard, München. 1972

Ulfers, Heike A.: *Der Consultance-Berater.* Publicis, Erlangen. 2004

Varakin, Leaonid E.: *Distribution of Incomes, Technologies and Services.* International Telecommunication Academy, Moskau. 2002

Warnecke, Hans-Jürgen: *Projekt Zukunft.* vgs, Köln. 1999

Waterman Robert: *Die neue Suche nach Spitzenleistungen.* ECON, Düsseldorf. 1994

Wenzlau, Andreas et al.: *KundenProfiling.* Publicis, Erlangen. 2003

Weston, Fred J./Copeland, Thomas E.: *Managerial Finance.* Dryden Press, Orlando. 1986

Wieners, Brad/Pescovitz, David: *Reality Check.* Midas, St. Gallen. 1997

Wind, Yoram et al.: *Convergence Marketing.* PRENTICE HALL, Englewood. 2002

Acknowledgments

In writing this book I repeatedly received guidance and assistance from a number of people, to whom I would like to express my thanks here. For linguistic suggestions and revision I would like to thank both Anita Koziol and Heike Schindler. Thomas Strobel contributed valuable comments and ideas and provided photographs from his archive. Dr. Gerhard Seitfudem was a constructive editor and publisher. I received informed advice on a number of subjects from Johann Breidler, Dr. Hartmut Raffler and Dr. Ulrich Eberl. Hans-Werner Hartmann and Anton Schmöller coached me in the subjects of controlling and organization. Dr. Stefan Kurze of the Institut für Mikrotechnik and Judith Egelhof and Lika Meissner of Siemens helped with the photographs and the rights to them.

I would also like to express my heartfelt thanks to my family for their tolerance of the additional workload caused by this book. My son Tobias also contributed many photographs.